Pause & Effect

the art of
interactive narrative

mark stephen meadows

New Riders | 201 West 103rd Street, Indianapolis, Indiana 46290

Pause & Effect: The Art of Interactive Narrative
Copyright © 2003 by Mark Stephen Meadows

International Standard Book Number: 0-7357-1171-2
Library of Congress Catalog Card Number: 2001091119
Printed in the United States of America
First Printing: September 2002
06   05   04   03   02   7   6   5   4   3   2   1

Interpretation of the printing code: The rightmost double-digit number is the year of the book's printing; the rightmost single-digit number is the number of the book's printing. For example, the printing code 02-1 shows that the first printing of the book occurred in 2002.

PUBLISHER
David Dwyer

ASSOCIATE PUBLISHER
Stephanie Wall

EXECUTIVE EDITOR
Steve Weiss

PRODUCTION MANAGER
Gina Kanouse

MANAGING EDITOR
Sarah Kearns

ACQUISITIONS EDITOR
Michael Nolan

DEVELOPMENT EDITOR
Richard Kadrey

COVER DESIGN
Gabriella Marks & Mark Stephen Meadows

GRAPHIC DESIGN, LAYOUT, COMPOSITION, AND PREPRESS
Gabriella Marks, Shelby Ring, & Mark Stephen Meadows

COMIC STORY, ANIMATION, AND CHARACTER DESIGN
Marvin Mann & Mark Stephen Meadows

CHARACTER ANIMATION AND ENVIRONMENT DESIGN
Marvin Perry Mann

PHOTOGRAPHY, ILLUSTRATION, AND PHOTOMONTAGE (AS NOTED)
Gabriella Marks, Shelby Ring, & Mark Stephen Meadows

PROMOTIONS MANAGER
Amery Calvelli

PRODUCT MARKETING MANAGER
Tammy Detrich

PUBLICITY MANAGER
Susan Nixon

MANUFACTURING COORDINATOR
Jim Conway

COPY EDITOR
Keith Cline

PROOFREADERS
Linda Seifert
Karen A. Gill

INDEXER
Chris Morris

2   Chapter 1.1 - Theory & Principle
The changing forms of narrative. Perspective as the basis of narrative.

6   Chapter 1.2 - Perspective
The evolution of dimensional perspective. The relationship between emotional and dimensional perspectives. Inside-the-skull and outside-the-skull interactions. The individual perspective as it shifted to social perspectives, then back to individual. Subjective and objective perspectives.

18   Chapter 1.3 - Narrative
The potential of narrative in emerging media types. Aristotelian definition of narrative. The Freytag triangle and the dramatic arc. How readers are becoming investigators. Computer applications seen as an interactive form of reading and writing. Use-case scenario considered as plot. Tropes and other forms of telescoped tales. Imagery considered as a non-linear form of reading. The emerging population of visual narratives.

37   Chapter 1.4 - Interaction
Forms of interaction considered. The roles of rules. Three principles of interaction presented. Four steps of interaction presented. Symbols discussed as the foundation of decision making. How different readers bring different times to what is being read. How time's role in narrative is changing. The tyranny of interaction design. The natural intersection of interaction and narrative. Television and the Internet's roles reviewed.

60   Chapter 1.5 - Interactive Narrative
Interactive narrative's episodic nature. Interactive narrative defined. Plot structures and how they can be used. Nodal, modulated, and open plot structures.

67   Chapter 1.6 - Summary
The nature of interactive narratives. The accelerations of narrative and interaction. Story as an algorithmic form of logic. Narrative considered as interface design. Non-interactive narrative presented as a subset of narrative.

72   Chapter 2.1 - Introduction
The various relationships of words and imagery.

73   Chapter 2.2 - Perspective
Points of view (first, second, third person), the role of the camera, the perspectivist approach. The function of different points of view. Different kinds of camera angles. The power of the abstracted image and the character. Time in narrative. Forms of telescoping perspectives in narrative and visual imagery.

93   Chapter 2.3 - Narrative
The line of sight and its importance in graphic novels. The narrative importance of saccadic and peripheral vision. Memory generates meaning. Composition in imagery. Eight examples of narrative imagery. The importance of symbols and redundancy. Developing new themes. Visual functions.

116   Chapter 2.4 - Interaction
Items that visualize interaction: microscopic and macroscopic; subdivisions; feedback; composition. The relationship of these items. Acquiring information. Discovering information. Redistributing information. The importance of image in interaction.

124   Chapter 2.5 - Examples and Interviews
Interview with Scott McCloud. Examples of AI Internet Game, Liquid Stage, Crutch, Jimmy Corrigan, Banja, The Devil's Tramping Ground, and Memex Engine.

154 **Chapter 3.1 - Introduction**
The longstanding relationship of narrative and architecture. The Acropolis and Holocaust Memorial.

157 **Chapter 3.2 - Perspective**
The spatial implications of perspective. How space influences story presentation. Perspective determines understanding. Buildings considered as narratives. First, second, and third person perspectives. Mimesis. The relationship between proximity and meaning considered. Theater and movie compared. How video games combine these narrative forms. Movement and space increase interaction. Why 3D is important.

170 **Chapter 3.3 - Narrative**
The architect considered as narrator. Architectural forms of narrative and vice-versa. Fort Scott, Kansas. Kelly Collins considered as technology.

174 **Chapter 3.4 - Interaction**
Walls presented as an important part of dimensional narrative. Walls as separators of information. Visual cues as joiners of information. Human interaction underscored. Acquiring information. Discovering information. Redistributing information.

180 **Chapter 3.5 - Examples and Interviews**
Interview with Marcos Novak. Examples of La Noche de Santa Inés, Deus Ex 2, God is Flat, Ultima Online, Top Agent, and Virtools.

212 **Chapter 4.1 - Introduction**
Formal rules and guidelines given second seat to impact on reader.

213 **Chapter 4.2 - Design Considerations**
IonStorm's system design approach. IonStorm's reality checks reviewed. Interactive narrative includes multiple forms of storyline. Banja's approach as an example of excellence. Software Requirement Documentation (SRDs). Approaches offered toward delivery and performance goals. Primary design constraints reviewed: Responsiveness vs. Resolution; Optimization vs. Ubiquity; Customization vs. Design. The role of metaphor.

223 **Chapter 4.3 - Narrative**
How character role combines literary, visual, and interactive perspectives. The importance of investment and interest in interaction and narrative. How design constraints steer story development.

228 **Chapter 4.4 - Interaction**
The history of the Interactive Media Festival and Construct Internet Design. Lessons learned from that process. Interaction and narrative must be concurrently developed. Forms of interaction that can later be added.

232 **Chapter 4.5 - Summaries and Outlook**
The adoption and hybridization of emerging forms of narrative. The Snowcrash Dream. The emerging trends of procedural development and artificial intelligence. The marriage of plot and interaction. The authors' new roles reviewed.

241 **About the Comic and Flipbook Narratives**

242 **Bibliography**

244 **Index**

250 **Image Index**

Credits and Thanks

This project couldn't have happened without Gabriella Marks, Michael Nolan, and David Dwyer. My personal thanks for all their great help over the years. Thanks also go to the excellent staff at New Riders, notably Victoria Elzey for helping fill in the gaps that we could have driven a truck through. Richard Kadrey brought insight and imagination to this project as my development editor. Specific appreciation needs to be sent to Carmen Hermosillo, Suzanne Stefanec, and Nathan Shedroff for their staunch criticism, insightful inspiration, and continued kindness for the better part of the last decade.

Interviews and Case Studies

Marcos Novak, Doug Church, Scott McCloud, Brenda Laurel, Harvey Smith and the IonStorm office, Ed Bain, Raph Koster, Linda Stone, Olivier Janin and all the folks at Team ChMan/Banja, Marc Lafia, Maurice Benayoun, Elan Lee, Adrian Hon, Anita Pantin, Nicolas of Paris, Michael Bovee, Michelle Citron, Hillary Goidell, Ludovic Duchâteau, Robin Hunicke, Marko Laukasto, Mitja Kurki, Teemu Huutanen, Janne Kouri, and Chris Ware.

Advisory Board

Nathan Shedroff, Brenda Laurel, Suzanne Stefanec, Paco Xander Nathan, Carmen Hermosillo, Jeannine Parker, Justin Hall, Anne Balsamo, Amy Critchett, Tony Parisi, Mark Pesce, and Jeffrey Veen. I owe a lot to each of these folks for being kind enough to review the manuscript, send feedback, and basically cover for me when I was less than diligent or more than pigheaded. And more than once.

Additional Appreciations

Kate Seekings (for her hawk-eye vision), Stinkfoot (for the elevator ambiance), Brenda Laurel (for the numerous levels of invaluable assistance), Shelby Ring (for providing foreign bridges and continuous help), Brian Lang (for the architectural leads), Nicolas Aubrun and Helena Fantl (for cinematic openings), Inga von Staden (for her germanic, definitive help), Christine Schoepf, Gerhard Schroeder and the Ars Electronica Staff (for time and guidance), Richard Saja (for exacto-knife-edits), Paul Mondani (for the rides to and from the airports), Jethro Odom (for his critiques and reviews), Kelly Collins and the rest of the Fort Scott crew, Ivan Almeida (of the Borges Center for Study and Documentation), Hillary Goidell (for her perspicacious editorial reviews), Désirée Hupy (for keeping the night outside), Betty Scott (for the southern cooking and editorial inspiration), Sally Meadows (for renaissance photography and a-priori initiations), GG & General Moore (for the place to sleep, sustained support, and immense kindess), Chris and Heather (for the lakes of inspiration), Bernice Vancil (for her patient advice), Kathryn Ross (and her gaming consultants including Colin Brimm, Ned Perry, Brendan Lavender, and Nick Forbes),The Colorado Rocky Mountain School (for the use of their library for several productive weeks), Lisa Goldman (for longtime friendship and assistance), Steve Dietz (for agreeing and disagreeing while crossing the Italian Alps), Sarabeth Sclove (for her reviews and assistance with theatre.theory), Susan Bukowski (for the ITv assistance), Sterling Stoudenmire (for the solid business sense), Ludovic DuChateau (for being the ever-vigillante intellectual watchdog), Christina Brodbeck (for acquisitions and permissions assistance), and to Mark Johnson at the Daguerreian Society (http://daguerre.org/) for his fantastic and speedy assistance finding images from a completely different world. Thanks also to Scott Allie, Irena Rogovsky, Kelli Richards, Joe Lambert, and Nina Mullen.

Tools used for this book:

A round peg, a square hole, a hammer, some elbow grease, and a pile of misgivings.
And the Internet, as the book was written primarily from the road.

Visit Our Web Site: www.newriders.com

On our Web site, you'll find information about our other books, the authors we partner with, book updates and file downloads, promotions, discussion boards for online interaction with other users and with technology experts, and a calendar of trade shows and other professional events with which we'll be involved. We hope to see you around.

Email Us from Our Web Site

Go to www.newriders.com and click on the Contact Us link if you

- Have comments or questions about this book.
- Want to report errors that you have found in this book.
- Have a book proposal or are interested in writing for New Riders.
- Would like us to send you one of our author kits.
- Are an expert in a computer topic or technology and are interested in being a reviewer or technical editor.
- Want to find a distributor for our titles in your area.
- Are an educator/instructor who wants to preview New Riders books for classroom use.

In the body/comments area, include your name, school, department, address, phone number, office days/hours, text currently in use, and enrollment in your department, along with your request for either desk/examination copies or additional information.

A Message from New Riders

As the reader of this book, you are our most important critic and commentator. We value your opinion and want to know what we're doing right, what we could do better, in what areas you'd like to see us publish, and any other words of wisdom you're willing to pass our way.

As Executive Editor at New Riders, I welcome your comments. You can fax, email, or write me directly to let me know what you did or didn't like about this book—as well as what we can do to make our books better. When you write, please be sure to include this book's title, ISBN, and author, as well as your name and phone or fax number. I will carefully review your comments and share them with the authors and editors who worked on the book.

Please note that I cannot help you with technical problems related to the topic of this book, and that due to the high volume of email I receive, I might not be able to reply to every message. Thanks.

Fax: 317-581-4663
Email: steve.weiss@newriders.com
Mail: Steve Weiss
        Executive Editor
        New Riders Publishing
        201 West 103rd Street
        Indianapolis, IN 46290 USA

Preface

This book is designed for anyone interested in narrative art forms. Narratives (also called stories) are everywhere. Movies, newspapers, books, television, conversation, and, with computing technologies, the Internet.

My first experience with the Internet was in 1982—a year or two before I would have a computer of my own. The Internet was approximately 14 years old and the infrastructure was still so thin it was invisible. Someone at my high school in Colorado Springs had given me a piece of paper with a seven-digit number scrawled on it. Next to it were the words "Satan's Phone Number." It was a local number, which didn't surprise me. Satan, as my friends and I well knew, lived somewhere just east of the high school (in fact, we suspected him to be a member of the administration).

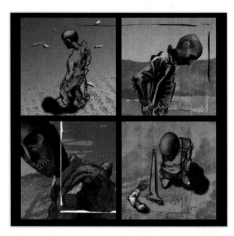

When I got home that night I rang the number. My hand rested on the receiver, ready to disconnect the line (I was an experienced prank caller, you understand). After two rings, the phone picked up on the other end. The sound I heard wasn't a human voice but a sustained screeching, like metal being ground against itself. It was as horrible as any noise I'd ever heard. I must have listened for a full minute, fascinated, waiting to be possessed, the phone a good six inches from my ear. Eventually the sound stopped and the line went dead.

At the time, I wasn't sure if it was Satan or not. But I think, today, it was a modem.

More than a decade later, in 1993, I was hired by The WELL, a bulletin board service in Sausalito, California, to help build their website (they had dozens of modems that were constantly squeaking). The WELL was, to our knowledge, one of the first three commercial websites registered with what was becoming InterNIC. During the following years, I co-founded Construct Internet Design, and after working there, went on to Xerox-PARC, where I spent time as Artist-In-Residence doing research on reading and interactivity. In 2001, I moved to Paris to look at art and interactivity through a slightly different cultural (and technical) lens.

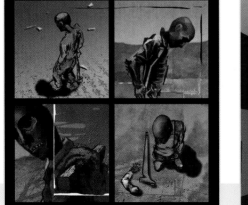

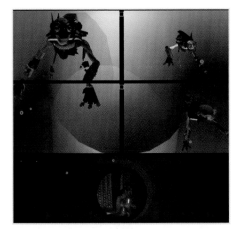

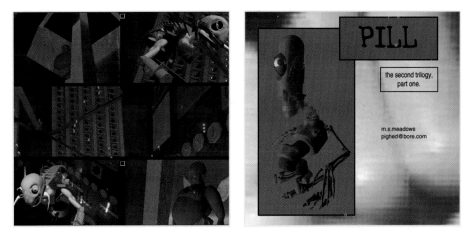

The point where imagery, narrative, and interaction converge has been the focus of my career. During these years, from Colorado Springs to Paris, the single thing I've called myself has been a painter. For me, the image has always been primary. I'm transfixed by television. I gorge myself on movies. I love comic books. And yes, I played Dungeons and Dragons back in the day.

The Internet became interesting to me only when imagery emerged from its muddy depths. If it weren't for computer graphics, I would never have been interested in virtual reality. Had it not been for the comics, I probably wouldn't have bothered publishing my own narratives to the web.

In some ways, this book has been almost 20 years in the making. My professional work has historically included image composition and animation, graphic design, interface design, character design, environment design, and information design. All of these I've done in both two-dimensional and three-dimensional image formats. During the last four years, my work has continued to migrate toward the world of fine art because artistic ideas sometimes take deeper risk than commercial ideas. And the rewards can be greater.

In working on this book, my own opinions about narrative didn't seem sufficient. In the interest of preserving a spirit of interaction, I've interviewed friends, co-workers, and associates who have significant experience in the field. This book isn't intended to be the final word on interactive narrative. If anything, it's another window, looking out onto an emerging landscape.

One: Theory & Principle

Authors have one thing in common: They have a perspective to convey. Playwrights, journalists, historians, fiction writers, and biographers all have a story to tell. Their story is their perspective.

If humanity were a building, each author would be a window. The view from that window would be the picture each author paints. It's a view that explains a little bit more about the confusing things we call "Life" and "Reality." A narrative is an individual's perspective of the surrounding landscape. It's one small view on the big picture. For millennia, we've used our perspectives and stories to find a larger perspective on what's been called "The Human Condition." And stories are what we rely on. Stories are what we use to explain the underpinnings of reality.

This is why narrative exists: to convey perspective.

Interactive narrative is the most ambitious art form existing today because it combines traditional narrative with visual art and interactivity. Strangely enough, these three art forms share an important feature: They each allow information to be understood from multiple perspectives. Traditional narrative has tools such as foreshadowing and epiphany. Visual arts rely on point-perspective and foreshortening. Digital Interactivity uses iconography and expanding menus. These are all tools that do the same thing: convey perspective. This book examines an emerging art form that relies heavily on the role of perspective.

The first goal of this book is to broaden current thinking about narrative. An "Interactive Narrative" is a narrative form that allows someone other than the author to affect, choose, or change the plot. The author, in writing this narrative, allows the reader to interact with the story. This changes the role of the author; it changes what an author does—and in the case of narrative, that's to narrate. Therefore, traditional narration begins to require an expanded understanding.

The second goal is to broaden current thinking about interaction design. Many forms of "content" that are distributed via electronic media are based in narrative or contain narrative elements, but few of them have recognized the means of integrating narrative and interaction. Fewer still have even recognized the inherent value in doing so.

The book's third goal is to illustrate the role of imagery*. As narrative shifts from the linear progressions of text and speech to a more nonlinear and visual mode of communication, new methods of narrative are emerging. These days we rely less on the linear process of the spoken word because images can often convey the same information in a faster, more precise, and—in many cases—nonlinear fashion. They're worth a thousand words.

Any traditional, noninteractive story might be thought of as a single path through a structure of an interactive narrative. Despite the changes we see in television, Internet, movies, radio, print, and other media, we're still, effectually, thinking in Elizabethan terms when a story was originally defined in a linear system of a "Dramatic Arc."

This book, in presenting some of the guidelines of an emerging art form, intends to offer alternatives.

Although other forms of communication lend themselves to narrative (such as audio and video), I have chosen to focus, for this book, on imagery—mostly from the western tradition.

Our methods of telling stories and presenting information are being welded together.

These days, if you walk into a modern movie theater, a video game is sure to be lurking nearby. Sometimes the movie is about the video game (or vice versa). As you browse web pages, you can see video and animation woven into the page adjacent to the text. We see more picture books—magazines, newspapers, graphic novels, and catalogs—than we did 20 years ago. Many of these are merely references to other forms of narrative. Examples of such referential work are *TV Guide*, movie-based websites, or projects like Dark Horse's *HellBoy* comic series, in which a book and a CD-ROM are intended to be read together as a single story. We see this most commonly with video games and movies. *Star Wars, Tomb Raider, Anarchy Online, Everquest, Final Fantasy,* and even televised sports such as football seem to have more than one public face. Contemporary ad campaigns invent billboards that begin to tell stories over the course of a month and encourage us to solve this mystery by visiting a website.

Perhaps one of the strongest indications of this is the fact that a multimillion dollar, multimillion user interactive narrative was distributed several months before the movie *A.I.* was released. The narrative, taking place in the same universe, but with a completely different plot, was used as a means of integrating the movie into the real world [2.5.2].

Meanwhile, the integration of traditional narrative and digital interaction are warming the relationship of the disparate languages of books and computers.

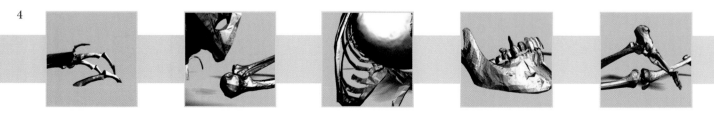

1.1.2: The Importance of Opinion and Perspective

All stories contain a perspective. In the case of movies, it's a camera. In the case of writing, it's the writer (consider Borges' short story of nested perspectives "The Immortal"*), and in the case of a narrative image, it is often the painter.

Until recently, narrative has been, most simply, a process of narration. A narrator tells us something—a story, information, etc. But these words and their meaning are, naturally, mutations from earlier languages. The word "narrate" itself originated from the Latin word "narrare," which evolved from the Indo-European word "gnarus" meaning "to know." Therefore, a narrator has knowledge about something and tells us about it. Perhaps a narrator can be thought of as an interface designer, as someone who is collecting information and determining the best method of presentation.

But none of us knows everything. We all have our perspectives and opinions. Even the "objective" news sources, such as National Public Radio or the British Broadcasting Corporation, hand-pick phrases that appeal to specific audiences. This means that, despite our best efforts to be objective, an opinion is implied. Historic narratives, too, are based in opinion. History is written (or so it's said) by the winners. All narration picks which events get presented, in what order, and how.

But that's okay. When we listen to someone tell a story, we listen to his or her particular perspective. We listen to what that person experienced or thought, and the personal angle that he or she brings to that small history is the part that's interesting.

Even a narration of simple events in a newscast requires some perspective to exist. A narrative in this way is almost like a kind of image—It can't exist without a perspective of some sort. The context of the person telling the story, the specifics of the way that it's told, and the pieces that are chosen to be relayed all inform the perspective. The particular relationship between the teller and the listener informs the perspective as well.

In the context of storytelling, perspective may be the only thing that exists.

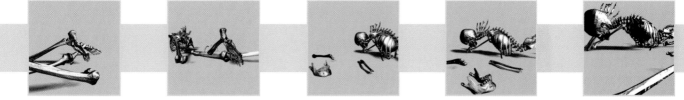

Jorge Luis Borges frequently built stories inside of stories, telling stories from the perspective of a writer whose work was being read by the story's narrator. One of the best-known versions of this idea was the revelation of the "Aleph," the mystical letter through which the whole universe can be seen. The entire universe can be found in this "Aleph." "The Immortal" is the first short story of this highly recommended work.

1.2: Perspective

Perspective is a critical characteristic of narrative, but there are at least two kinds of perspective: emotional (or cognitive) and dimensional (or visual).

If you look at most buildings made with 90-degree angles, the lines that are parallel with the ground appear to be angled to one side. When you look at these angles, you know they're made of 90-degree angles but, if you hold a protractor out at arm's length, they don't look 90 degrees. And as you look down the street you notice that the roofs of the buildings are slanting toward a single point on the horizon where everything seems to collapse into itself. That "vanishing point" is a strange place. It identifies where you are standing. This is where your "perspective" ends.

The vanishing point is a point in linear perspective at which all lines that are parallel in an environment collapse and at which all elements in that space cease to exist.

It's also a place that we learned about only relatively recently.

1.2.1: A Genealogy of Perspective

At the end of the 13th century, a painter named Giotto di Bondone would sit with his teacher Giovanni Cimabue, spending their afternoons on street corners in Rome, staring at buildings, stretching strings in the air, and drawing.

When Cimabue and Giotto looked at the buildings across the street—wood and glass boxes made of 90-degree angles—they saw roofs that appeared to be twisted and bent to the side. Despite the appearance, they knew these buildings were made of right angles. As they held string in the air and followed these angles, they began to see spatial relationships, and their understandings of what they were seeing was sharpened.

This invention (or discovery) of perspective had a deep impact on Giotto. While he was painting the fables and myths of his time, he was doing something very new with the discovery (or invention) of vanishing point from both a dimensional and emotional standpoint. He was depicting the physical and geometric location he was standing in, which put the viewer in Giotto's dimensional perspective while he was painting.

Prior to this time, paintings of the Western tradition lacked this sense of location, the visual vocabulary to achieve the relocation of the viewer, and the sense of actually being there as a witness to the events. Putting the viewer in a new dimensional perspective also affected the viewer's emotional perspective.

This is something we still see today in most forms of image presentation. Traditional western movies, such as *The Good, The Bad, and The Ugly*, or *Shootout at the OK Corral*, show characters from knee level. Clint Eastwood towers over the camera, a giant of a man, dust on his boots, six-shooter in his fingers, twitching for battle. But he's seen at these moments from a specific dimensional angle. These camera angles present a character who's meant to be seen as important or dominating when viewed from a lower dimensional perspective. We're meant to think, "He's bigger than me," which then gives the character an emotional perspective of importance or power. Mystery, another kind of emotional perspective, is also built this way. When we can't see around a corner, we're left wondering.

Thus dimensional perspective affects emotional perspective. This is old news for most film directors, architects, and sculptors.

Giotto, born in Tuscany circa 1267, lived until 1337 when he died in Milan. Cimabue, his instructor, died circa 1300, but his birth date is not known.

Giotto spent a tremendous amount of time painting facial expressions. So, while putting the viewer in his own dimensional—or visual—perspective, he was also putting the viewer in his own emotional perspective.

Doing this increased viewers' participation in the work on both an emotional and visual level. There is a relationship between them. One is outside the skull—it's what's presented on the canvas or screen. The other is happening inside—it's what the viewer is imagining or feeling. Both relate to what is being seen.

Meanwhile, as Giotto was working in churches, busily mixing his paints, other inventions were crackling into existence. The glass mirror was discovered, spectacles were invented, block printing was the hip new trend in Italy, Thomas (The Bull) Aquinas was quietly scribbling the *Summa Theologica*, and highway tolls were making a big comeback in England. Things weren't so different then as now—change was underfoot and mainstream society was fascinated, watching it unfold.

What was different then, though, was how people—and specifically visual artists—viewed people. Giotto was working at the sunset of the Medieval Ages, just prior to the dawn of the Renaissance. He was working at a time when the invention of stories mattered less than their interpretation. The people of this era were interested in the retelling of stories (rather than the invention of new ones, as we are today). The Annunciation or The Passion, for example, were stories that had been interpreted and re-interpreted thousands of times by as many people. Each interpretation presented a new angle on the story they already knew.

Giotto was obsessed with individuality and the pathos of the individual. These ideas give his painting a subtlety that's still touching and somehow both familiar and alien. The faces of his characters are soft; sometimes a lower lip is pooched out, a hesitant hand is lifted, or a forehead is wrinkled.

The perspectives being painted are those of both the painter and of the subject. In this way, Giotto was both inventing and interpreting.

Giotto wasn't simply interested in the visual perspective of an individual in a story—he was obsessed with it. Giotto was equally obsessed with the emotional perspective of that individual. For him the dimensional and emotional perspectives were linked and even informed one another.

It's worth looking at the Church of San Francesco, in Assisi, where Giotto did some of his best work. His obsession is most evident here. Each bay of each nave in the church is divided into three sections by columns that stab into the ceiling, dividing the architectural space that Giotto put to use as a painting surface. It's a physical division. When seen from an angle, the paintings appear to be scooped or slanted, resting at an odd angle. If you stand about two meters in front of the painting, with your head in just the right location, the geometry of the painting aligns with the geometry of the church. Suddenly the oddly angled lines snap into a horizon, walls lift out of the jumbled geometry, and a virtual space falls back into the wall in front of you. It gives the distinct impression of looking into a series of virtual rooms.

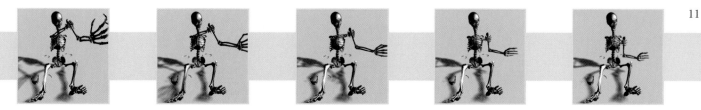

But you have to adjust your head—quite literally. These spaces are about the size of a shoebox. It's a specific location where you need to stand to see it, but it's clearly what the painter had intended. It's as if Giotto's ghost is there, standing behind the visitor, guiding them, telling them where to stand, his fingers gently on their temples, his voice whispering in their ear, "Fermi li, rimani in piedi li."*

It was this approach—let's call it a Perspectivist Approach—that allowed Giotto to depict for the viewer both the dimensional perspective and the emotional perspective of the people in these stories he was painting. But it's a four-fold perspective: the point of view of both the subject matter and the visitor, represented dimensionally and emotionally. This crossroads of architecture, the church, painting, and mathematics, were the crossroads where Giotto worked. And it was at these crossroads that Giotto, sitting with his strings in the air, next to his teacher Cimabue, discovered the vanishing point.

And vanishing point gave us perspective.
And perspective is a point of view.

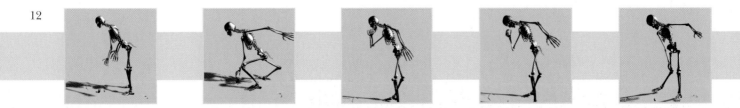

The curtains rise on the 16th century. We're still in Italy, though now a bit north, in Florence. Booksellers, printers, and type foundries are now distinct industries. The postal service is the new privilege of the middle class, and a German sailor named Martin Behaim (an interface designer) has made a spherical map of the earth called a "globe."

The greatest hits of Aristotle and Aristophanes were making a big comeback with their recent reprints, and italic print was invented to facilitate the new burst of translations. In 1504, Raphael Sanzio, a painter and a contemporary of Michelangelo, used mirrors and a primitive photographic device (called a camera obscura) to shed enough light on the mysteries of perspective to continue the work Giotto had started. These events changed how people saw the world, and inventions such as the globe, camera obscura, and mirror were the tools that have since affected our modern perspectives.

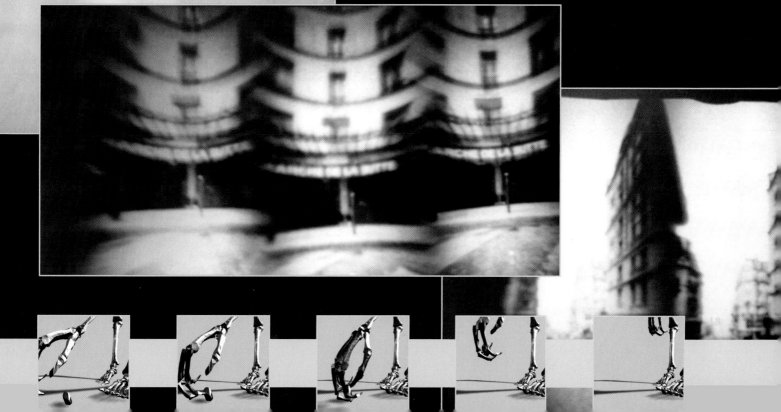

In retrospect, the work of these people and
the effects of their technology is evident:

Despite the bouts of famine, syphilis, and plague, this was a reassuring period. First, this dramatization of linear perspective and vanishing point put the observer on par with the observed. This was risky business when you stop to consider that the mother and son of God were the images being depicted as if the viewer were somehow in the same room or on the same level. The church was known to have severe reactions to unapproved methods of interpretation. Second, because the observer was being considered by the painter as the painting was composed, or laid out, it also gave the observer the perspective of the painter, which was, in those days when painting was in some cases actually prayed to, quite powerful. Third, and most importantly, the invention of linear perspective gave humanity an appropriate point-of-view where everything could be seen at once. With this introduction of perspective, the entire world that was depicted in the painting was presented from the best possible vantage point to provide the densest information at an appropriate moment.

It was the beginning of a kind of telescoping. It was the beginning of a compression of information—a form of interface design that allowed the most important information to be presented at the most appropriate time from the appropriate angle. That's what everyone still wants: to be able to see it all, from our single point of view, at just the right time, and know that we "get the picture."

These trends that developed out of the first half of the millennium influence how we see the world today. Our modern means of telling stories are the children of these parents of perspective.

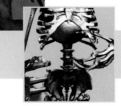

1.2.2: Objective Linear Perspective

By the 1700s, interest in the perspective of the individual shifted to interest that was outside of sense-based perception, such as sight and sound. Communicating this perspective was, at the time, one of the primary roles of mathematics. The three Laws of Motion* had been published, the pendant barometer invented, and the Rococo period was in full bloom, filling the Western world with the cloying trends of domesticity, mathematical harmony, and the taming of nature. Times were changing, and our interest in control was increasing.

This interest in control and mathematical rigor had much to do with a perspective that belonged to no one in particular, but everyone in general. It was an objective perspective. But, ironically, it's the individual perspective that allows perspective to exist at all. Millions of people can't all stand in the same place and still view the world from the same perspective.

It didn't seem to matter—we had new inventions to keep us busy. In the mid-1800s, Monsieur L.J.M. Daguerre was dabbling with silver-coated plates of copper and capturing—as if by a butterfly net—actual light.

But something was missing through the 18th and 19th centuries. It was something that Giotto had started to introduce hundreds of years earlier, something to which we're only now returning—the importance of the individual's perspective.

Isaac Newton's Laws of Motion: LAW 1: Every body continues in its state of rest or of uniform motion in a right line unless it is compelled to change that state by forces impressed upon it. LAW 2: The change of motion is proportional to the motive force impressed and is made in the direction of the right line in which that force is impressed. LAW 3: To every action there is always opposed and equal reaction; or, the mutual actions of two bodies upon each other are always equal and directed to contrary parts. Less notably but of equal importance for some of us, billiards was introduced just a few years later in bars and coffeehouses of Berlin.

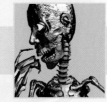

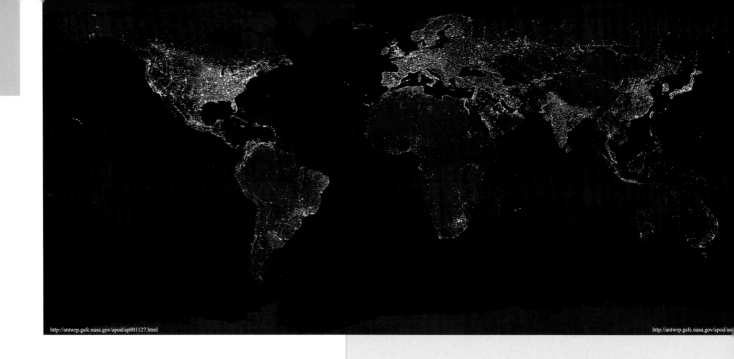

1.2.3:   Subjective Linear Perspective

The more things change, the more they become their opposite. First, Giotto helped push the Medieval Ages out of a period of authority and objective authorship (namely, that of the Church's) into a period of humanism in which the individual perspective came to be seen as an entity of its own. Then the Renaissance took advantage of that shift and, by extension of those ideas, pushed it into increasingly extreme arenas until the clergymen and clerics became scientists and mathematicians. The objective approach to perspective came back in fashion at that time of the 1800s. Fast forward another two hundred years, and now, a population of more than six billion people, flying over the planet's surface, communicating across massive distances at instantaneous speeds, delivering addresses over the television, firing TCP packets back and forth across continents, are all presenting individual opinions.

And it's happening in a way where there no longer appears to be a single authority, author, or authorization needed to get the opinions and point of views across the globe. We now are all authors and readers in a tangle of communication and multiheaded interaction.

The arrival of new technologies and their use in our culture has seen, especially in the course of the last 50 years, an increased emphasis on the perspective of the individual.

We know about this. This is the time is where contemporary—and interactive—narrative begins.

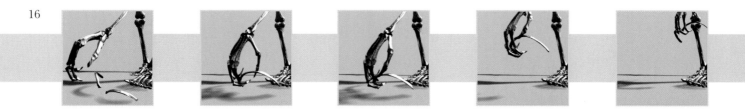

1.2.4: The Perspectivist Approach

Earlier we called Giotto a "Perspectivist." This is to say that Giotto had an approach that allowed him to consider the painting's multiple viewers from both an emotional and dimensional perspective. The painting was then composed with that person's specific emotional and dimensional perspectives in mind. These perspectives were not separated, but parts of the same unit.

The Perspectivist Approach is the fundamental mindset of any author of interactive narrative. This approach comprises two principles.

First, it bridges foreground to background. It resets the spatial relationships between people and their surroundings. The integration of the imagery with the walls of the church is as good an example of this as any. The place is a part of the experience. This is a way of looking at dimension and image from a holistic point of view. It doesn't necessarily separate the painting from the wall, but considers the totality of the environment as a single mode of communication.

Second, it bridges context to decision. The Perspectivist Approach looks at the environment and its context as being a thing that braces the actions of the occupants of that environment. A fish swims because it is in the water. A bird flies because it is in the air. St. Francis expels the demons because they're inhabiting Arezzo.

If you have foreground, background, context, and decision, you have the bricks of which the plot structures of interactive narrative are built.

1.3: Narrative

Literature is language charged with meaning.

—Ezra Pound

Surprisingly, both the denizens of the Internet and their fearless leaders remain largely clueless about the currency of their medium. Most websites understand the Internet as being little more than a globally distributed brochure. The interactive, social, and narrative capabilities of the web remain unexplored, so the return on the investment that most companies made is still simply an investment that's burning fuel on the launch pad. This lack of understanding contributed to the Internet downturn of the late '90s. The majority of the sites that have returned revenues have usually involved a synthesis of commerce and community.

The Internet is fueled by two commodities: Attention and Reputation.

America Online, for example, has managed to convince its users to pay for what others are giving away. In fact, they've convinced their users to pay for what others are paying to give away. Due to the fact that the money-meter is always running, AOL users pay to upload their writing while other users are paying to download that same content. So, in effect, the users pay to allow AOL to profit from their contributions. Additionally, AOL managed to convince these same users that all of the rest of the content of the web should follow this same commodity model. Their users quite literally bought this story and assumed that AOL, a subset of the Internet, subsumed the Internet and was their gateway, or "portal" to it.

AOL's approach is a vitriolic and intelligent commodification of the users of the service (or, more accurately, those users' attention and reputation). In fact, it was an intelligent commodification of the unassuming public and our markets of stock and trade in that the company was able to use Internet stock funny-money "assets" to buy Time-Warner, and most notably their flagship subsidiary, CNN.

But AOL could have done much more and, currently in league with Time-Warner, it's positioned to take advantage of the benefits of interactive narrative in the coming decades. The recent integration of *Harry Potter* movie releases and the interactive vignettes that have appeared on America Online are early indicators that they're waking up to these capacities. It seems likely that they will distribute largely narrative-based content. But how they integrate this with their previous model is the interesting question of "How do we use interactive narrative to make us some money?" Simply, we will soon see "AOL users" becoming "AOL writers." More so than we do now. This might be among the reasons AOL Instant Messenger was so important. The ways in which writing is becoming interactive will surely affect narrative's future.

We'll have to wait and change.

Those sites that featured some form of narrative (occasionally named "Content") relied on traditional modes of impression-based advertising and "click-thrus," assuming that their audiences would tolerate this outdated form of informational pollution called "Advertising." In many cases, they've been right; users, specifically American users, have tolerated this. But if the authors of these sites understood the value of narrative in their "Content Offerings" and how interactive narrative works, they might have changed their financial models and means of making money.

The model is very much like the BBS, or bulletin board service. As some users build, more users are interested and the guy in the middle collects the coins. Ultima Online and other gaming systems understood the Internet well enough to take advantage of these approaches. This is the commodity of attention.

We'll see this sort of approach become increasingly common. AOL and other "portals" will begin to integrate large-scale multi-user environments that are narrative based. Users will feel more emotionally connected to what they are uploading and will include their friends and associates in the process. It's a matter of integrating projects like *Simnet* or *Everquest* ith the cultural models of the bulletin-board service, or BBS (on which AOL still relies). This is the commodity of reputation.

Banja won the 2001 Ars Electronica Golden Nica, the highest international award for digital art. A few months later, it also received the Europrix 2001 for the best interactive fiction and storytelling. Banja can be found at http://www.banja.com.

In the small town of Lille, France, this traditional BBS model is being cracked. Team ChMan—the producers of labyrinthine and a very rich narrative named *Banja**—has done an excellent job of pointing a direction for communities that integrate narrative and interaction. *Banja* is a story about a character (named "Banja") who lives in a world with a population of other characters. Although there is a consistent metaphor, storyline, and interface to the entire community, there is a series of services, games, and online community activities that make this a promising competitor for a system like AOL.

Corporations—whether they're online gaming companies, interactive television networks, wireless networks, or Internet conglomerates—would be well advised to provide large-scale metaphors (such as e-world or Ultima online) that encourage their audience to come and assist in the building process. This process made the web successful in the early 1990s, and it wasn't because of the technology.

Meanwhile, as far as storytelling is concerned, we should get set for a long maturation cycle.

Consider the four major trends that literature has seen so far: Epic, Gospel, Romance, and Essay. It began with the Epic (stories about battle in which the individual embodies social values). This was the first major trend in literature. Epic literature is about the hero's fight to freedom in books such as *The Iliad*, *The Odyssey*, or *The Aeneid*. This first literary trend was followed by Gospel (stories about religion that served as moral instructives) and marked the second major trend of literature. Examples include the Old and New Testament, Thomas Aquinas, and, perhaps, Machiavelli. The third trend in literature was Romance (stories about human interaction with nature in a realm of magic). And, in the last few hundred years, we've seen the emergence of the most personal of perspectives and, in many ways, an inversion of EpiczEssays. These are personal perspectives in which, as an inversion of the Epic, the social values embody the individual. Montaigne's *Essays*, Boswell's *Life of Samuel Johnson*, or James Joyce's *Portrait Of The Artist As A Young Man* are each healthy examples of this latest trend.

So it's not surprising that, at this nascent stage, shootem-up video games are the primary form of interactive narrative. They're the Epic form of the interactive narrative. If Gospel doesn't follow, then Romance might, but projects such as *Banja* show us that we have options other than slash-and-stash video games.

1.3.1: The Changing Definitions of "Narrative"

Here, in the tradition of the Western world, narration has come from the single voice of the narrator. It has been a spoken tradition of narration. But what if there are multiple people working on it? What if it's a visual narrative? What if it's entirely silent and nonlinear? What if it's a play in 18th century London, or a movie in 21st century Los Angeles, or TCP/IP packets from Quebec? People talk about "High Narrative," "Episodic Narrative," "Guttural Narrative," "Multilinear Narrative," and "Narrator's Narrative." What do these things mean?

In order to know what interactive narrative is we need to clarify the term

"narrative."

Narratif (ve), n.m.. Récit, exposé détaillé d'une suite de faits.

Narrative (n): 1 : something that is narrated : STORY 2 : the art or practice of narration 3 : the representation in art of an event or story; also : an example of such a representation

Erzählung <f,; -, -en>
1 <i. w. S.> Bericht, Beschreibung, Schilderung von wirkl. od. erdachten Begebenheiten; jmds. ~ mit Interesse zuhören; die ~ ist frei erfunden

Aristotelian Definition

The Poetics, oneof the very first serious treatises on narrative and dramatic structure, was a series of lectures and writings delivered by Aristotle*. *Poetics* defines the plot (this important part of narrative) as an imitation of an action that has a beginning, a middle, and an end. Aristotle explains it like this:

> *"We've considered that a tragedy is an imitation of an action that is complete in itself because it's a whole of some quantity (because a whole doesn't have to have a quantity). Now a whole is something that has a beginning, a middle, and an end. A beginning isn't necessarily after something else but is followed by something. An end naturally follows something—either as necessary or as consequential—and has nothing following it. And a middle follows something and is followed by something else. Therefore a well-constructed plot cannot begin or end at any point the author would like. Beginning and end have to follow the forms described."*

—Book 7, *Poetics*

There aren't many guidelines for what makes a story interesting, exciting, or unnerving or how a story begins or ends. But this passage does identify that there are parts that work together to form a beginning, middle, and end. Aristotle points out that, basically, there are causes and effects that occur over time.

It's worth noting that Aristotle was considering a world in which stories were occasionally read, but more often orally narrated.

Freytag Definition

We can also consider the analysis of Gustav Freytag*, the German novelist, dramatist, and critic who invented a familiar diagram commonly called the Freytag Triangle (or Curve, Arc, or Pyramid). This 19th century gentleman, apparently dissatisfied with Aristotle's holistic approach, sliced the classic plot into three primary servings. His rework of Aristotle's definition pointed to the increase, culmination, and decrease of the plot. Plot is expressed as a function of time along a horizontal axis. The density of plot, or the interest that the reader has, is expressed along a vertical axis. This "thickening" of the plot is a reader's (and author's) concentration on a problem that is being solved. Perhaps feeling some pressure from the abstraction of Aristotle's definition and living in a time when narrative was beginning to change, Freytag broke the structure of narrative into three primary movements.

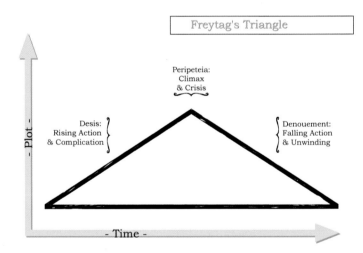

Freytag's Triangle

Peripeteia: Climax & Crisis

Desis: Rising Action & Complication

Denouement: Falling Action & Unwinding

- Plot -

- Time -

Freytag (1816–1895) wrote a book called *Technique of Drama*, which was published in 1863. He outlined his famous triangle there and presents the different angles of narrative with it. In his exposition, he used the actions of the main character to determine the rise or fall of the plot.

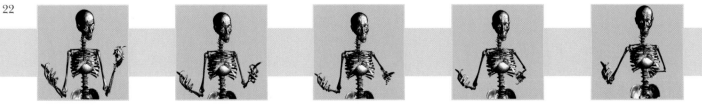

The "Peripeteia" is the problem and the "Denouement" is the process of solving that problem. This implies that every narrative will have (in addition to Aristotle's beginning, middle, and end) a series of time-driven events that hit a "peak" at which the complexity of the plot is a maximum along a continuum of time.

The Freytag Triangle makes some sense because it can represent very complicated narrative arcs. One of the defining characteristics of a novel is that it contains multiple plots. For example, Dostoevsky's *Brothers Karamavoz* contains at the very least three simultaneous plots, and each of these contains subplots that have their own pyramid structures, making Freytag's Triangle into something that can be continually subdivided.

But this basic diagram of the Freytag Triangle hasn't been emblematic of all narrative since Elizabethan times. The diagram is great for linear narrative or narrative that is interested in presenting a problem and then solving it. Edgar Allan Poe, however, as one inventor of the Mystery Genre, wasn't as interested in presenting the problems as presenting the solutions to them. Poe simply lopped off the "Desis" and the most revealing portion of the "Peripeteia," allowing the gradual solution of the problem to serve as the story itself. He was interested in what cause produced which effect. If the effect is the characters looking for clues to the crime, then the crime was generally committed early in the story. This isn't true of his work universally, but it does help to see into the heart of narrative literature structure as it's been evolving over the centuries: Readers tend toward a process of investigation.

Poe wanted to bring his readers closer to the story. To do this, Poe turned the reader into an investigator. This brings us one step closer to interactivity.

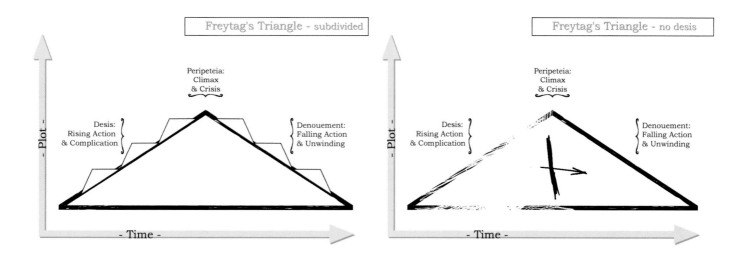

The Crisis, or Problem, of Narrative

For an author, the plot determines the actions that appear in a linear narrative. The plot doesn't exist if there is no time in the story (a series of actions can't exist if there is no time, so the plot couldn't either). Time determines speed, pacing, suspense, and movement. Plot is there for the what and how. Time is there for the when. But it's the coordination of these two that make an interesting story.

The problem, or "conflict," of a story is the heart of the dramatic arc. The nature of the problem, when it occurs in the story, and how it is solved are the things that determine the quality and quantity of a narrative. The problems or "conflicts" most authors choose tend to be something universal because it becomes a story that appeals to a larger population. It also becomes a story that addresses important issues because these are problems that humans have been struggling with throughout history. Fear, Struggle, Love, Desire, and Society are all issues that are both universal and personal, and it's the specific relationship of the personal to the universal that makes them so poignant for a reader.

The "problems" and their solutions are told from the perspective of a narrator. This is the basic approach of the story. The specifics of the problem and the perspective can determine the story's success. Regardless of the choice of the story material, stories are generally structured as Freytag and Aristotle point out because this is how writers have traditionally been able to captivate their readers. This is because they are writers. Ironically, the writers are mimicking the orators. But it works. This is how Shakespeare is able to turn the description of love into a feeling of love, through a familiar process of oration. It's one thing to read about the love of Romeo and Juliet. It's a different thing to feel it on a personal level.

Or maybe not. But there is something going on inside of our skulls when we read this. There is a symbology and imagery that we, the listeners, generate. This symbolism and imagery create feeling from the linear process of reading and listening.

How camest thou hither, tell me, and wherefore?
The orchard walls are high and hard to climb,
And the place death, considering who thou art,
If any of my kinsmen find thee here.

With love's light wings did I o'erperch these walls,
For stony limits cannot hold love out,
And what love can do, that dares love attempt;
Therefore thy kinsmen are no stop to me.

If they do see thee, they will murther thee.

Alack, there lies more peril in thine eye
Than twenty of their swords! Look thou but sweet,
And I am proof against their enmity.

I would not for the world they saw thee here.

Writing and reading is a very detailed relationship of symbology, even a layering of symbols. In this example, the symbology practically flies in your face. Love has wings, it has flown into a dark place where it may be killed, and, as an overall metaphor for the story, this symbol is how Romeo and Juliet first confirm their love for one another. The symbols and the relationships of the symbols are the very heart of the writing. The symbology that is used represents the actual problem, or crisis, of the story. The writing is often, as is the case with Shakespeare and hundreds of other authors, a symbology of symbols. Thomas Pynchon, for example, uses the arc of the story to represent the arc of missiles that are discussed in *Gravity's Rainbow*. In "The Aleph," Jorge Luis Borges uses the image of an infinite library to describe a story he tells about the same. The symbols are a layering process. The author relies on this foundation of the simplest symbols—letters—to then build more symbols through words, phrases, paragraphs, and chapters, introduces a layer of context to that symbology, and, finally (as with epiphany, foreshadowing, and foreshortening) provides a particular perspective on a particular plot.

And so a narrative is built, symbol by symbol, brick by brick.

1.3.2: Reading, Writing, and the Blurry Lines in Between

Writing is an interface between the medium and the message, and between the author and the reader. Humans are adept at this basic process of turning symbols into meaning. Text is a very old interface. Therefore, authors and illustrators bend it to new uses whenever the opportunity is available. Software designers, also, have relied heavily on this in their work.

Software development is similar to writing. It's a generation and presentation of symbols for the sake of communicating a more complicated series of relationships. A programmer writes lines of code, in a language, "authoring" a particular executable.

Simply put, running an application is an interactive form of reading.

When reading a book or even a sentence, there is a beginning step. A book and a sentence both have a beginning that is formally denoted. There is a middle and, hopefully, there is a solution to a problem that is posed. The reader is recognizing symbols and making associations. The reader controls the pacing, the level of participation, and the dwell-time (that is, how long he spends with the text he is reading). But the part that interests the reader are the symbols and the solution of the problem set. Consider the desktop metaphor. The symbols of the desktop represent relationships between other things. These relationships inform the user of the software's function and their capabilities as a user.

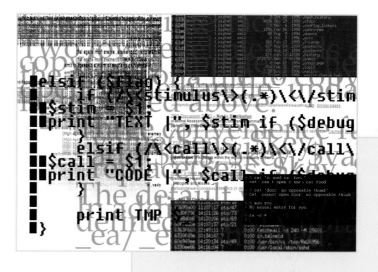

Or consider Microsoft Excel. Launching an application follows the same steps as reading: a beginning step is followed by the middle, which offers a solution, and then the process is closed. In formal programming terms, these are referred to as ("init"), ("run"), and ("quit"). In Java, this is formalized literally as a part of the language, in, for example, the "applet" structure. The user of the program, however, recognizes symbols for the sake of solving a problem. The user determines the pacing, the level of participation, and the "dwell time," or length of time he spends using the application. In the end, he or she is most interested in the solution of the problem or set of problems. A user, after launching an application, ends up participating in a form of reading.

It's no real stretch to say that running an application—specifically applications that include an interface of symbology, such as a GUI (Graphical User Interface)—is a form of reading. With that idea in mind, we will, in this book, refer to all video game, web, and computer users, in general, as "readers."

An interface designer or a programmer may be considered a writer. Interface design relies on symbology, signs, metaphors, and codes. These are the same tools that a writer uses. This is certainly the verb that is used in some software development circles: "writing code" is a term commonly used. The product of their effort is written lines of text, and the person at the other end of the line is a reader. Steven Johnson*, in his book *Interface Culture*, rightly points out that the interface sits between the medium and the message. This is as true with a book as it is with a software application.

What is more is that the reader—or user—acts as a kind of secondary writer while he is participating in this form of interactive reading. The reader, in the case of applications that require input (such as Excel), is also adding information and meaning. Subsequently, the reader becomes a writer as well. The roles of the reader and writer get blurry because both roles (reader and writer) are adding information and meaning to a dataset.

This blurring of roles is one of the inherent characteristics of interactive narrative. This is also what makes it difficult for us to understand.

But, there doesn't appear to be a whole lot of "plot" in Microsoft Excel. It's staid, boring, and mathematical. It's missing soul and passion compared to a work by Dostoyevsky or Poe. The interactivity has little soul or meaning to the process of running an application; therefore, this notion of "reading" Microsoft Excel or "writing" to the spreadsheet is an anemic form of creativity.

Is plot what's missing? We want, when we read, some form of story, or plot. This makes the material being read relevant to our lives.

The Plot and the Use-Case Scenario

The word "plot" comes from the early days of French and means, as it's still used in English and French, "a portion of land." Why would the idea of a plot be used to represent a story? Is a story a kind of topology?

As we've pointed out, a plot is the author's planned organization of the events of the story. Plot, in determining What and How, is a topology, but it's a planned topology that has an implied opinion and perspective. A story's organization is essentially the author guiding the reader through the solution of the problem that the narrative presents.

Let's assume that there are three parts to any plot (as per Aristotle and Freytag, et al) 1) the "Desis" (beginning) or the introduction of the problem, 2) the "Peripeteia" (middle) or the problem itself and 3) the "Denouement" (end) or process of solving the problem. Mixed in here we have all of the symbology that makes the plot interesting and allows the reader the ability to understand what's happening.

In software development and documentation, there's a concept called "Use-Case Scenarios." These charts are interesting because they diagram the function, flow, time, and interaction between a user (or reader) and a particular piece of software. An example of a simple use-case scenario might look like this:

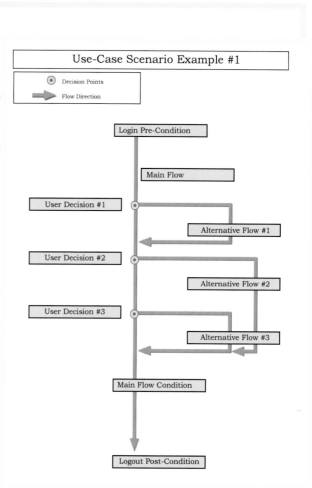

The equivalent to plot, in the interactive world of software design, is the use-case scenario.

Just because all use-case scenarios don't follow the Freytag or Aristotelian structure doesn't mean they aren't a story structure any more than ending a piece of music without a tonic note indicates that it's not music. Dessert doesn't have to be served for a meal to exist. Liturgies don't need to be played for someone to die, and a denouement doesn't have to exist for a story to be compelling.* Calling a use-case scenario a plot is an over-simplification, but the basic function of tying events together as a function of time is the same.

A use-case scenario and a plot are similar. They're both read, both present a problem to be solved, both work by using symbologies that are used to generate larger meaning, and both are authored environments that are meant to be read by another party.

Whether it qualifies as classic drama is not our concern. Whether it qualifies as potentially compelling narrative is.

New art forms change old rules.

We're getting closer to understanding a kind of narrative that can be interactive. We at least have possibilities to consider. A use-case scenario, like a spreadsheet, still doesn't feel like a narrative because it lacks a sense of story that is being told by someone. We might be able to apply a use-case scenario and tease out a form of interactive plot, but this still doesn't mean that it's worth reading as an engaging narrative.

Microsoft Excel doesn't "imitate life," as Aristotle explains a drama should. The imitation of life (and the interpretation of that imitation from a reader's perspective) is what differentiates a narrative from other forms of writing. This is why characters are such an important part of a story. Characters, be they protagonists, antagonists, or narrators, offer perspective, deliver opinion, provide interpretation, and generate a kind of emotional foundation the story is built upon. The plot alone, regardless of how carefully it's diagrammed, gives little to the story as it's perceived by the reader. To return to a previous example, this is another method Shakespeare uses to turn the description of Juliet's love into a feeling of love: through the characters.

A character that is present in an environment, someone who cares about something, someone who has some form of opinion, perspective, or passion, is something that gives a narrative a life.

The Moral of the Story

We've been referring to the development of applications as writing and the use of applications as interactive reading. Narration can play a role in this. The key difference between narration and this software-related writing is the opinion implied in the story—the individual perspective. The human element of interpretation needs to be present for writing to become narration.

A piece of writing requires an opinion—call it perspective or call it point of view—before it becomes a narrative. If this isn't self-evident, read the output of an Excel spreadsheet. If you still see a narrative line (such as the birth and death of a company), then it's worth recognizing that it's the opinion of that data that instills a sense of narrative. If you still see a narrative you're working too much.

Narrative requires opinion. But we're not suggesting that the opinion has to be of the narrator or the reader. This is a big swerve from the course of traditional narrative because, traditionally, the narrative opinion is the opinion of the author. Sometimes, with narrative that contains interactivity, the interpretation is made collaboratively (or simultaneously) by both the author and the reader.

A moral that concludes a story is generally a summation of the opinion of the story; it's a distillation of the story's purpose. Without it, the story wouldn't exist. The moral of our story here is that all narrative needs an opinion. This might also be called a perspective. Finally, this function of personal perspective and interpretation is more important to interactive narrative than is the curve that Gustav Freytag outlined. The Freytag diagram could contain the process of using Microsoft Excel. But we all know that this is not a narrative form. It's the human element of the perspective that's significant in stories, not the quantities or its charts.

Stories seem to be a way in which we report to one another on the events of life. We don't need machines to do that. We need individual opinion and perspective.

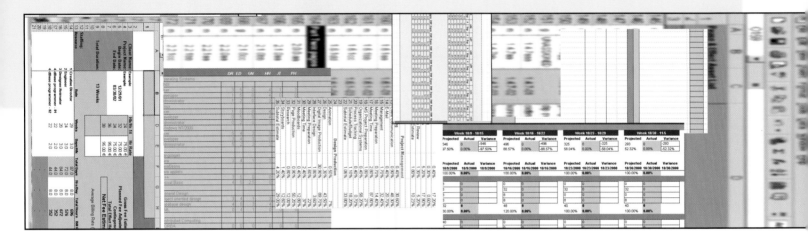

1.3.3: Tropes and Other Figures of Speech

"The greatest thing by far is to be a master of metaphor. It is the one thing that cannot be learned from others; it is also a sign of genius, since a good metaphor implies an eye for resemblance."

—Aristotle, *Poetics*

Metaphors are the foundation for visual design, narrative, interaction design, and fine art. A metaphor is a set of symbols that has enough redundant information that a new meaning emerges [1.4.4]. A metaphor is a pattern that provides a telescoped perspective on a different set of information.

Metaphors don't care whether you know the equation or not—they just give you the sum. Metaphors build on an assumed basis of knowledge and they also include a strong emotional punch being both more concrete and direct than maxims or aphorisms. What's more interesting is that they rely on both the author's and the reader's imaginations to fill in the gaps. Metaphor informs us on how to modulate our action by influencing our thinking and perception. Metaphor magnifies implications, sorts the clutter of imagery we carry around in our heads, and connects pieces that weren't. By placing a metaphor between two ideas, the reader gets a whole new picture. A metaphor is another kind of lens. A metaphor adds information by comparison.

No man is an island.
- John Donne

You ain't nothin but a hound dog.
- Elvis Presley

I am the bread of life
- The Book of John 6:35

The best graphic design, story, or interaction design contains a metaphor. The metaphor can be explicitly spelled out as "desktop" or "dungeon," or it might be something that is implied through the continued use and interaction with a system. The more it is implied, the more it is abstracted. Abstraction almost always needs to be used for any metaphor to exist. Abstraction of metaphor, as long as it has some form of self-consistency, is fine, provided it serves the reader with increased amounts of information and redundancy. Just as a desk was considered an environment that facilitated information management, so it was used as the metaphor for the modern computer.

More than 10 years ago, Ted Nelson, one of the pioneers of hypertext design, pointed out some flaws with the desktop metaphor, saying,

"We are told that this is a "metaphor" for a "desktop." But I have never personally seen a desktop where pointing at a lower piece of paper makes it jump to the top, or where placing a sheet of paper on top of a file folder caused the folder to gobble it up; I do not believe such desks exist; and I do not think I would want one if it did."

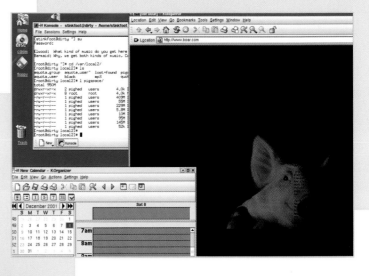

His point is that the more a metaphor relies on an example, the more it should follow that example's characteristics. That's not entirely right because we, as humans, have the ability to separate and contextualize meaning from information. Nelson is pointing out that a high degree of consistency should be used in metaphor. He's pointing out inconsistencies in the design metaphor of the desktop.

Finally, for our use here, a metaphor is a consistent relationship of symbols, as are fables and myths (the most complicated form of figures of speech and an advanced, narrative form of metaphor). A myth generally has an invented, original metaphor. This opinion, this invention, is what makes it a myth.

Fables, allegories, and myths are another step up the ladder of implied meaning, but they also differ from metaphors because the context isn't generally implied and, because of this, the real meaning of the narrative usually comes last. In some cases, in more complicated fables, the meaning and context don't become clear until the very last sentence. "And they lived happily ever after" is a classic.

So finally, it's all in your skull. And the author's. Somewhere between the two of you there's an interface of symbology, perspective, and perception of meaning. The interpretation of the meaning is what makes reading a story worth the effort.

Oddly enough, this is the case with literature, paintings, and, these days, interface design as well.

1.3.4: The Relationship Between Imagery and Narrative

It's natural that interactive narrative includes imagery. Narration is not limited to text. Narration originated in speech and has been neatly transferred to text, but text is a close cousin of image, and an image can be a kind of "non-verbal text" (as it's called in many educational and academic circles). The relationship between text and image now ranges from complementary to competitive. Magazines, television, the Internet, newspapers, dashboards, money, clocks, comics, packaging, advertising, clothing, maps, games, and even the email that we send frequently offer examples of text and image, set next to one another.

Using images and text together is as natural as combining words and music. But this wasn't the case back in the days of Queen Elizabeth or Gustav Freytag.

The frequency of marrying image and text has increased as publishing technologies have become more available. It seems to be something we've been waiting to get our hands on, as if there were a kind of barrier to image communication (which there is, be it a photograph or an illustration). The barrier to make an image—the costs of many sorts—is higher than for writing. This is part of the reason why more people write and part of the reason (I'm guessing here) that imagery is used less than words in western society.

The computer, however, makes image production easier and simpler. Desktop publishing, digital photography, and photomanipulation are all powerful tools. Copying and pasting are sacred. The stuff gets easier by the day. The image is important in its own right, and the increased presence of imagery in our daily lives can make text that accompanies it more personal.

The coupling of imagery and text is one of the most trusted bullhorns of professional communicators. Marketers and advertisers want to speak as directly and as personally as possible to the reader. These are the fulcrums of influence.

The presence of imagery becomes the crowbar. Newspapers know that they're trying to transport you to the scene of a crime, so they show you an image of the location. Television, inherently image based, uses text to represent more general and abstract ideas that are not image based.

These days, it means that images are used for general representation, and text for specific.

There is something very immediate in the communicative power of the image (the phrase "worth a thousand words" comes to mind here). I have a friend named Sarah whose child, at the gurgling age of 13 months, is already communicating "Hungry," "Tired," "Sleepy," "Finished," and "Thirsty" through hand-gestured American-style sign language. It's easy to understand how this happens since sign language is simpler and easier to learn than spoken language, but in this case no less communicative. Children can learn it faster than the phonetics, intonations, and syllabic subtleties of the spoken word. This mother and daughter have learned to communicate through the spoken word of imagery faster than if they had waited for speech to arrive.

The image is a powerful thing when it comes to communicating ideas, and it's been coupled with text—even being able to replace text entirely—as a means of telling stories.

1.3.5: The Role of Narrative Today

Narratives seem as common as the buildings we live in. No matter where we turn, we see some form of narrative nearby. The meat and potatoes of any television diet is narrative. Newspapers contain substantial doses of narrative by relaying stories of what has happened in the last day somewhere else. Books, magazines, essays, pamphlets, and posters generally represent a narrative. Movies certainly are narrative based and now, with the trailers and even the advertisements that often precede them, we see even more narratives. When we meet people on the street, we exchange narratives. When the telephone rings, a narrative is often waiting for us on the other end.

Narrative serves to inform, educate, and entertain. It provides meaning, background, and context, and it incites interest in what's next. In the past two decades advertising (to pick an example), because it uses imagery, has become more aggressive, more interactive, more personal, and more metaphorical. It has also taken on increasingly narrative components. This is because advertising's goal has been to fold the viewer of the ad into the ad itself. By reflecting the desires of the viewer, the ad not only is able to tell him or her what to do, but when to do it. This is usually done in the form of a command coupled with an image. It's a gossip gone gospel.

The liquid surface of the television is not one to be watched lightly. 483 scan lines flashing at roughly 32 frames per second isn't only hypnotic, but downright dangerous. It has a deep impact on the somatic and peripheral nervous systems (including, in some cases, dizziness, nausea, and coma).

Despite the watered-down content of most television programming today, narrative writing took like fire to the deadwood forests of the broadcast world. Newscasters, sports announcers, and meteorologists all have their story to tell. Writers of sitcoms, episodic series, and advertising spots aggressively broadcast carefully designed non-interactive narratives. This is why the sitcom, series, and episode have come to be the primary modus operandi of broadcast/network television.*

Regardless of how people are convinced to invest their time and attention in these forms of content, the roles of plot and character are central to all of these because, finally, what else are we really interested in?

1.4: Interaction

The most engaging interactive narrative relies upon flow; that is, uninterrupted participation in the unfolding action. Poor interaction design can interrupt flow and degrade the experience.

—Brenda Laurel

Interaction can be described as many things. Catchwords abound: "Engaging," "Immersive," "Participatory," "Responsive," and "Reactive."

Interactivity is a continuing increase in participation. It's a bidirectional communication conduit. It's a response to a response. It's "full-duplex." Interaction is a relationship. It's good sex. It's bad conversation. It's indeterminate behavior, and it's redundant result. It's many things, none of which can be done alone. Interaction is a process that dictates communication. It can also be a communication that dictates process. It provides options, necessitates a change in pace, and changes you as you change it.

1.4.1: Interactivity Isn't a Feature of a Medium

This is why, like smoke and fire, communication is implied wherever there is interactivity.

Interaction operates on something. It's a form of dealing with pre-existing material. It's modification, not generation. This means the role of the author, or the person who is generating material, is both more difficult and more important than before digital interaction because increased attention has to be paid to what is being generated. But it's also formalistic and, because it operates on something, it is governed by rule sets.

Interactivity requires rule sets and constraints in order to function smoothly. Consider the rules of driving: traffic lights, street signs, sidewalks, dotted lines, and speed limits. We interact, ultimately, with one another while driving, and it's always a curious lesson to see who is flipping off whom for what reasons.*

As Nathan Shedroff, design consultant, founder of Vivid Design Studios, and author of the recent publication *Experience Design* puts it,

> "… interactivity (so far) can really only occur between two people, whether or not they use a device between them to aid in the experience. This, then, is the key: interaction is what people can (and get to) do. It's not about things moving on screen. It's not about a particular technology…"

With any good interaction, the rule sets are iterative and often unconscious, providing a framework for minimizing damage and maximizing meaning. In the case of traffic lights and the interaction of driving it's getting from point A to point B. The stoplights don't tell you where to go; they just tell you when. The constraint of the grid of the street isn't there as a means of dictating generals, but specifics. If you want to get from the northwestern corner of town to the southeastern, it's perfectly possible; you just have to take lots of little 90-degree turns.

The fact that you can conduct general decisions within the framework of specific guidelines is a key trait in good interaction design. Interaction isn't a feature of a medium. It's a process of communication that, like any form of communication, follows a set of rules and guidelines.

These may also be named "Interaction Design Constraints."

In the Middle East, drivers generally honk to say "I am here" and in North America, drivers generally honk to say "You shouldn't be there." These are unspoken rule sets of interaction just as shaking right or alternately kissing on the cheek are rule sets for introduction. They govern our interactions.

1.4.2: Three Principles of Interaction

Interaction, like any other form of communication art, can be informed by a set of principles. These principles guide the quality and depth of the interaction. If the principles are considered in the process of development, the quality of the design can be improved.

Three principles of interaction are:
1. Input / Output
2. Inside / Outside
3. Open / Closed

The first principle, the principle of Input / Output, says that input should create output and the output should create input. It's the interaction cycle's ability to add information that defines the interaction's quality.

First, the response time between the input and the output should be quick enough for the user to have a clear sense of what change he is affecting on the system. In the early days of the web, Stanford, Microsoft, and Xerox-PARC all spent many hours showing that a person won't wait more than 20 seconds for a page to download. After 20 seconds, he or she clicks to another page or stops the download. This is because there was a need to know that some change was being affected to the system—within 20 seconds.

Second, the ability to control the input should be present. If you push a button next to a door, you expect someone to answer. The input should facilitate more input. And the input should provide the user with a new capability. As this happens, the line between stimulus and response thins. And as the line between stimulus and response thins, the depth of immersion increases. This is why you can't do something else if you're immersed. This is why, if it's really interactive, it's consuming.

The second principle, the principle of Inside / Outside, says that a dialogue should be created between the internal and external worlds.

"Inside-outside" refers to the relationship of two sorts of interaction. I also call this the difference between "inside-the-skull" and "outside-the-skull" interactivity.

Inside-the-skull interactivity is a process of extending what the user already knows. It is the world of the reader's imagination. Take, for example, reading. It works with existing iconography (the alphabet) and metaphor (little red riding hood) and relies on the reader's interior understandings to build a visualized and emotional suspension of suspicion. "Inside-the-skull" is the world of meaning. As William James puts it, "Fantasy or Imagination are the names given to the faculty of reproducing copies of originals once felt." Inside-the-skull is the art, metaphor, and subtle cues that build things like dreams.

Outside-the-skull interactivity is based on what we are experiencing on an empirical, or experiential, level. The framerate of the video game, the haptic feedback of the joystick, the hues of the colors, or the 32-bit stereo depth are all elements of craft, not art. These timed and physical elements are the components of interactivity that many authors think are the only pieces worth paying attention to. This is a mistake because technology is not only an extension of ourselves; it is a reformation of the world around us. Authors of interactivity who are not paying attention to both the subject and the object of an interaction (the subjective and objective perspectives) are missing one of the key values of interactivity. This key value is the proportion of inside-the-skull and outside-the-skull information that makes the art of interactivity interesting.

The writers of the video games *Tomb Raider* and *Final Fantasy* have done a marvelous job of capitalizing on this by increasing their out-of-the-skull narration. They released movies. They increased their audience's understanding of the "backstory"— the implied narration of the video game—but also, by making Lara Croft a living character on the screen with a photorealistic environment (and, uh, topology), they increased the visual depth of the video game for game players.

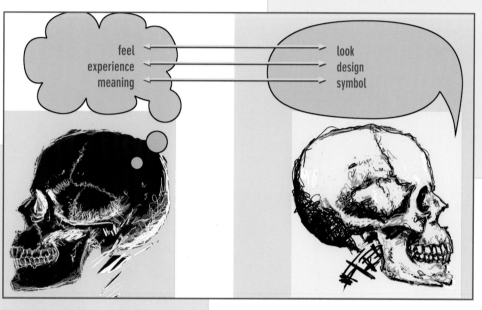

feel → look
experience → design
meaning → symbol

Inside the skull　　　　　　**Outside the skull**

In 1992, Paul Sermon, an installation artist who had worked at the edges of digital technology for more than a decade, was commissioned to produce a project he named "Telematic Dreaming" in which there were two rooms. Each room contained a bed, a camera that was above the bed, and a projector that was next to the camera. One museum visitor was in each room, lying on each bed. The result: Two people were seen lying next to each other, but, of course, only one was physically there. The other was a projected image from the other room.

The success of the project was based on its ability to work with both inside-the-skull and outside-the-skull interaction. If you were lying on the bed, your external world was being immediately informed that there was an image of a person there next to you. The power of this project was that the sight of the projected image of the person overlapped with the intimate meaning of the bed (the internal, inside-the-skull world).

The third principle, Open / Closed, says that the system should get better the more it's used.

Closed systems are boring. Open systems have something to give back. This can be tested by going outside and kicking two things. First kick a brick. As soon as you kick it, the brick will move. It's a response that is expected (and potentially painful). Next, go kick a person.

The reason why the interaction with the human is more intense than the interaction with the brick is because the interaction with the human gives something back that is unpredictable. The human is independent and unpredictable. The human is an open system. The brick just rolls over—it's a closed system.

The real indeterminacy is in how the person will respond, not whether he knows he has been kicked. This introduces second-order effects because the person might just jump away or will try to kick you back.

As many software programmers have learned, indeterminacy is the characteristic of a system that gives the system its independence. If you have a system that has a kind of dynamic equilibrium, it will be more robust, more capable of handling change, and, therefore, more interactive and participatory. These are characteristics of its independence.

Open systems are more complicated, less predictable, and more interesting than closed systems. Algorithmically generated geometry, such as 3D-flythrough landscapes, are a good example. Algorithmically generated personalities, such as high-end artificial intelligence systems, are an even better example. But what remains the most unpredictable, independent, and captivating of all interactions is other people. There is no predicting the behavior with certainty, but there is almost always a context that defines the response.

This is the reason why multiuser gaming environments (an example of interactive narrative), such as the movie *A.I.* online component, [2.5.2], or multi-user games such as *Ultima Online* [3.5.5], have started to take such a share of the time we spend with interactive systems.

These principles of interaction, Input / Output, Inside / Outside, and Open / Closed, can be used to guide authors as they develop narratives that use interaction.

1.4.3: Four Steps of Interaction

Interaction is composed of steps that, like dance chore-ography, music notation, rhetoric, or any other form of communication art, can be outlined to better understand its basic process. These steps guide the form and shape of the interaction. If the steps are understood prior to designing an interactive system, the quality of the design can be increased. To clarify, these are steps, not (as in 1.4.2) principles. These are actions that a reader follows. These steps are intended to complement and work with the principles listed previously.

The principles are a means of guiding development. The steps are a means of evaluating the result of that development.

Interactivity is, like plot, based on fascination and captiva-tion. It is how people get pulled into a process that continues to draw them deeper and deeper. Interaction can be broken down into four steps which, if the interaction design is done well, generates an increased interest in further interaction. The steps go like this:

1. Observation
2. Exploration
3. Modification
4. Reciprocal Change

Note how each of these steps drives the following.

1. Observation: The reader makes an assessment.
In any system, a simple level of familiarity is necessary to act. And, before any action takes place, a kind of awareness of first-level options is necessary. First-level options might include the identification of things like buttons or levers or stairs. The reader might ask, "Do I move or does the environment move around me? Do images or text represent some kind of code or set of codes? What is possible?" In *Myst*, an interactive narrative published by Broderbund and authored by the Rand brothers, readers experience this very effect. They are dropped into an environment in which they need to use their skills of observation to determine their abilities in the environment.

2. Exploration: The reader does something.
After first-level options are discovered, a second level is then moved to in which capabilities are explored. The reader finds out what she can and can't do and, effectively, stretches out her hand and finds that she can make a change. But it's a process of unintentional discovery, not conscious change.

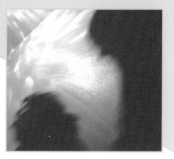

3. Modification: The reader changes the system.

If a reader has made an assessment and done something based on that context, the reader will change the interactive system. The reader bridges context to decision. This is the leap from unintentional discovery to conscious change. At this point, the reader knows at least some of his or her abilities and uses them with intent to modify the system. The modification was created for the user by the author, and because it was allowed (and sufficiently motivated), the level of interaction in the system is increased.

4. Reciprocal Change: The system tries to change the reader.

And if it's interactive and the reader is engaged, the system changes the reader's actions. The fact that there is reciprocal change is one of the defining steps of high-latency interaction. Without reciprocal change, the system might as well be a brick or a doorbell rather than a person who has the ability to be somewhat indeterminate and interactive.

1. Repeat: The reader makes another assessment.

By this time, the system is rolling, and by going back to step 1, the process deepens and the interaction increases. If all goes well, the system then begins to improve for the person, the inside-the-skull and outside-the-skull worlds start to mix, and input creates more output.

Let's go back. Interactivity is an increase in a reader's participation. It's a bidirectional communication conduit. It's a response. Interaction is a relationship. It's mutually executed change. It's indeterminate behavior, and the redundant result. As far as narrative is concerned, it amounts to providing the reader with the ability to alter specifics in the plot.

1.4.4: Designing Information for Interactivity

Redundancy and Context: Cues of Interaction

You open your eyes and it's completely black. One of those dark situations where you almost feel the blackness pressing on your head… completely numb and silent. Ahead of you is a point of light. You have a piece of information because you have a piece of difference. Difference generates information.

Next imagine that the piece of light—this small, yellow pinprick in the fabric of the darkness—begins to get taller. There's change, therefore more difference, therefore more information. The line breaks off another to its side, and another, spilling out so that it looks like this:

The width of the lines—there seems to be fat and narrow—and the spaces between the lines give us more information.

Two narrow, two fat. Space. Three narrow, two fat. Space. Then it repeats.

It might look familiar to you but I doubt that you can read this without a barcode scanner. Here's the same information in a different context (in this example, a different iconography or alphabet):

TTFSS

The repetition begins to generate a pattern. How we interpret the pattern, however, is another issue. We can recognize this more clearly because we might read it as Greco-Roman if not English. It's the same information, but in a different, more familiar (and therefore more informative) format. The ability to predict the pattern is based first on its redundancy and second on its context. In this case, its context seems to live in the Greco-Roman alphabet, so probably a romance language, but beyond that we don't have much more information (because these things are just floating in space).

A clue: 2 3 4 5 6 7
And the same pattern in its most easily recognized, and most redundant, state:

two three four five six seven

This would have been easier to recognize had the context of the Greco-Roman alphabet been transcribed in a little more familiar (and, in this case, more iconographic) method. Because the letters have a context, they make it more iconographic. An icon is a contextualized image.

These precepts should be intuitive to any interface designer, storyteller, graphic designer, or interaction designer worth their picture. The precepts run like so:

· Difference provides information.
· Repetition provides redundancy.
· Redundant information (a.k.a. "repetition with variation") provides context.
· Context allows prediction.
· Prediction allows participation.
· Participation is the cornerstone of interaction.

I've found that people get very excited when they learn they can predict things because this allows them to participate. They suddenly have a grasp on time that they didn't before, the world seems more manageable, and their role in it comprehensible.

But finally, these are all simply means of building a metaphor's launch pad. A metaphor is a super-set of symbology. It's a meta-message that allows for very complicated forms of communication. We rely on it whenever we tell a story.

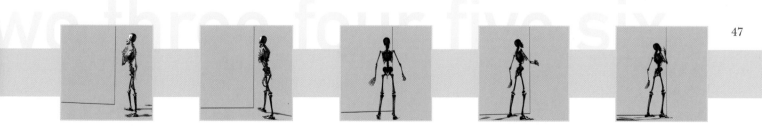

"In truth, our life is such that
its unconscious components
are continuously present in all
their multiple forms. It follows that
in our relationships we continuously
exchange messages about these
unconscious materials, and it becomes
important also to exchange meta-
messages by which we tell each
other what order and species of
unconsciousness (or consciousness)
attaches to our messages."

- Gregory Bateson

The adage "information is not knowledge" is one way of representing this idea. But in the world of interaction design, this adage can be pushed further. Really, knowledge isn't worth much more than information if it doesn't allow for action. In the world of interaction design, action becomes the reason for information.

"Meta-messages," as Bateson calls them, come in all shapes and sizes. Their key characteristic, however, is to convey meaning that reaches beyond their information.* Adages, metaphors, and fables all do this, and so they serve as strong guides for ways to develop interface and narrative and to design elements of interactivity that help readers better understand what they are able to do, what the effects will be, and how they can do it.

The key is relying on the inside-the-skull world of the reader.

1.4.5: Designing Time for Interactivity

The Spectra of Permanent and Temporary Times

Writing on cave walls, sending letters, scrawling in books, pecking at a keyboard, and scribbling up a diary are all methods we use to make time and the stories of our lives permanent on parchment, paper, and monitor. Writing is an effort to escape death, perhaps, or a recognition that time is the stuff of life, but despite writing's best efforts, it still generally lacks the luster and the shine of the moment it describes. It's still a description.

There are strange moments in most reading when we realize that a chunk of time is missing, is repeated, or is looping back on itself. Literature has an arsenal of tools to facilitate this process. "Foreshadowing" and "Epiphany"* are two of them.

The act of writing, narrative's corpus primus, has always been—at least on some level—an attempt to escape time.

We don't always notice it, but some experiences seem more susceptible to time. Dreams quickly fade in the morning, we keep mementos as physical kinds of memory (hence the word), and spoken stories seem barely solid enough to weather the winds of change. So we make efforts to write in a way that is permanent. Consider some examples: The tablet of Isis [2.3.1], a kind of topology of narrative built into stone, has lasted for thousands of years. Pioneer 11, launched in 1973, continues to float through cold space as you read, and will probably continue to do so until it's either read by extra-terrestrial eyes or gets sucked into the nuclear center of some unmapped sun. A plaque on the space probe contains a compact narrative outlining our position in the solar system, who we are, and when Pioneer 11 was launched. The engravings and the stories it holds are intended to outlast the perspectives of the writers and the readers of the story.

*"Epiphany" comes from the ancient Greek, *epifanos* or *epiphanos*, which loosely means "to make manifest." Epiphany is a term that James Joyce coined to express the moment when the reader understands the entire arc of the story as a single thought. It's a foreshortening of the story and a compression of information that, according to Joyce, is an act of authorship. This is a foreshortening of the story and a compression of information that, according to Joyce, is an act of authorship.

Some narrative has only a temporary existence. The ancient Greeks used to have huge tracts of narrative they would repeat in a lyrical voice that would last for many night-times of around-the-fire singing with each epic continuing for many nights. In fact it's assumed that Homer never actually wrote the *Iliad* or the *Odyssey* but that he, like most schooled Greeks of the day, simply recited the epic from heart. Homer was just the guy who finally took the time to distill these cultural songs into a format that made it more durable to listeners from a culture of only a few degrees difference from our own. And he did it with a guitar.*

Bob Dylan pulled the same stunt in covering the old blues tunes of the American South. The Irish are alleged to have kept their stories, called "finger alphabets," in the tips of their fingers. They memorized them by assigning different syllables or letters to different parts of their fingers.

These forms of narrative are as lost as the breath of the dead that sang them. Like the Oroborus that chews its own tail, these stories that used time were eaten by it, and their death forced a kind of change in the way the stories were told.

Homer, really, didn't use a guitar. The guitar was invented some 1,500 years after Homer's day, following the Moorish invasions of Spain. The guitar is a child of the tar, which, depending on the number of strings and shape might be (and sometimes is) named tar, dotar, ektar, setar, etc. But Homer probably played the lyra or kithara.

The Spectra of Slow and Fast Times

We don't always notice it, but time, like a flock of birds, can move in radical and unpredictable ways. Time flies quickly when you're having fun, it drags an hour before the workday ends, and sleep washes it all away.

Narrative has some sharply honed tools for articulating the elements of time that go slowly or move too quickly for us to consciously map. In most narratives, sleeping isn't generally detailed (though video artist Bill Viola has done a fine job of investigating this strange space of time), nor are the long moments of silent solitude in which our protagonist might be staring off, bored and thoughtless, at the toe of his shoe, waiting for the train that will carry him to the battlefield.

If you've ever noticed how your brain accelerates with a healthy shot of adrenaline, it will make some sense as to why narrative increases detail at moments of greatest conflict. Events that require solutions warp the weft of time. Narrative moves slower or faster, depending on the kind of problem being addressed. The speed at which time appears often has a relationship to the place we are when it happens.

Our subjective experience of time is often dilated at moments of intense choice. When we are on the stage in front of an audience involved in improvisation, performance, reading, or speaking, the "length" of time seems shortened and severely protracted. Suspense, for example, is just that—a suspension between two events that are further apart than you'd anticipated. Expectation and surprise, likewise, rely on the relationships of points in time. Suspense is just one of the aspects of time that is commonly used in narration.

But the use of time in narrative is a complicated thing, and when we introduce information display—and specifically interactive information display—nonlinear choices need to be allowed within the context of the linear story.

Narrative has traditionally followed a linear path. Because narration comes from a verbal tradition, linguistic communication is necessarily bound in linear time, making linearity the strongest influence on how we've told stories.

This is changing because more and more stories are told visually. Consider Chris Ware's comics [2.5.5], a glance at a newspaper's photos, or the links that are highlighted on a web page. None of these forms of storytelling is necessarily linear, but they all tell, from a perspective, what happened.

The job of writing has been far easier for historic authors than it has for authors of science fiction or fiction authors like James Joyce, who have made the brave choice to toggle back and forth between events at different points in the story. People like Joyce were pioneers in considering how to use time in other than linear fashion and might have unintentionally invented hypertext.

Because interaction includes decision making, and because decision making is not necessarily linear, we need to learn how to tell stories that facilitate this approach. Like Joyce, we need to invent new modes of thinking about time.

Time, as a tool that a writer uses, can move in strange ways. And digital media, with things like back buttons and the ability to accelerate, decelerate, link, and close, changes how time is used in narration.

Events in narrative generally follow what came before, and can often precede them that same way. If this seems confusing to you, it's because emerging forms of literature are encouraging us to think differently about time.

I walk up to a door and push a button. A doorbell sounds inside. I push it again. The door opens and an old man answers the door.

1. Time does not need to be ordered in a sequential fashion. But that's our perception of it. I push the button, the bell rings, and someone answers the door. We're inclined to say the bell rang because I pushed the button, but we might never know whether I pushed the button because the bell rang. Maybe the bell rang because the man was about to come to the door. The cause doesn't need to precede the effect.

2. Time does not need to be universal, but we perceive it as such. Please imagine everything has already happened at once. In the preceding fable, an old man answered the door because I pushed the button. Maybe in another time, he wasn't there at all. Or maybe he was and didn't feel like answering. Let's consider that there are at least three different tracks of time that exist—we just happen to be experiencing only one of them. Imagine all of the possible tracks of all the possible events running smoothly along simultaneously—you just happen to be riding on one of them.

3. Time does not need to be ordered in a linear fashion. Assuming the preceding is plausible, then why wouldn't it be possible for a single cause to split into several effects? Or, vice versa, we can mix in the first two examples with this forked approach in which the old man's cause might become my effect as well as the door's effect—both of which preceded the cause. In other words, maybe I rang the doorbell and someone answered—both because the bell rang. Multiple effects might have a single cause, or multiple causes might have a single effect.

4. Time might be considered as a volume. Imagine yourself as someone who has no sense of space as a surrounding entity. Your first perception of space is as a camera that's mounted on someone's shoulder. You would see space moving toward you as the person moved; then it might slow down and stop altogether, slide sideways, and then suddenly move toward you again. It's possible that we understand time this way—in an apparently linear way, not because it is time's nature to behave this way, but because it is our nature to perceive it like that.

So much for that; there are a lot of different possibilities. Forms of interactivity need to take this into account at least as much as forms of narrative have over the past century. It's an issue of plot as much as an issue of use-case scenario. Our process of considering and deciding impact one another, as do reaction and action, within the framework of cause and effect. These are principles that inform any structure of interactivity, but because narrative and modern literature use time in ways that are not always as we perceive (or even understand) them, sequence and reaction can get unorthodox, let alone incomprehensible.

This is one of the primary arteries of interactivity: It's about understanding new methods of articulating time and human decisions within that framework and how we can relate to them both conceptually and spatially.

Let's return to our use-case scenario, still considering it as an interactive kind of plot. This is an expression of events that takes place over a period of time. That period of time is determined not as much by the author as it is by the reader. The reader carries his or her own sense of time into the interaction model. He or she controls the pacing, and it's up to the interaction designer to see that the reader is still conducted to the appropriate step at the appropriate time: when he wants.

Notice that time is represented as a spatial arrangement of decisions and that it can be moved back and forth along the line of the main flow. This is surprisingly similar to the Freytag Triangle. But the author of this system has a great deal of influence over how the reader reacts to it.

The Tyranny of Interaction Design

There are differences of opinions among designers of interactive narrative. Some authors I've spoken with rant about the influence that a designer can have over the interaction of a game. In some cases, readers have said that they are not playing a game, but rather jumping through the hoops that the game designers have put in their way. This "hoop jumping" is an example of the kind of design that is implicit in many interactive systems. The design of the interaction and the influences the designer has can become excessive and force readers to spend time doing things they may not otherwise choose.

Consider the video game that has levels. To get to the next level, you have to perform some simple function or you have to repeat a single function within a prescribed error margin. This might be jumping Donkey Kong or Super Mario from a barrel into a hole, for example.

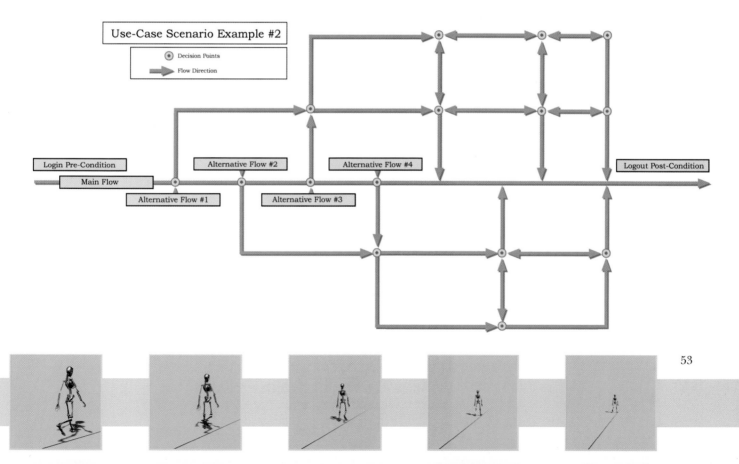

Use-Case Scenario Example #2

- ⊙ Decision Points
- → Flow Direction

Login Pre-Condition
Main Flow
Alternative Flow #1
Alternative Flow #2
Alternative Flow #3
Alternative Flow #4
Logout Post-Condition

But it becomes frustrating if, after several tries, the goal hasn't been reached and the player is still there, sweating over the split second that will either allow him to go forward or put him back to where he was five minutes previous.

This is a form of tyranny and poor interaction design. It should be avoided when possible.

In most cases, it should be considered that the goal of an interactive narrative is not to author the narrative, but to provide a context and an environment in which the narrative can be discovered or built by the readers of that story. In this way, designers and authors of interactive narrative are far more like architects than they are like writers. The author considers the interactions and movements of readers of the story and works to accommodate that reading that can happen from many different sides.

As Doug Church, one of the most respected game designers in the United States, puts it:

> *"Those of us doing 'immersive simulation' strive to make the game the player's, not the designer's. While we, as designers, are clearly creating the environment and rules, we hope to allow the player to act, plan, and decide. Working on a talk several years ago, I was talking to a co-worker (Marc LeBlanc) at Looking Glass about this and defined it as "getting the designer off of the stage, and pulling the player onto it." He described that as 'abdicating authorship,' not feeling like we have to be 'in control' of everything. It is important to realize this doesn't mean 'abdicating responsibility,' for creating the rules and procedures of the world is an act of authorship that defines the space. But at the same time, a carefully authored environment can abdicate the specific control to the player, who can then make and fulfill their own plans and decisions. Done well, this leads to more investment from the player, as they realize that the world is about them, and that they matter."*

1.4.7: The Emerging Forms of Interactivity in Communication

As we've seen, most entertainment and communication toolsets have adapted quite handily to the digital medium. Video, audio, photographs, text, and most communication technologies that originally relied on the airwaves of the analog have found comfortable homes in the wires of the digital.

Electronic technologies, and specifically the emergence of color television, have brought us closer and closer to the hallucinogens of imagination and story-telling. Television in particular has helped each viewer to participate in that comfortable space of collective awareness and distributed narrative that happens when millions of people are all seeing the same sound, watching the same image, and dreaming the same dream. It's a powerful thing. It was electronic technology, and the fact that this technology could now live with us in our homes, which first introduced us to a new narrative space of technologic interaction.

Before electronic media was distilled into its digital form, television channels and radio stations were some of our first opportunities to choose the evening's entertainment in our own living rooms. My first impressions of Robert Louis Stevenson were through a battery-powered radio in the northern wintertips of Maine. It was 1977 and anachronous, to be sure. We would huddle around the radio and listen to *Treasure Island* through the tinny, rattling speaker, and a massive ethereal cornucopia of words and images would spill deserted beaches of white sand, huge clipper ships with full-thrown sails, sharpened sabres dripping with hot blood, and the occasional mocking parrot spreading its wings in the bright sun into our remote, wintertime cabin.

There was, strictly speaking, some choice: We could listen to *Treasure Island* or we could hear about the coming snowstorms.

Then, maybe six or seven years later I spent time watching how people watched television. Not having grown up with a television, it has always had a severely anesthetic and hypnotic impact on me. Consequently, I've always been a keen observer of viewing behavior. After trying to watch Lee Majors defeat Sasquatch, I would become infuriated with Billy Reidel as he would change the channel in the middle of the battle royale. For him, as someone who had grown up with television, the channel switching was part of the program experience. "Surfing" (as web usage has lately, and ineptly, been dubbed) seemed to involve a persistent entering and exiting of the material being watched. The dwell-time and form of attention for traditional network television was very different from radio partly because of the speed with which channels could be accessed.

The remote control had something to do with this. It was the convenience of pressing a single button as opposed to getting off the sofa and twiddling a dial that, at least partly, facilitated this change in concentration and attention. But other things facilitated interruption and mode-shifts. The volume could be turned down, the box was small and could be looked away from, and the signal could get interrupted. But even more than the remote control, the presence of broadcast commercials (full-volume mini-narrative advertising interruptions of the larger narrative) at high-tension points in the story caused us to restructure the way we considered stories and the attention span we brought to them.

The remote control and the ever-intruding advertisement facilitated a different kind of attention in viewers of television. It facilitated a nesting of narrative and a kind of attention that was very facile with mode-switches, context-swapping, and interruptability. This form of intertwined and entangled attention span of the television viewer fast revealed itself in the graphic design of television content. Camera cuts, character introduction, music pacing, color contrast, volume, and even story structures themselves were built to grapple with the viewer's need to flip over to something faster and more hypnotic. Watch any music video on VH1 or MTV; compare *Weakest Link* to poor old Vanna White; or watch a batch of contemporary Saturday morning cartoons and you'll soon see that the drum that these shows march to is increasing its beat.

The tradition of the interruption that binds together a larger narrative has been inherited by digital media. Early BBSs—the greenhouse nurseries of MUDs, MOOs, MUCKs—and electronic mail systems were built, from the ground up, to be a thing that you could enter, use, be interrupted in the middle of, use again, and leave. Unlike a radio-based narrative, the participation wasn't dictated by a set amount of time. It was left to you, as when reading a book, to decide how long and how much. This was already implicit in most electronic media—but digital media in particular held nonlinear participation, interruption, and resumption as part of its assumed capabilities from the start.

This idea of interrupt-and-resume is deeply embedded in the command line. Konrad Zuse*, a German researcher and engineer, was 31 when he completed a prototypical programmable calculator he named Z1. It was automatic, it was mechanical, and it was digital. But it was the first binary machine based on Boolean algebra, which was an important step. The command-line input used something we might recognize as a keyboard and the output was displayed on electric lamps that hung overhead.

By this time, IBM (then awkwardly named Computing - Tabulating - Recording Company) had manufactured almost 1,500 punch card machines. Seeing what Zuse had done, the company was quick to adopt this interface innovation. By 1940, Bell labs had teletypes running with multiple, remote input keyboards chained to a single machine. Only one could be used at a time, and when it was, the output was displayed at the same location. Only nine months later at a mathematics conference, a teletype keyboard in Hanover, New Hampshire was connected to that same machine in New York. Conference goers were able to use the machines remotely.

These innovations in interaction happened because the computer, unlike the television, is always waiting for you to tell it what to do. Its time is determined by your presence (at least for now).

Konrad Zuse also developed of a basic programming system known as "Plankalkül" with which he designed a chess playing program. A copy of his first digital binary computer is on display in the Museum für Verkehr und Technik in Berlin.

The interactive capabilities of the command line are massive because it was developed as a means of providing users with remote-controlled actions such as "Run," "Print," and "Copy." The command line is far from dead, and its implications are still being explored today. Mode-switching is implied with a command line. At a primitive level, the computer presented the idea of switching channels of concentration—of switching modes—with the command line. But there were other ideas in there as well.

The integration of the graphical frontend with the computational backend has been a recent development in interactivity that's introduced a realm of possibilities that we see in contemporary interfaces, such as the Macintosh and Windows operating systems. Xerox-PARC and several other research institutes were working on a graphical pointing system during the 1980s, and the invention caught on as soon as the cognitive leap from "Data" to "Image" was made. The idea of graphical computing didn't initially include a mouse, but was later added because the authors sensed a need for a new way to interact with the space other than the keyboard (which hardly considers space at all). It wasn't until Apple integrated this new interface convention—this hardware-based form of interaction named The Mouse—that computers really discovered any commercial success. But the leap from data to image is not a difficult jump for us to make as we look back, but certainly something that was a little hard to see if you were there as it was happening.

Command lines are fascinating because, like tropes, they require cognitive participation. The graphical interface is probably an improvement to human-computer interaction because we don't need to remember as much to get the same task done, but I wonder if this shift from command-line to graphical-user interface is a bit like the shift from radio to television. The radio was a trickle of static interspersed with words. The task of listening to the radio was more focused, demanded more of the listener, and its smaller flow of information forced listeners to pay more attention over a longer time. It was an inside-the-skull interaction mode. The command line is like this. There are always help systems to remind you of what's there, but you only begin to work with those systems of interaction once you've remembered them. And the act of remembering can be difficult.

The graphical user interface, or GUI, came along and we could see where on the screen a particular thing—be it an action or an object, a verb or a noun—lived. When using a GUI, you might remember that, in the menu at the top of the screen, one slot over and two slots down is the Copy command. Or, as your command-line capabilities increased, you might remember that a combination of two buttons is the copy command. The web, the graphical version of the Internet, simply took this basic idea and extended the metaphor out of the command of the individual computer to the command of multiple computers.

Web publishing and chat rooms have largely defined our understanding of interactivity. Chronologically and commercially, the Internet followed the Internet prototypes known as CD-ROMs. And CD-ROMs were the commercial leveraging of data storage devices such as the hard-drive or floppy disk. But the transition from data storage to CD-ROM to Internet has been one that has allowed access to more data in a faster and more convenient way. The curve is simple, really—it's entirely quantitative at this point. And, as I sit at my desk and wait for data to arrive onscreen, it's easy to see that this trend will continue. Now that the Internet has gone through the same suspiciously similar curve of high-acceleration accompanied by tremendous collapse that the CD-ROM publishing industry went through in the early '90s, we may begin to understand that this is part of the cycle of these technologies. We can anticipate mobile technologies and, later, ubiquitous computing, to follow the same path.

Enhanced television, too, has followed this trend of relying on data storage to increase its commercial heft. The trend, again, will be predictable in the coming decade: More is better. It's the whole idea behind video on demand. Store more data so customers have more choices. The only real challenge that most enhanced television manufacturers face is how to make that data accessible to the customer when he or she wants it.

These trends of quantitative increase show us which features of interactivity are inherently digital. Issues of access, mass storage, and transport are not the inherent issues of interaction. The interactive is not contained within the digital—it's the other way around. We're just learning how to make the digital medium more interactive.

But trying to provide access while viewers are switching modes, stopping, starting, speeding up, slowing down, leaving, entering, getting bored, excited, confused, and progressively poorer with each tap on the button is difficult. These are interaction design problems of a different sort that will continue to evolve far past the coming decade.

1.5: Interactive Narrative

There is nothing wrong with games which decide to place the designer center stage, and task the player with "discovering" the will of the author. However, I believe that if we learn to effectively involve the player we can create more satisfying experiences, unlike anything offered by other media. A work in which the player must figure out how to turn the prewritten pages can be fun, but one which the player writes the pages seems far more likely to be transformative.

—Doug Church

1.5.1: The Generation of Additional Understanding

Interactive narrative generates a set of multiple perspectives.

The episodic story structure changed the face of narrative forever. In the 1960s and 1970s, the injuries, antics, and love affairs of the television show *Bonanza* would entertain us every Wednesday night at its expected hour. The story was framed by a context that we, as viewers, already knew. We didn't have to relearn every week why the Cartwright Family lived at The Ponderosa or what motivated the characters of Little Joe, Adam, or Hoss. The episodic structure was an interface we were somehow familiar with because it not only reduced emphasis on the protagonist of the story, but simultaneously gave us more characters with which to identify.

As television stories have grown more complex, that same narrative interface has changed and grown more complex as well. Consider the multi-valent perspectives of soap operas such as *Days of Our Lives*, *As The World Turns*, or today's television shows like *The X-Files*, *The Sopranos*, or *Dark Angel*. Although not interactive, these shows continually push the boundaries closer to being a movie interspersed with weeks rather than a television show interspersed with ads.

In the United States, the advertising is even designed to match the show. The designers of the advertisements are aware of the preferences and interests of their viewers and regulate the content and pacing for that audience.

Episodic narrative is often thought of as a lower form of narrative because it doesn't develop story arc to the same depth or breadth that something with more space and time might.* The argument goes, "Tolstoy has more time with the reader than does Stan Lee; therefore, the quality of the story is better."

Nevertheless, it's interesting to notice how many episodic stories were framed with some other larger context that helped to lend them a level of realism and solidity in the real world. The story of Spider-Man, for example, originally appeared as an episodic installation in not only Marvel's comic books, but in newspapers and a full-length book of written, text-only narrative as well. These days, as a movie is being developed, video games are made available, and a host of other media have sprung from these humble episodic beginnings.

Episodic forms of narrative might be more powerful than originally thought. Episodic television changed narrative forever. By now we're accustomed to interruption in the tale. Perhaps, like a denouement, we're coming to expect it. This is interesting to consider in light of the rather abrupt endings that many video games choose to deliver. While I hesitate to mention it, I hope we don't begin to see commercial breaks in video games and other forms of interactive narrative.

* This author does not, by the way, endorse these views. Neither the quantity of authorship nor readership time determines the quality of the story.

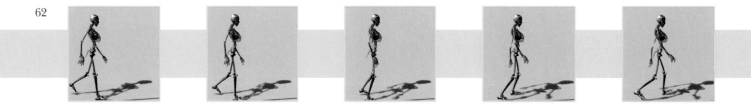

1.5.2: Interactive Narrative Defined

An interactive narrative is a time-based representation of character and action in which a reader can affect, choose, or change the plot. The first-, second-, or third-person characters may actually be the reader. Opinion and perspective are inherent. Image is not necessary, but likely.*

Thanks to Brenda Laurel for her assistance with this definition.

Interactive narrative is, in many ways, about the process of narration and its implied perspectives, but as we noticed before, interactivity fractures the perspectives of the individual author, places new perspectives in the hands of the readers, and accommodates a relationship between reading and writing. In developing interactive narrative, the plot has to accommodate a more flexible structure that allows for multiple perspectives into multiple viewpoints, each of which work together to assemble an overall and cohesive worldview, or opinion.

Interactive narratives vary in shape, size, and fur color, but there are means that we can use to determine their quality and form. These may include:

1. Interactive narrative is a form of reading that contains representations of character and or opinion. This representation of character is generally something that follows a schedule of development that takes place over a period of time that can be determined either by the reader or author. In this way, interactive narrative is very similar to traditional forms of narrative.

2. Because interactive narrative contains a character (generated by the author) and a reader, it is an intersection of multiple perspectives. These perspectives might be the author and the reader, simultaneous readers, or simultaneous authors. In this way, interactive narrative differs greatly from traditional narrative, and it is in this space that we find the greatest potential for interactive depth and form.

3. Interactive narrative generally follows our steps of interaction:
   · Observe
   · Explore
   · Modify
   · Change

4. Interactive narrative generally follows our principles of interaction:
   · Inside / Outside
   · Input / Output
   · Closed / Open

Some forms of interactive narrative more closely follow these criteria than others. The more of these criteria that are followed, the higher the level of interaction and the deeper the degree of narrative.

Interactive plot structure is more of a system of connections than it is a curve or arc. What follows are three models that are intended to be general approaches. The visualization of plot structure can be more useful for interactive nonlinear narrative than for traditional linear narrative. Plot structures are, however, an analysis tool and don't have much to do with emotional punch or aesthetic interest.

In some ways, the plot structure of interactive narrative can be thought of as music notation. An author may write the basic structure, but it's the participation and interpretation of that structure that makes it come alive. Music scores give rough guidelines (Con Brio, Fortissimo, etc.), but are intended as a forum for active participation in which the control of the author is second to the participation of the musicians.*

Plot is a function of time. It is the plan of the action. The plot is the series of events. In interactive narrative, plot continues to be a function of time, but here is its one main difference from traditional plot: The timing of the events in a plot are determined by both the author and reader. In many cases when the interaction is of a high quality, it is determined more by the reader than the author.

In most stories, authors introduce skips, folds, or omissions in time. A phrase such as "The next day" might be used to point out that a night has passed and anything that has happened since the last activity of the story was uneventful. We're comfortable with these forms of compression and foreshortening in literature, but what is new for people in our era is the idea that this can be determined by the reader of the story.

Raph Koster, the lead designer of *Ultima Online*, the first pervasive multiplayer game that had a true graphical front-end, claims that there are two primary forms of interactive narrative: Impositional and Expressive [3.5.5].

Though other people use different words to express it, this seems to be a common form of thinking among most developers of interactive narrative. The thinking runs like so:

An author or designer has some control over the story. The story, however, because it's interactive, needs to provide control to the reader as well. A heavily designed story, such as one of the 1980's *Choose Your Own Adventure* books, conceived and invented by Ray Montgomery, is heavily impositional. It guides you with strict sets of individual rules that only allow the reader a narrow margin of decisions. Another example is *Liquid Stage* [2.5.3], in which the viewer of the show has only particular moments of interaction available and the rest of the show is a dictated and sequential story.

Expressive, in contrast to this, relies less on the series of events and behaves more like architecture: The visitor is allowed to roam freely, explore, investigate, and make changes in the environment. The specifics of a narrative plot are far less defined and, as a result, the breadth of interaction is much wider. Examples of this generally show up in 3-dimensional interfaces and narratives such as *Ultima Online*.

The challenge, of course, is finding the appropriate balance between the two.

Plot structures for interactive narrative will continue to evolve and will most likely become increasingly simple and homogenized as history allows us to normalize our bellcurve of examples. However, now, at this early stage of the art, we will look at three different types of plot that represent both Impositional and Expressive plot structures. We will start with the most impositional and move toward the most expressive.

*It is worth mentioning that the interaction that musicians share when producing their work is similar to the roles that readers share when participating in many forms of multi-user interactive narrative. A "wizard" or "host" conducts the orchestra.

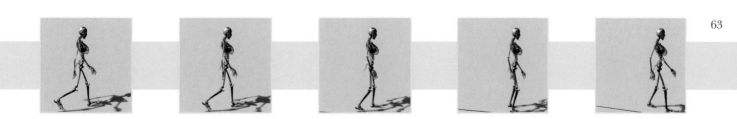

The following diagrams are some examples of interactive narrative plot structures. The black line is the progression of events or time (as dictated by the reader). The red lines are the different points at which the story will end—generally this follows an event of interaction. The diamonds are interactive moments.

Nodal Plot Structures

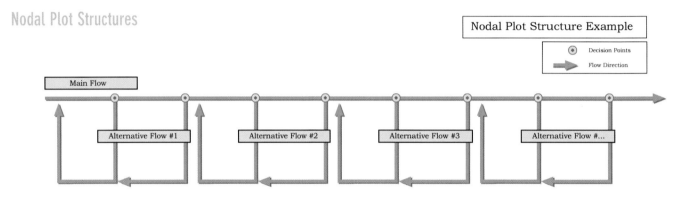

Nodal plots are a series of noninteractive events, interrupted by points of interactivity. This plot structure, which provides the most potential support for the classic dramatic arc, has been referred to as a "string of pearls." Games such as *Sonic the Hedgehog* and *Deus Ex* follow this pattern but fail to capitalize on its dramatic potential because the switch between modes of active and passive participation lacks integration and smooth transition. Michael Bovee's *Liquid Stage* roughly matches this type of plot, deviating in the fact that his story has a specific ending.

The benefits of this form of plot allow strong backstory, clear character development, and deep environment, but subsequently runs the risk of limiting the breadth and form of the interaction. This is more "designer focused" as Doug Church might put it. One

solution to this problem is to make sure that the interactive components of the plot are there as a means of exploring elements of the main plot and, if possible, generating additional backstory.

Nodal plots have a single beginning and usually at least two endings. It's important to note that although the event of the ending will be the same, it does not need to happen at the same time in the story. In some cases, there is a goal at the end of the story. This is generally the case with games.

Again, take IonStorm's game *Deus Ex* as an example. There are two possible endings, one of which is seldom seen by the reader. The most likely ending is that the character dies. This ending happens to everyone, but it happens at different times. Most readers will never know the other ending. And, oddly enough, it's in the interest of the authors who this conclusion remain unattainable.

Modulated Plot Structures

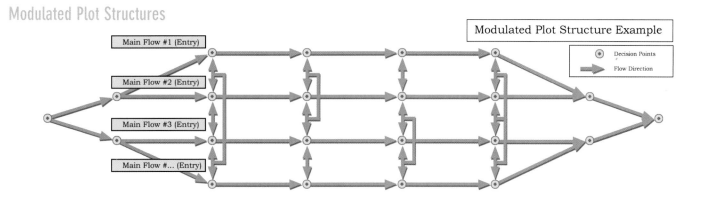

Main Flow #1 (Entry)
Main Flow #2 (Entry)
Main Flow #3 (Entry)
Main Flow #... (Entry)

Modulated Plot Structure Example

Decision Points
Flow Direction

   Modulated plots are plots that still support the dramatic arc, this time to a lesser degree, but do not necessarily dictate the order of events that are being followed. Transitions may be made to an earlier point in the story, and time can often be looped back on itself. This is a challenging plot to develop because it represents a middle ground and compromise between two trends in design.

   Marc Lafia's *Memex Engine* [2.5.8] is a plot that allows a reader to follow different events in the narrative but which still maintains a dramatic arc: The diva is lost, a mystery is afoot, and the reader needs to face specific challenges to solve a specific riddle. (This story is not played as a game, but it is interesting to note that as we move toward the more expressive forms of plot, the gaming sensibilities emerge.)

   The interaction of a modulated structure is more plot based than in a nodal structure. Modulated plots will, ideally, provide a reader with the option to bore straight through and avoid interaction, or to take a more leisurely route and increase the interaction and participation.

Open Plot Structures

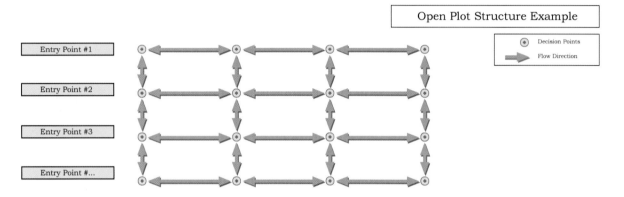

Open Plot Structure Example

Entry Point #1

Entry Point #2

Entry Point #3

Entry Point #...

⊙ Decision Points

→ Flow Direction

Open plots can resemble a roadmap. There are points of decision that then carry a reader along to another point of decision. Open plot structures are the most expressive for the reader, far less so for the author. Often the dramatic arc is completely abandoned for the interests of exploration, modification, and investment. This form of narrative has no specific starting point in the sense that there is an event that begins the story. The story is usually one that is based on the development of character (such as *Ultima Online* or *Everquest*) or the development of environment (such as the *Sims* or *Age of Empires*). There is, of course, overlap and development of character and environment.

Let's return to considering an open plot structure as a series of intersections in a city. If you are driving, your individual decisions are what allow you to get where you are going. This process of getting there is what is valued in this plot structure. The journey is, itself, the goal and so it's up to the author to see that the ride is a smooth one for the reader. Because there are so many opportunities for interaction, the frequency, scale, and form of interaction are usually found at their most developed here, making this form of narrative a complicated and expensive production process.

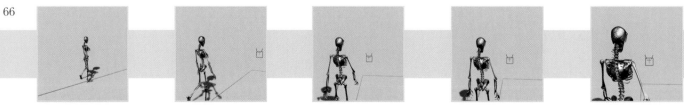

1.6: Summary

Politics will eventually be replaced by imagery. The politician will be only too happy to abdicate in favor of his image, because the image will be much more powerful than he could ever be.

—Marshall McLuhan

1.6.1: The Crossed Lines of Design

Interactive narrative is an emerging art form that borrows from multiple disciplines. Most emerging art forms grow like this; they're fruity. Emerging art forms will often take methods and approaches that were developed by previous forms, copy them, alter them, and drop from the vine before taking the role of seeding a newer art form that follows.

The practice areas of experience, visual, and communication design are being integrated so that we understand what makes, finally, someone change television channels. It's a reflex to an altered state of attention span. It's a curiosity that is induced by a desire for a change for change's sake. Like the video game player's interest in seeing returns, any executive who's responsible for a firm that is doing this kind of development wants returns on the company's investment. The video game development world is ferociously competitive, the pace of work is crippling, and the demands on the software are unknown. Consequently, the resulting products are, like the fractured and harried world of the television commercial, wound up and dumbed down. But these harried developers stand on the shoulders of existing art forms to build new rules, new roles, and new ways of thinking.

The internal world of the reader and the external world of the viewer continue to weld themselves together, and we're still learning how to draw these two personalities closer. There continues to be a distance between the movie-goer and the programmer, between the remote and the joystick. The executives of firms involved in some form of digital design recognize, at least on an intuitive level, that these media share narrative as a common thread and this recognition pushes those firms to innovate. Some of them begin prodding the soft body of the public for that nerve cluster that, when pinched, induces relaxation, catalepsy, hallucination, and a greasing of the desire to buy (to make little mention of a dilation of the wallet).

The external world of entertainment and video is slowly splicing itself onto the internal world of coding. It's at this splice point that interactive narrative is coalescing into its contemporary form. The arc of development in digital design tends toward increased interaction, increased stimulus, increased response, faster feedback, richer narrative, deeper throughput, and far-flung networks that follow us, sheep-like, wherever we may go. It's a trend that is easy to anticipate if we look back over the past 30 years.

As any arc, the change in the rate of change is the characteristic to watch. At a certain point it's no longer us who are driving the change, but, instead, the relationship changes at the epicenter of the arc, and suddenly the roles are reversed; the change is driving us. I'm not referring to an issue of control that developers, readers, viewers, and users of digital media have, but rather an issue of their investment of attention.

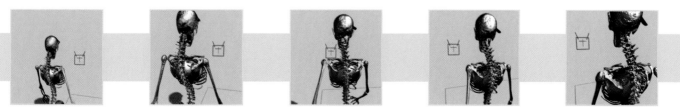

What is it about interaction that makes it so addictive? What is it about the high-latency interactivity—and specifically digital interactivity—that causes, for example, gaming trends to give so many parents so many wrinkles in so little time?

It is the change in the rate of change. This is the source of the addiction of video games (to speak both culturally and individually) and the interest of attention. Narrative will play an important role in the Internet's development in the coming years. This is important to consider in light of the fact that the two commodities of the Internet are attention and reputation.

Play a good video game for a few minutes and you'll experience this rate-of-change arc on a tiny, momentary level; after you've contributed a small amount of yourself to something that is really interactive, after you've spent just a few minutes with your head in that box, you'll find you've lost more time than you had intended. Your initial investment saw returns, but not of the sort you had imagined. The change of your attention span is the intoxicant—far more than the content or design of the product.

Some neighbors of mine recently bought a computer and they bought with it Microsoft's *Age of Empires*. The husband spent several days playing it while the wife complained that he was spending too much time killing Carthaginians and building Wonders. For whatever reason, he stopped long enough to give her a chance to play and, as you can imagine, the rest of the story is that two weeks later, they got rid of both the video game and the computer.

In short, it has to do with the return on investment of attention that the person at the end of the line feels. And that investment is entirely based on the interaction of the material they're engaged with, what the narrative is, and how it appeals to their individual interests.

"How Could the Butler Have Done It?"

There's something else, however, that's worth noticing. Interactivity allows a reader to bring his own sense of time to what he is reading. This is the nature of interaction. This is also a progression in literature that has been happening for ages—probably before Poe made such bold contributions to the genres of mystery and the short story. As with mystery novels, the reader of an interactive narrative takes on a role that is more closely aligned with that of an investigator, or perhaps of someone engaged in a conversation. In many computer games, the reader takes on a role of debugging, as it were, the underlying structure of the story. The reader becomes the investigator, vested with that perspective, making efforts, meanwhile, to understand the perspective of the author. It's a process of reverse engineering. But different people will solve the same problem at different speeds, so when problem-solving accompanies narrative, the amount of time the narrative takes to read changes.

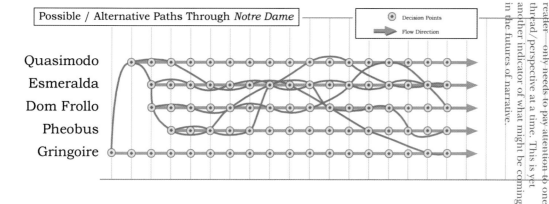

Possible / Alternative Paths Through *Notre Dame*

Quasimodo
Esmeralda
Dom Frollo
Pheobus
Gringoire

⊙ Decision Points
➜ Flow Direction

In multiprocessing, there is one CPU acting as an executor of sequential machine code instructions. Forking allows for several threads of nonlinear narrative to be active within the context of the GUI and its background processes, but then the CPU—as reader—only needs to pay attention to one thread/perspective at a time. This is yet another indicator of what might be coming in the futures of narrative.

This consideration is a key factor in narrative and game design because it lies at the intersection of intention and interpretation.

The similarities between this form of reading and the basic form of algorithmic logic—the semantic and tautological properties of computer programs—are suspiciously similar.* Both are a sequential interpretation of a series of events that were already there. This is the point where a use-case scenario and a plot converge.

Consequently, we can think of writing a narrative as interface design. It's a telescoping and a presentation of a series of events. Some events are important, and some are not. Some events are engaging, and some are not. The author's job is to decide which are which. And how to make this clear.

Consider Victor Marie Hugo's work about Notre Dame and the hunchback. Hugo had to choose a perspective to tell the story from. However, that story could have also been told from the single perspective of one of the characters, resting only in the first person, and been, under the guiding hand of a skilled author, an interesting perspective on the same story. Consider the different perspectives of Esmeralda, Frollo, Quasimodo, and Phoebus. Hugo combines them, in many ways, and in doing so has chosen a single path through a complicated field of interwoven possibilities and overlapping worldviews.

From this perspective of authorship, narrative's shift to interaction seems natural. Any traditional, noninteractive story might be thought of as a piece of a larger interactive narrative.

The story that is told is one of a number of possible ways to interpret and present the data of that world-view. The role of the author in traditional narrative is to generate both the world-view and the particular perspective that looks into it. He has to pick the path through a garden of infinitely forking paths to discover which path is the most beautiful. The role of the painter is the same, as is the role of the interface designer.

The author of interactive narrative has to present all the forking paths by telescoping information and offering perspective. So the art of interactive narrative lies in the author's ability to simultaneously imagine (and illustrate) each of these views and make all of them accessible for the reader. It's a difficult task of schizophrenic design.

Interactive narrative's potential future and its current success lies exactly here: It's the point at which these different forms of design—writing, imagery, and interface—cross and spark a new kind of attention in an emerging art form.

Two: The Second Dimension

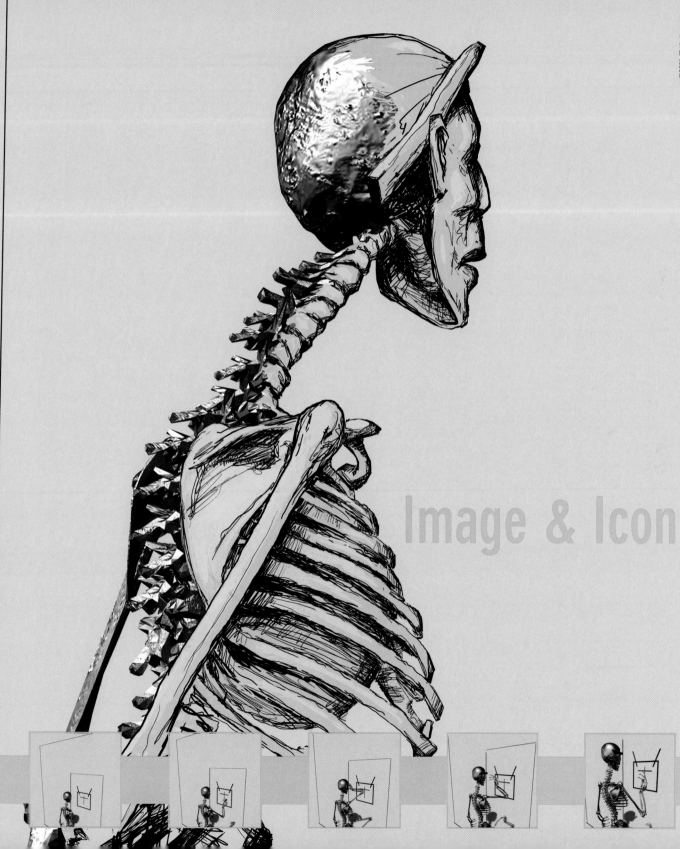

Image & Icon

2.1: Introduction

I think that what makes a photograph so powerful is the fact that, as opposed to other forms, like video or motion pictures, it is about stillness. I think the reason a person becomes a photographer is because they want to take it all and compress it into one particular stillness. When you really want to say something to someone, you grab them, you hold them, you embrace them. That's what happens in this still form.

—Joel-Peter Witkin

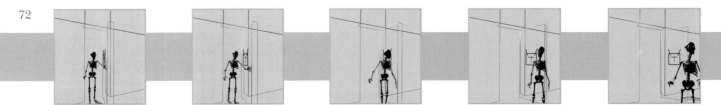

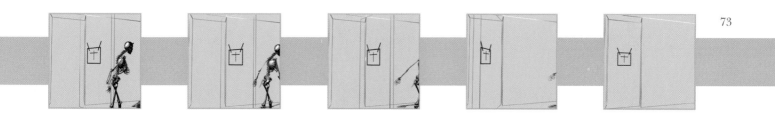

2.2: Perspective

The way a story is told determines how it's understood.

If we look at the existing media of television, movies, books, and the Internet—and specifically the stories that float on the rivers of these media—we learn a great deal about how to design interactive narrative. Dialogues have sprung up around how to present these forms of story and languages with advanced vocabularies that exist to explain the techniques and ideas that fuel them.

Much of what follows is not new. Most of the following material is borrowed from the world of literature, television, movies and "IF"or "interactive fiction" (a rather ill-defined term that includes Choose-Your-Own-Adventure games, hypertext narrative, and a broad base of MUDs and traditional (or semitraditional) text-based adventure games. See *Zork* as an example of this).

Consider three primary points of view: first, second, and third person. These are classically accepted aspects that are used by playwrights and novelists to express different levels of tension, attachment, and passion. These points of view also map in a strange way to graphic storytelling, as we'll soon see.

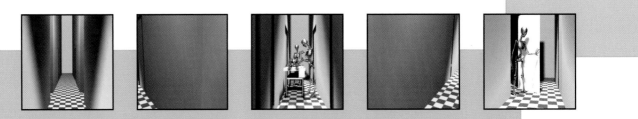

First Person

Think of this as "I." The term "first person" comes from movies and literature and refers to someone seeing the world through the eyes of the protagonist. The first-person point of view is a method of most closely identifying with the protagonist, or main character, of a story. "I run down the hallway, slide to a stop in the middle of the intersection, and look left. I see two doctors pushing a gurney. I looked right. Someone is opening a door and stepping out into the hallway."

There are at least five first-person images implicit in the preceding paragraph:
    Run down hallway
    Look left
    Two doctors pushing a gurney
    Look right
    Someone stepping into the hallway
And, if we include the skidding to a stop before looking,
    Slide to stop
We have six.

The equivalent passages, in something like a comic, graphic novel, or storyboard for a movie or animation, might get represented something along the lines of this:

Gaming examples of first-person perspective include *Doom*, *Deus Ex*, and *Everquest*.

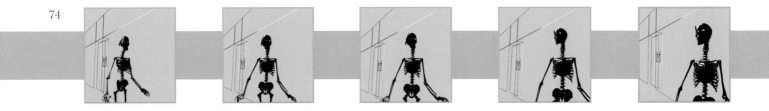

Second Person

Think of this as "You." The term refers to someone seeing the world through the eyes of the protagonist, but this time with a slight level of removal and even control. The second-person point of view is a method of identifying with the protagonist but simultaneously introducing a degree of separation because the voice of the narrator is coming from outside "your" head. "You run down the hallway, slide to a stop in the middle of the intersection, and look left. You see two doctors pushing a gurney. You look right. Someone is opening a door and stepping out into the hallway."

Again, we have the same number of images implied:
> Ran down hallway
> Looked left
> Two doctors pushing a gurney
> Looked right
> Someone stepping into the hallway
> Slid to stop

But they start to look different as the amount of information being represented is increased:

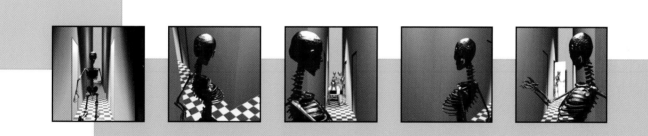

Gaming examples of second-person perspective include *Dungeons and Dragons* and *Sega Snowboarder.*

Third Person

Think of this as "She" or "He." The term refers to someone seeing the world through, not a pair of eyes so much as a series of understandings. The third-person point of view provides a knowledge that allows a reader, in some cases, omnipotent understanding. In others, it provides only a few ideas, but still leaves the reader far more aware than a person or any individual character in the story.

This is the god's-eye perspective, the removed, floating overhead, watching-and-waiting perspective that gazes down with detachment and a comparative calmness. "He runs down the hallway, slides to a stop in the middle of the intersection, and looks left. He sees two doctors pushing a gurney. He looks right. Someone is opening a door and stepping out into the hallway."

Again, we have the same number of images implied:
Runs down hallway
Looks left
Two doctors pushing a gurney
Looks right
Someone stepping into the hallway
Slides to stop

Gaming examples of this perspective include
Age of Empires, Sims, and *Broodwars.*

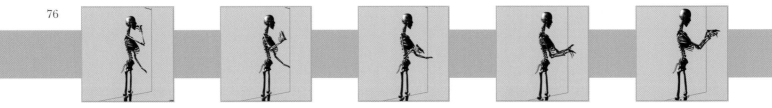

How the story is presented determines how the story is understood. This is something that impromptu actors and excitable participants of role-playing games have known for years (*"You walk into a dark, musty room behind the secret door..."*).

77

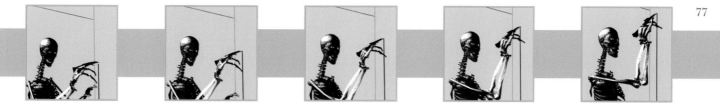

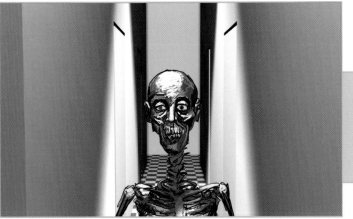

The ability to read the character's face is most important for second-person graphical presentation. The author of the narrative would either want to show what the character was seeing, and sacrifice the display of the character's reactions to what they were seeing…

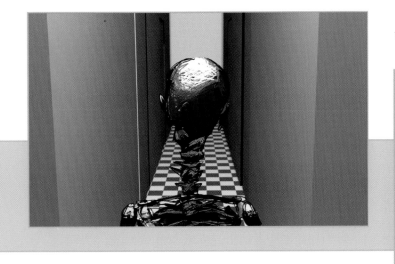

… or show how the character is reacting at the cost of showing what it is that he or she is reacting to…

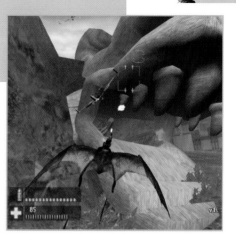

In several games, such as *Turok Evolution* (for the XBox) and *Star Wars Rogue Squadron*, players have the ability to move the camera to different locations in order to see what is happening at different times. This makes very good sense because it allows the player to see not only reactions, but what is being reacted to, giving a stronger sense of environment and interaction.

The perspectivist approach necessitates that each point of view be considered so that the different windows into the narrative provide a different view. In multi-user environments, such as *Ultima Online* or *Everquest*, the readers of the story are all contributing, adding their own perspectives. It's a gentle blending that provides a cohesive narrative but with enough freedom that it allows increased interaction in the narrative.

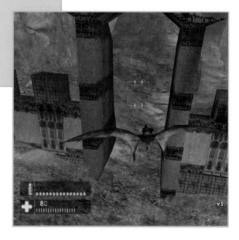

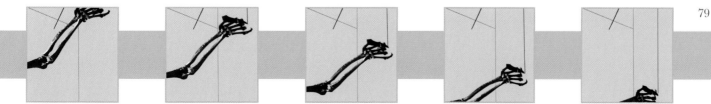

2.2.2: The Position of the Camera

Personal Perspectives and Social Scenery

Although there have been efforts to bridge this gap with modified and modernized versions of the third-person omniscient, third-person limited omniscient, third-person objective, and third-person closely attached, for the sake of this study, we will focus on the classic three-part distinction of merely first, second, and third person.

While the graphical and textual points of view are similar, there is a subtle shift that has an important effect on interactive narrative—and specifically the visual design of interactive narrative. Some cameras are appropriate for personal interaction and others for group interaction.

Consider, in literature, the distance between our three points of view.

We use the words "I" and "You" when we are speaking directly to or about the person in question. They are present there at the time that word is used. "He" could be someone on the other side of the planet or "She" might as well be pushing daisies and we'd speak of him or her in the same way. There is an immediacy to the first and second person in classic narrative that doesn't exist in the third person.*

The difference between first and second person seems smaller than between second and third person because in each of these, the point of identity, or agency, is the individual protagonist that is present at that time. In other words, "I" is closer to "You" than either of these are to "He" or "She" because the individual in question is the central focus of activity and concentration at that time. He or She just won't be there.

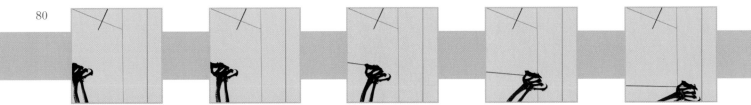

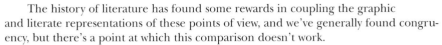

The history of literature has found some rewards in coupling the graphic and literate representations of these points of view, and we've generally found congruency, but there's a point at which this comparison doesn't work.

Graphically, if we look at the previous examples, we can see that this isn't the case, but rather that the second- and third- person perspectives, which both include the subject in the scene (as if we were there, speaking), are the second- and third-person perspectives.

This may indicate that social interaction is best left to second and third cameras from a visual perspective and to first and second person from a literary, or textual, perspective.

Consider Microsoft's 1998 project, *Comic Chat*. There were several successors to this project, but *Comic Chat* was an early form of interactive narrative that will most likely establish a genre because it solved so many problems simultaneously. *Comic Chat* did several things very very well. First, the producers of the project had the intelligence to hire Jim Woodring—an insanely brilliant and mildly mad comic illustrator—to do the illustration for the project which, alone, was a wise choice because this illustrator already had a solid understanding of the language of comics. Second, the camera used was generally second or third person, which allowed multiple people to be framed in the imagery. This built a kind of visual frame around the social interaction of the comic narrative and provided a sense of depth and background that is much harder to achieve from a first-person camera.

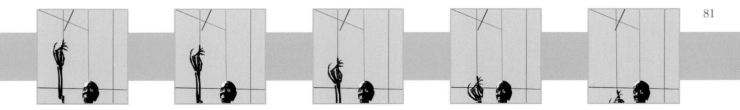

Virtual Places, *Worlds Chat*, and Time-Warner's *The Palace* were all, essentially, the same basic interface. There was minimal metaphor in each of these places, which gave them a slightly trashy feel. The design was relegated to the reader, and this was a trade-off that they felt they needed to make in order to allow readers the ability to feel more invested and increase the perception of participation. But they were all wheels without a motor. None of these really had a significant backstory, and while they presented an image that had narrative components, conversations usually ranged from the mundane to the moronic.

Banja [2.5.6], however, followed a similar approach with a slight difference: They have a narrative that sits behind the chat interaction. It's the same interface approach to chat, but with a "raison d'être" narrative. People who are involved in the chat spaces have a shared reason for being there. The chat might still be mundane and moronic, but readers have something in common: the story of Banja. Not only do they have a richer metaphor and a stronger narrative (which gives people a reason to be there in the first place), but they also have given readers the ability to configure their characters. This makes the visual design much richer and the narrative aspects of the environment stronger, still.

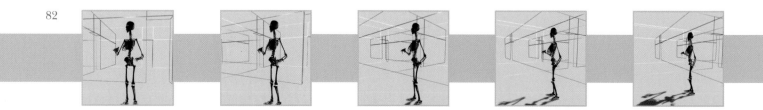

The Fixed and Floating Camera

There are some other cameras that appear in interactive narrative as well. One is a fixed camera. *Comic Chat* uses a fixed camera because the camera doesn't move. The focus is on the specifics of the interaction rather than on the change of scenery. Fixed cameras are well suited for conversations, and less so for exploration.

A floating camera, by distinction, is one that is used in games such as *Doom, Quake, Deus Ex,* or *Ultima Online.* A floating camera changes from scene to scene more like a movie camera. It's useful for representing first-person perspective. Most virtual reality applications rely on the first-person perspective, and it's interesting, when one begins to look into the side effects of virtual reality, to notice the frequency of nausea, headaches, and disorientation. It's as if there were something deeply powerful and, perhaps inappropriate, in representing what a person sees directly to the brain without the accompanying input that it is accustomed to getting from the legs, ears, and other parts of the body. Notwithstanding, no one can deny, when going into a video game arcade and watching someone lean into turns in front of a stable machine, that it has a powerful and addictive capability when coupled with even minimal interaction.

2.2.3: The Benefits of Image & Icon

Text Is Linear

We experience a text-based story as a linear process. It's part of the nature of that kind of reading (and writing). The linearity of the spoken and written word has forced multiple conventions in narrative structure. Many of the conventions that written or spoken forms of narrative employ are efforts to utilize or circumvent this characteristic. Consider tools such as foreshortening, simulacrum, allusions (references to things in other places), foreshadowing (references to events that will happen later in the story), expositions (a brief passage that gives background information), prolepsis (a form of anachronism in which a future event is treated as having already happened), and even tools such as soliloquy (in which a character, alone, "thinks out loud"). These are all linguistic hacks. Most of these, within a context of appropriate narrative that includes a different, nonlinear approach, become far clearer. Even simple transitional terms (such as "meanwhile, back on the ranch") have been handily dealt with by the native capabilities of the video arts.

We talk about circular arguments and intersecting paths—narrative forms that take on linear shapes. We tend to think spatially about narrative, yes, but it is generally not very dimensional (because, so far, it hasn't been presented that way).

By using imagery, we have increased communicative capabilities not only in terms of story structure, but also in terms of the content being presented.

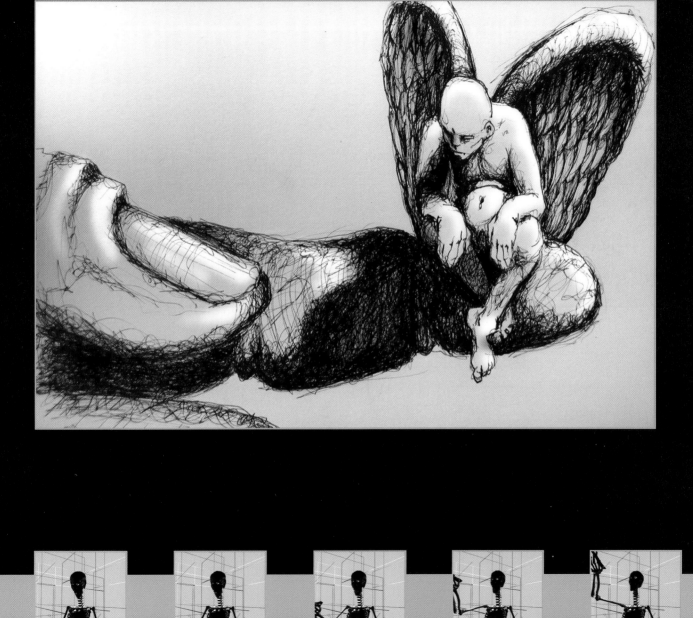

The Familiar Seen Abstractly

For the past several years, I have taught a character design class. One of the activities of the class is to draw, on paper, several characters and to use some level of abstraction to emphasize a theme or metaphor. When these drawings are done, the students go on to model the character in a 3D modeling application.

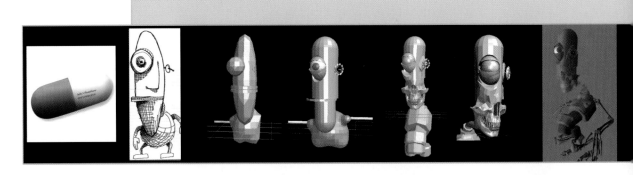

It's a strange thing that the face is the most often abstracted part of the characters. This part of the human form is the area where we get the most information and see the greatest response during conversation. It is the area where we tend to see the most detailed personality. It is also the part that is the most likely to be abstracted by students. In thinking about this, it seems that it's not the information but the method of identification that makes the image of the face so difficult to accurately reproduce (and, therefore, difficult to abstract). Here's an example.

In 1956, in the *American Journal of Psychology,* two researchers named Ryan and Schwartz conducted a series of tests on subjects to analyze their image recognition capabilities. The test changed itself from being about the subjects to being about the method of portrayal. They presented the subjects with a series of images, each subject being given a different image, and each image being shown to the subject who was then timed until they were able to recognize what the image was. The images ranged from photographic to abstracted cartoons.

Interestingly enough, the subjects more quickly identified the illustrated versions of the hand than they did the photographic. Ryan and Schwartz conclude that this was because of an economy of visual information. The subjects were not being overwhelmed with the tasks of winnowing depth cues such as shadow contour. I suspect also that it has to do with the redundancy of the information that is being shown and so metaphor steps in for a guest appearance. We implicitly understand that this is a hand because there is a basic proportion and interpretation that matches our own experience of the hand. Because the image has this kind of redundancy [1.4.4], but because it is also different from our own hands, it offers information and meaning more immediately than a photographic image. This is an important issue for anyone who is developing abstracted or semi-abstracted characters.

But why would the students place the emphasis of abstraction on the face of their characters? If abstraction facilitates a kind of meaning that is implied by the author—and is simultaneously easier to identify—and if we're trying, as character design students, to articulate the meaning of a personality through a drawing, then what else would make sense?

The character of a character is in the face.

On a general level, we can say that images become more meaningful and personalized if an appropriate quantity and form of abstraction are used—and this is true for both the author and reader. Appropriately, abstracted imagery allows user identification and increased perspective and participation.

There is an important issue under the carpet, however, and it is that the image needs to be appropriately abstracted. It is here that we again fall off of the cliff of design into the abyss of art, but gratuitous abstraction does little more than obscure meaning, distort intent, and ruin communication. Abstraction is like a kind of drug; it must be used with care.

In the worlds of narrative, character development and identification are so important, they might be said to be the most important methods of telling a good story. This would mean that learning how and when to abstract characters is at the very heart of narrative quality.

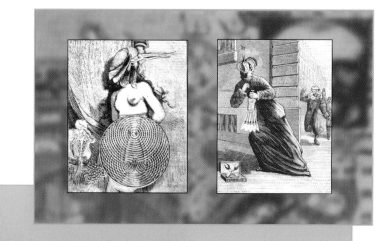

Likewise, these images all use forms of abstraction to convey opinion. Abstraction should be used for communication, not confusion.

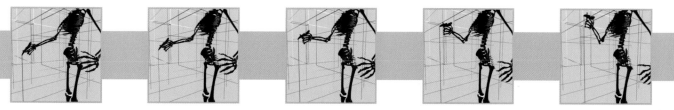

The Presence of Time and the Passage of Time

But imagery is often abstracted to represent time as well as personality and story. Consider the gutter in between comics panels. It is generally a representation of a passage of time. Scott McCloud [2.5.1], in *Understanding Comics*, proposes six categories for the gutterspace of comics: Moment to Moment, Action to Action, Subject to Subject, Scene to Scene, Aspect to Aspect, and non-sequitur. Even in still imagery such as comic books, there is a sense of time.

Let's consider the aspects of time in flat imagery. This seems important if narrative is to exist in imagery.

Perspective has the curious capability to foreshorten things, to show more than would normally be possible to see, but only from a particular position. This is one of the primary strengths of point of view—to give an overview and an understanding that extends beyond our everyday perceptions. Anamorphosis is the opposite of foreshortening. It requires that the viewer move to a particular location to view an undistorted version of an image.

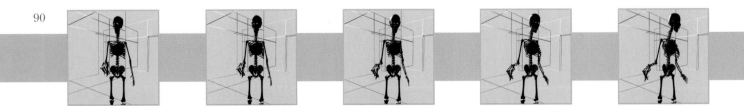

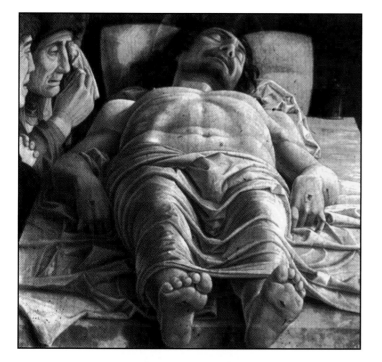

As noted earlier with regard to cameras and the first-person perspective, most graphical conventions that employ perspective also have narrative equivalents, and vice versa. Let's start with foreshortening, which is usually given through some kind of protracted perspective that allows an overview.

The equivalent to this in traditional narrative is epiphany, the term that James Joyce coined to explain the feeling of understanding the entire plot in one thought. And, surprisingly, anamorphosis has an equivalent as well, although it is far better known than either anamorphosis or epiphany. It is called foreshadowing. It is a particularly abstracted view of what is ahead in the story line, a hint at things to come. But anamorphosis and foreshadowing are there as clues and neither is intended to serve as a primary perspective.

Foreshortening, anamorphosis, epiphany, and foreshadowing all give protracted perspectives. Foreshadowing jumps ahead temporally just as foreshortening does spatially. Because of this protraction, both are narrative elements that enable us to understand things from more than one perspective.

So time and space seem to dwell comfortably together in forms of visual narrative. At least, the tools are in place to allow for this cohabitation.

As far as narrative is concerned, space and time work toward solving the problem that a narrative has implicit to it; they build the context that allows narrative to occur. This is fortunate because for a narrative to exist, something that takes place over a period of time needs to exist. This problem (generally referred to as conflict) must be solved.

But, as Chairman Mao once said, "In order for a problem to be solved, it has to be recognized first."

This process of recognition is not, fortunately for story-telling and the narrative art, always conscious.

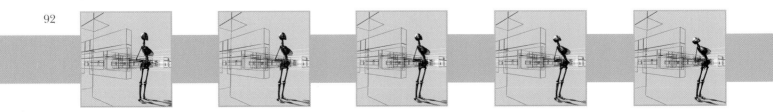

2.3: Narrative

*Works of art are not mirrors but they share with mirrors
that elusive magic of transformation which is so hard
to put into words.*

—E.H. Gombrich

Images tell stories. Certainly comic narratives tell stories, but
also most single-frame images, such as paintings or interfaces,
contain elements of narrative as well. Images provide us with a
strange kind of inside-the-skull interaction as our eyes trace the
lines and composition of a composition.

Any art student worth a half a can of gesso will tell you that
there are "lines of sight" that the eye traces when it looks at a
canvas. Our eyes register detail within only a very small foveal
area of the cone of vision. Foveal is the opposite of peripheral.
Foveal is the part that stays in focus. It subtends less than one
degree—less than a third of a percent of what we are able to
see. Consequently, as far as the rest of the image is concerned,
there is a blur and something of a mystery outside of that
foveal area. But our peripheral vision, inaccurate as it is, leads
us forward.

2.3.1: Principles of Narrative in Image & Icon

Our eyes
track to
new loca
to clear
blur of
peripher
percepti
This kin
moveme
called sa
cadic.
Saccadic
moveme
are a kin
moveme
that is m
tally targ
well before the crosshairs
the eyes are aligned wit
them. We know wher
will look before the
sharp, machinelik
movement of o
eyes look the

Our eyes track to that new location to clear the blur of peripheral perception. This kind of movement is called saccadic. Saccadic eye movements are a kind of movement that is mentally targeted well before the crosshairs of the eyes are aligned with them. We know where we will look before the sharp, machinelike movement of our eyes looks there. Like a page to be turned in a book, the eye determines the next area on which to focus. This decision is based on the categories of movement, contrast, and color (as discussed shortly). Snapping into its new position, the eye usually traverses areas that are adjacent and then retracks to spots that need to be confirmed—and made redundant—after most of the image has been stitched together, like a cognitive quilt made of visual patches.

It is not reading. It happens far faster and far less cognitively, staying below the radar of conscious understanding. da Vinci knew this well.

This temporal process of seeing, as fast as it is, is one of the things that allows a narrative aspect of imagery. This is a temporal process that is implicitly narrative because it provides for a beginning and an end, and it's this motion of the eye that many authors of narrative are able to manipulate and control for the sake of telling a story.

Consider comic narrative—the kind of sequential imagery that is running along the bottom of this page. Comics are a medium that take advantage of the foveal aspects of the eye. The eye tracks to one position, scans the image, snaps to the next, predetermined area, scans across lines of contrast and color, panning for a new spot of light or dark, and then tracks to the text to shift into a different mode of perception altogether.

In our days in the crib, we stare off, gradually learning how to use our eyes well before we can talk. Saccadic eye movements then begin and we learn to move from point to point, panning the landscape as we see. Then moving from the crib to the schoolhouse desk, the reading of text is learned. It's a difficult process at first because the student is working hard to read each letter of the alphabet as if it were something life-sized and unfamiliar. Eventually, as we get better at reading and seeing these strings of images, we learn to scan words for individual letters and eventually, words and phrases. This familiarization is one that takes years, but soon, colloquialisms and even whole sentences can be parsed in a glance, almost saccadically, because we know what to expect. The redundancy of the information allows us to move easily through it.

But this redundancy is also where the meaning comes from. Any image, even if it's completely abstract and offers no context or redundancy, will cause the eye to move across its surface this way. The narrative component of an image comes from that image's ability to generate meaning, opinion, and some sense of beginning, middle, and end.

The Generation of Meaning

What does all this mean? It means that most of what we "see" is really just what we "remember" because at any given moment, the majority of the image will not be seen, merely remembered. The cognitive quilt that was sewed by foveal vision is thrown over the cognitive map we have, both obscuring and defining the shape of the real image that lies beneath. This is a mental perception that functions in many ways as the figures of speech we looked into earlier [1.3.3]. These are often important in understanding how it is we find narrative in imagery.

The foundations of a narrative image should include some sense of the opinion of the author (some moral). Likewise, a context needs to be offered so that there is some kind of internal conflict, problem, or series of events. The decisions of how to solve these problems are part of the art of narrative—part of the sensitivity that an author of narrative needs to bring to plot to make it an actual story.

So, this is part of how imagery can generate narrative. There is a tiny narrative that takes place and, as far as the brain is concerned, it happens all at once.

Oddly enough, just as we learn to parse sentences and build on expected letters, words, and phrases, so we interact with the nearby world. As we age and grow accustomed to the visual input of the world, we adopt mannerisms that accommodate rapid perception and increasingly efficient comprehension. Most of us are in the habit of placing our heads in certain ways and framing images with specific, repeated mannerisms. Strange recurrences reinforce this. For example, 70 percent of all portraits painted from the chest up center one of the eyes in the vertical axis of the canvas.

This seems to be a desire to center our world as our eyes see it, with our own particular perspective guiding us through the world, composing it in the same way a painter composes a canvas. The composition of the canvas is, after all, that visual author's attempt to mimic the way we each view the world.

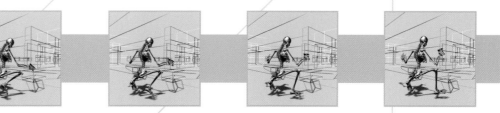

Examples of Narrative Imagery

Let's take a look at some examples of how this process of visually relating a story works. We'll start several thousand years back, in Egypt, and move toward early interpretations of video and time-based narrative. Note how in most of these examples, the narrative being told also indicates what behavior should be engaged in by its viewers at that location. The paintings are the exceptions to this because, by the 1500s, paintings were considered mobile and not as easily associated with specific architectural functions.

An Explanation of Worship, Example 1: The Tablet of Isis

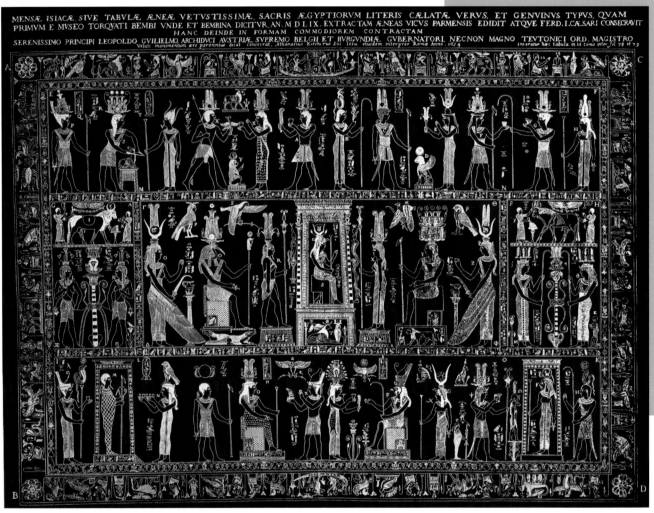

Before Rome was sacked in 1527, there was no mention of the Tablet of Isis. In 1559, Aeneas Vicus of Parma Italy made a reproduction of the small tablet—roughly 50" by 30"—and noted that it was made of bronze and decorated in encaustic enamels.

This image has been an intractable read for many people and is laced with such significance that we won't go into detail here other than to point out that this is actually a kind of recipe for rites of sacrifice that were extremely specific and elaborately detailed. Those familiar with the fundamental principles of Hermetic philosophy were able to recognize it as an intricate key to Chaldean, Egyptian, and Greek theologies (yes, all on the same tablet). In brief, the twelve houses of heaven are the twelve figures, divided into four seasons. The relationship between the fixed and mobile zodiacs is also represented as well as an elaborate key to The Scroll of Thoth.*

Portions of this tablet were specific instructions on how to carry out worship. For example, the figure in the center of the tablet is of particular instruction as the figures that surround it are the ones that indicate how and when sacrifices should be performed and of what sort. Additionally, the tablet indicates which of each of the gods had a particular set of ornaments, gestures, and symbols and specifies how and when to use them. Through these rituals, the priests who read this narrative believed they were able to foretell the future, interpret the past, and maintain some limited control of the world around them.

The tablet can be read from multiple directions, starting from any one of 12 entry points around the perimeter of the main composition.

This form of visual narrative was not only instructional and an intriguing combination of imagery and text (a large number of the images we see here are actually phonetic symbols, not icons), but it was actually something that affected the behaviors of the priests who used it. Its method of being read was based on the actions that it asked for in response to the reading. Whether this is a form of interaction that is based in active response to a form of reading is worth considering in the light of today's technologies.

*More than one accomplished writer about Hermeticism has confirmed with me that the current opinion about Levi's writing on The Tablet of Isis ranges from "occultnik dreck" to "demonstrable hoax." One of these scholars went on to say, "IMHO, Crowley and Levi (from whom the former claimed to be reincarnated) were largely extra-horny poets/dramatists, more so than historians."

An Explanation of Intervention, Example 2: The Annunciation

Approximately 200 years after Giotto, many of the stories that were familiar to the Christian Church were, of course, still in existence, and it was the interpretation of these stories that lent them a sense of individual perspective and transformed the visual representations into imagery. It was a moment of tilting from a Gothic past into a Renaissance future.

Originally named Guido di Pietro, Fra Angelico (formally known as Fra Angelico Giovanni da Fiesole) was a friar of the Dominican order who was born sometime around the turn of the 15th century in Tuscany. At the age of 35, he was commissioned to develop some frescoes that were painted onto plaster walls that were still wet (a relatively archival method of manufacturing a painting in those days). These were intended to be literal translations of the text of the Bible, but at the same time, they were also intended to inspire prayer and meditation among the clergy.

One of the primary themes that Fra Angelico focused on was The Annunciation, or the moment when Mary was informed that she would be bearing the son of God. We have multiple versions of this same idea by the same painter. The changes between these images are not great. The subtleties in where the viewer is located, what is in the background (be it a room or a man), the themes that surround it (such as the Garden of Eden) and the expressions and positions of the figures, tell us that Fra Angelica had a particular vision that he felt was closely communicated the first time.

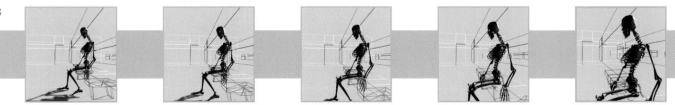

It's an old story told by many people. Before Fra Angelico, there was the curious comic-like integration of text with the image in Simone Martini's 1333 version of the Annunciation (left). And at approximately the same time that Fra Angelica was painting his version, Jan Van Eyck was working on an interpretation of his own (right).

Hundreds of years after these painters were dead, Leonardo da Vinci continued to carry the torch and shed light on an otherwise mysterious subject by producing two different interpretations of the story, both from relatively early in his life.

The similarities and the symbols of these paintings are what lend them a narrative aspect, giving a redundancy and a meaning to what the viewer sees, based on the icons and understandings of their times. This element of redundancy that was touched on in the first chapter [1.4.4] is what allows meaning to be generated. Tiny differences come to mean something with such repetition; repeated icons (such as a lily and an enclosed garden) come to carry their own representations (of virginity) in our culture today.

The number of times this story has been repeated points to its power. A small army of painters have depicted this story, including those pictured here: Boticelli, Solario, Vasari, Baldovinetti, Braccescom, Weyden, Daddi, Bouts, Reni, and Carracci. This tradition was carried on for more than 1,300 years.

But the repetition and generation of meaning through redundancy was just one of the tools of religious iconography. As we saw with Giotto, it was also the integration of that imagery with a physical location. Consider the Ravenna Baptistry, also in Italy.

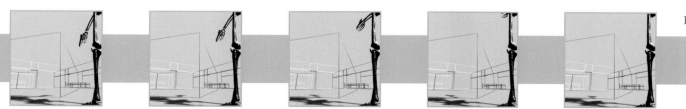

An Explanation of Ritual, Example 3: Baptism of Christ

The Arian Baptistry in Ravenna, reconstructed from its Roman origins in 520, contains a narrative on the ceiling. Looking up like this seems to be a source of inspiration for many forms of visual narrative.

The context of the room is what makes this interesting; it's a narrative about something that is happening both in the walls of the building and outside. The image on the ceiling, intended to be seen by a person being baptized, was of Christ being baptized by St. John the Baptist. The twelve apostles walk grimly toward the throne of Christ. The image can be read upside down or downside up.

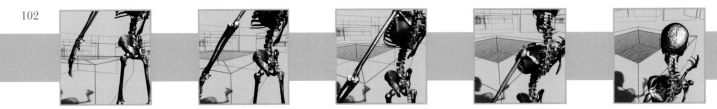

Hieronymus Bosch, a man in close touch with strange dreams and phantom worlds, is well known for his painting *The Garden of Earthly Delights. The Garden* falls into an almost standard format for Bosch in the way that it tells a story. What is generally overlooked is the form of narrative and reading activities that this painting asks of its viewer. It's a hell of a painting, but almost falls more into the category of an interactive form of painted sculpture. The triptych was intended as a kind of book with a cover, a beginning, a middle, and an end. If the two wings of the triptych are closed, the front panel shows the world as it was being created by God with the words "He spake and it was done; for he commanded and it stood fast" (Psalm 33:9).

When the wings of the triptych are folded back, the left-hand panel shows the Garden of Eden and a quotation from Genesis 1:28 ("Be fruitful, multiply, and replenish the earth"), the middle panel shows, simply, a carnal party of a fantastic nature, and the right-hand panel shows the subsequent punishment for this kind of partying: cards and musical instruments are scattered about while the devil makes a pact with a man who has legs growing from his helmet.

This story, already well known and packed with allegory for anyone familiar with Christian mythology, appears as a warning to us all. It's this form of allegorical stacking that makes the painting interesting. If it were simply an image that Bosch had conjured from his fevered imagination, the impact that it would have had on its viewers would have been minimal and, given the day, Bosch would have been in big trouble.

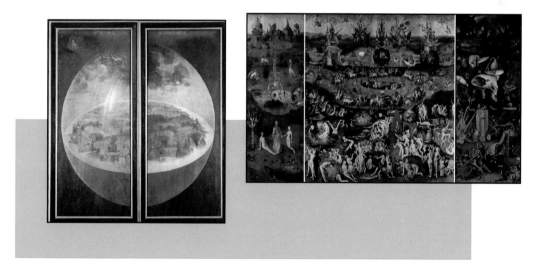

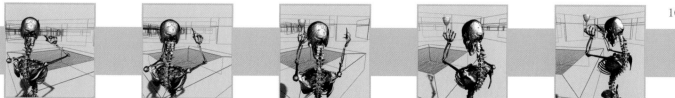

Hieronymus, born in the backwoods of Holland in the middle of the 1400s, came from a family of painters and started painting professionally when he was in his early 30s. His works generally have some inherent element of narrative. Many of them are read from left to right or from top to bottom. These are moral stories that were from an imagination with few limits. The synthesis of machinery and humans with animals and actions makes it relevant even now, 600 years later.

In each case, the individual panel of the tritpych frames the scenes of the narrative, but the panels don't so much depend on each other temporally (as words in a sentence do), but rather they support the general metaphor and context of the story as a whole. They're not terribly linear. The reader can move from left to right, but there isn't necessarily a need to do so to understand the whole world-view, or story, that Bosch is painting.

More than most narrative painters, Bosch relies heavily on foveal vision and the reader's ability to keep track of a bizarre battlefield of details which, because there's so much imagery that's all so dense, makes the paintings somewhat claustrophobic. Unlike Da Vinci's compositions that guide the eye along an informative line, the direction of the read is left to the eye that's looking at rather than the hand that painted it.

The Last Judgement combines a few different approaches. More than *The Garden of Earthly Delights*, the triptych presents itself as a left-to-right read because the color of the left-hand panel is so different from the other two. We're attracted to the difference and so start there, but the story is also one that's better known and has, traditionally, had a beginning, an end, a cause, and an effect. It has a linear component to it more so than *The Garden*, but it still isn't as strict as the Da Vincis, for example.

These are many of the same basic approaches that modern comics use: Time and change are presented, and each panel has a consistent metaphoric relationship with the other panels near it.

An Explanation of Redemption, Example 5: The Crucifixion

The Last Judgement is no less revealing when read from left to right, top to bottom, or bottom to top. Because it is in a triptych, this panel-by-panel read works with many of the same basic approaches that modern comics use: Time and change are presented in each of the three panels.

This book-based presentation of tortured souls was an apparent crowd-pleaser in the early 1500s. Matthias Grünewald, following a similar format but working with far larger materials and simpler individual compositions, chose to build his stories with icons that are a little easier to recognize. They're just more classic.

Grünewald shows a more complicated narrative when the complete altarpiece, with all of its wings and fold-outs, is seen together (though Bosch certainly has more complicated scenes). Because of the sequence of the structure and how Grünewald used it, he comes down a little closer to being a traditional book author than does Bosch (and, considering the size of the paintings, which tower over you if you stand in front of them, he might come close to a movie, or VR author, today). Saints Sebastian and Anthony occupy their well-known posts on the two wings that, when folded in, cover the entire image save for Jesus and a preliminary image of Mary kneeling near the cross.

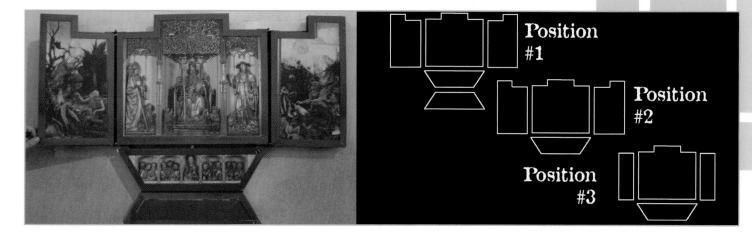

Position #1

Position #2

Position #3

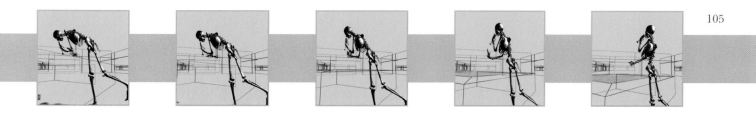

On opening the panels of the altarpiece, another image of Mary appears on the left and a third on the bottom of the painting, where a second image of Jesus, after the descent, is shown.

The narrative, again, is well known, but the means of depicting it is strange. The eye knows where to begin (even if the cover is opened) because the image of Christ in the middle of the painting is the highest point of contrast. The eye lands there first. The guest appearance of John the Baptist, pointing to the brightly lit shawl of the larger version of Mary, leads a viewer's eye left. It is as if John were saying "No, no, that way, dear reader" to us. The passive and sad expressions of Saints Sebastian and Anthony on the side buttress the painting with a kind of frame, and the composition of the wood panels sends the eye down to the bottom of the painting because of the third highest point of color and contrast. We know that, as far as the story of The Passion goes, this event of the descent happens after the crucifixion. Finally, the eye then returns to John the Baptist and the curious little anthropomorphic sheep that has its front leg wrapped around the cross as if to lend a poetic moral to the story and soften the impact of elements such as the outsplayed fingers.

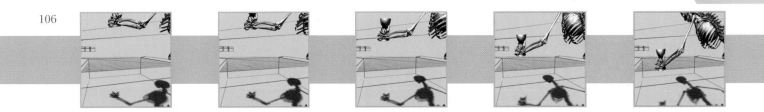

An Explanation of Perception, Example 6: Las Meninas

In 1656, Diego Velázquez started to push imagery and narrative into new depths of view. Although it was done 141 years later, *Las Meninas* (Maids of Honor) is similar to *Crucifixion* in that there's a distinct line for the eye to follow. Again, it is based on receding values of contrast, detail, and color.

The panel that, presumably, Velázquez is painting on, is foreground. Then, based on the light falling from the window on the right, we can tell that the two dwarves, one of whom is about to poke the dozing dog with her foot, are at a secondary plane. The princess, the focal point of the painting, is third. Velázquez and a couple of attendants are fourth. Then we have the gentleman standing, framed by the door. Then, after our eye has traveled all the way to the back of the room, we see the curious painting of the king and queen. But it seems so brightly lit that it might be a reflection in another mirror, and we are actually seeing the entire image through the eyes of the king and queen.

The point of view in this image is what starts to get complicated and lends it a strange story that almost reads like a mystery. Who is where? Whose eyes are we looking through? The princess looking at her reflection? She appears below the horizon line. Velázquez? He appears to the left of the vanishing point; so if the mirror were perpendicular, it wouldn't be him. The king and queen? They, like the princess, are below the horizon line as well.

Whichever, Velázquez has built a kind of virtual depth that causes this strange painting to hold at least six levels and a mysterious narrative of perception, perspective, presentation, and royalty.

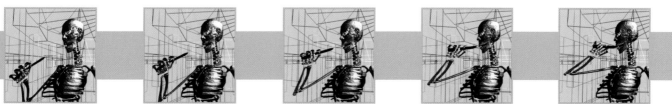

An Explanation of Movement, Example 7: Nude Descending a Staircase #2

By 1912, the world of painting was beginning to feel pressed upon by the emerging technologies in the world of photography. Perhaps it was a reaction to this series of events, perhaps it was independent innovation, but Marcel Duchamp put together a composition (perhaps it is more a composition than a painting) about a woman walking down stairs. It is very simple once the eye adjusts to looking at it. Small details, such as the dotted lines just above the center of the canvas, indicate that Mr. Duchamp wasn't entirely certain his idea was working. The panels of the figure overlap in a series that progresses to the right, however, so it is clearly a success after a few seconds of study.

What's significant is that this, like Velázquez's painting, concerns itself with depth, but has added on a component of time. The narrative form here starts to shift from the immediacy of the impression to an actual presentation of time and movement.

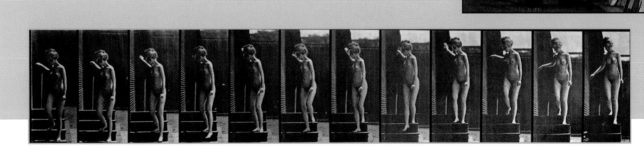

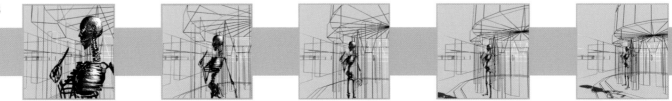

Gustav Rodin (perhaps the most perceptive sculptor who ever lived) was asked by Rainer Maria Rilke (perhaps the most perceptive poet who ever lived), "What is the creative process from its beginning?"

Rodin answered: "First, I have an intense feeling which slowly becomes more concrete and asks me to give it a solid shape. Then I begin to plan and design. Finally, when it comes to execution, I again abandon myself to the feeling, which may prompt me to modify the plan."

This is to say that the metaphor for any form of design, be it interactive, narrative, or graphic, can be guided, but that it is the ultimate judgement of the feeling (not the plan) that makes for a success.

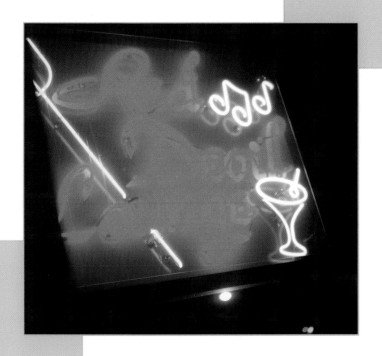

Building Metaphor

As we pointed out [1.3.3], a metaphor is a consistent relationship of symbols. Each of the previous examples of visual narrative use this: The symbols not only look similar in their style and their characteristics of production, but more importantly, the activities that these images represent build a world of internally consistent believability. In some cases, the metaphor is a conceptual one, as with Velázquez's painting; the metaphor has to do with the spatial differences. We can determine whether we've hit on the proper metaphor by testing its relationship to the other parts of the image. We can ask, "What spatial differences exist in this painting?" and begin to see emotional space among the members of the image; consider the princess' removal from the scene. To her right is the small girl offering the princess the apple; to the princess' left, the girl curtsying. That gives us three instances of separation. Is the symbol consistent? The answer is evident when we consider that everyone seems in a state of silence and deep class difference. The metaphors, as the symbols they are made of, may change over time, but it's the consistency within the entire affair that generates the metaphor. The metaphors inform our knowledge of the overall meaning of the work.

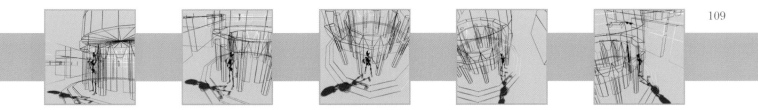

Building Redundancy

As just noted, the ability to repeat the symbols—and most importantly the relationship between the symbols—is important. A visual metaphor should be sustained by an author, just as an actor on a stage should not break the fourth wall. The redundancy is what allows the metaphor to take root in the mind of the reader or viewer. It's the repetition of the idea that serves as a suspension of disbelief.

In the Arian Baptistry in Ravenna, the image of Christ and the disciples maintains the metaphor of the ritual of baptism, and so the metaphor becomes increasingly strong as the person that is there, being baptized, sees a confirmation of this image on the ceiling above. This is a very powerful form of redundancy because it extends outside of the image and the architecture and into the very activity of the already charged religious ritual.

Redundancy in metaphor begins by being very fragile but is accepted as we continue to understand the relationships of the symbols. But it can be easily broken. Suppose, for instance, that there we are, nose to the wall, eyes squinting, carefully studying brush strokes of *Nude Descending Staircase* and we come across a tiny silhouette of Mickey Mouse. Suddenly, everything inside of the space of the canvas changes and we're left with this mysterious piece of information.

The Mickey Mouse silhouette would amount to a presentation of difference (a poor one). A better example can be seen in Velázquez's painting, or in the image of John the Baptist, pointing.

Presenting Difference

The difference that sits inside of a metaphor generally takes the form of instructing the viewer or reader of that metaphor to do—or consider—some part of the metaphor differently. In the case of John the Baptist and the small lamb at his feet, it seems a call to piety. By very slightly breaking that magic fourth wall of the narrative within the image, there is a need for participation on the part of the viewer or reader.

Generating Meaning

As soon as that difference is introduced, meaning appears. In the case of Grünewald's painting, John the Baptist, in pointing back to the central figure of Christ, starts to function like the ancient Greek chorus. He and the strange little lamb are adding commentary, as if to say, "Look back over here and think about this situation some more." And the lamb, at the bottom, echoes this. "Yeah. What he said."

It's a direct interaction with the viewer—a breaking of the fourth wall—that Grünewald is creating. He does this through building a metaphor and causing that metaphor to become redundant so that it sinks in. (Metaphors do not, after all, weigh much; it's the interpretation of the metaphor that is heavy.) At that point, difference is introduced, and, if the difference is intentional and well done, meaning may be generated.

This is the basis for most visual forms of narrative.

The similarities with figures of speech should be clear, but the main issue at hand is that the viewer participate with the metaphor on some level. We have called this inside-the-skull perspective, which is to say that a world of internal meaning is generated.

Legibility, Contrast, Color, Movement

Meaning, metaphor, and the internal world of dreams aside, there are some basic principles that can be useful when designing any form of imagery for interactive narrative.

What is the function of the task at hand?

This is the role that the architect is in when beginning his work, as well. The specific answer, of course, comes from the specific circumstances (be it a baptistry or a bronze tablet).

Four general factors affect the functionality of any graphic design. These factors are founded on how the eye is built and where foveal perception is led by peripheral input:

Legibility
Contrast
Color
Movement

Legibility should be evident. The basis of visual communication—be it image or text—is founded on legibility, and without it, narrative can't exist.

But the appropriate level of legibility is worth considering. Mick Jagger has quoted Muddy Waters, the great blues singer from the Mississippi delta, as saying, "If the audience can understand every word, then you're singin' it wrong."

Apparently, this was an adage that was followed by the Rolling Stones during their early years. It is about legibility. An appropriate level of legibility.

Aside from legibility, the other factors (contrast, color, and movement) are there to direct the eye into the appropriate portions of the composition. Consider the following:

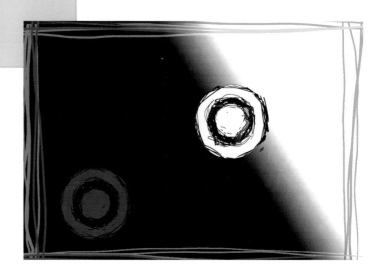

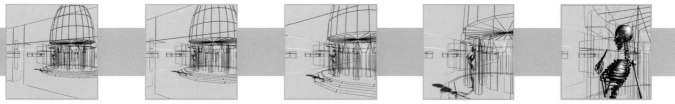

Because the eye, for reasons of survival, is attracted to contrast, we first see the dot in the middle, and then move down to the lower left, where the second point of contrast is highest.

Color is like this as well. And, as the impressionists taught us, some colors sit next to one another more easily than others. There are many forms of color contrast and usage (several of the Impressionists identified more than 12, including hue, light/dark, cold/warm, simultaneous, saturation, value, and others), but there can be simple relationships that, again, are based on how our eyes are built. Goethe (the same fellow who wrote *Faust* and made significant contributions to the early schools of genetics research) developed a rough system of quantifying complementary pairs.

As can be seen here, the relationships between reflected light and projected light differ, and a contemporary designer should know both models.

Yellow = 9 Orange = 8 Red = 6 Purple = 3 Blue = 4 Green = 6

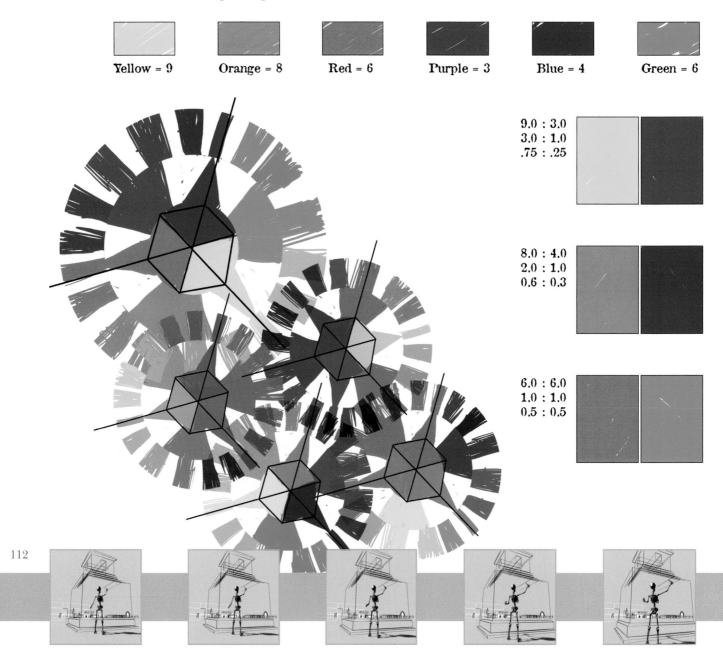

9.0 : 3.0
3.0 : 1.0
.75 : .25

8.0 : 4.0
2.0 : 1.0
0.6 : 0.3

6.0 : 6.0
1.0 : 1.0
0.5 : 0.5

Subtractive Color Model
(pigments and reflective colors
where all colors added together
tend toward a darker value)

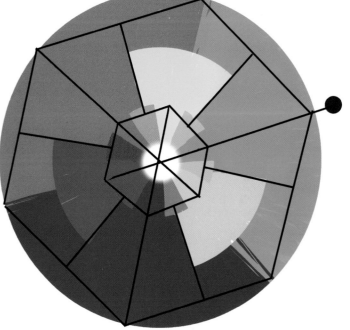

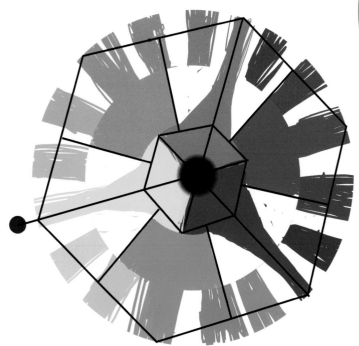

Additive Color Model
(lights and projected colors
where all colors added together
tend toward a lighter value)

Strange effects can be produced with color. Cover up all but one of the following panels and stare at the gray patch in the middle of each square. Watch for a color to appear and keep track of which colors appear in which gray boxes.

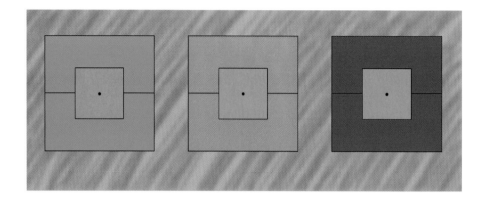

The eye adds in the complementary tinge to the gray patch. Our eyes do a lot of thinking for us. The eye considers blue to be a background (probably because we have a blue sky). It sees saturated colors as darker (something da Vinci realized during his chiaroscuro studies), and specific colors incite physiologic reactions. (Ask yourself why so many fast-food restaurants have orange signs.)

Likewise, depth is easily added with particular color combinations. Here is an example of z-axis color interpretation:

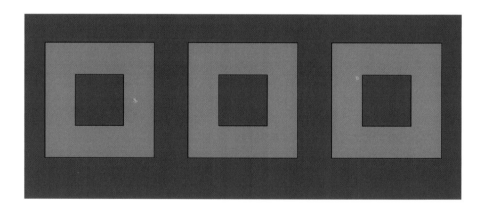

These things amount to simple tricks, but can be applied to a wide range of possibilities. Consider the colors in Mr. Bosch's *Garden of Earthly Delights* with these same principles. See what you can find.

Movement (we can easily consider this animation) is, as each of these, a subject for deep study, and we'll only skim it so as to understand its application for graphic design of narrative. In sum, place animation or any movement in a flat image to redirect an eye to that location, not as a means of embellishment or beautification. Later in this chapter, you'll see an example of this in Ed Bain's work [2.5.7]. Mr. Bain uses animation to direct the reader to the next point of interaction.

We instinctually respond to movement as if there were some possible threat or promise in front of us. It's how our eyes work. Our peripheral vision is highly sensitive to light, and it is worth considering alternative ways to present animations to the ones we see on the Internet so far. On web pages, the dancing banner ads do nothing other than distract from the site content. Which is fine, if you happen to be the advertiser; but, as a reader, the ads make the page uselessly polluted with inappropriate design.

Movement is best used if there is an interactive component involved.

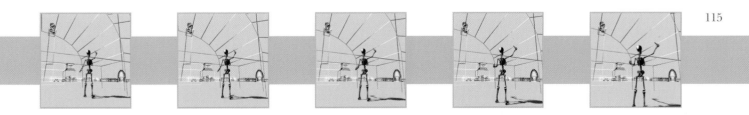

2.4: Interaction

For more information on the Shakespeare Programming Language (a very interesting approach to interactive narrative that allows the author to write a story that the computer interprets and compiles), see http://shakespearelang.sourceforge.net/.

```
{
Act II: Determining divisibility.
Scene I: A private conversation.
Juliet:
Art Though more cunning than the ghost?
Romeo:
If so, let us proceed to scene V.
Outputting Input Reversedly.
Othello, a stacky man.
Lady Macbeth, who pushes him around till he pops.
}


—Jon Åslund and Karl Hasselström,
     Authors of the Shakespeare Programming Language*
```

2.4.1 Principles of Interaction in Image & Icon: Separating and Joining

Composition, like color, works best when it's informed by design guidelines. Generally, I ask myself, "What is the function of that?" whenever an image is involved. Balancing a composition is an important element of traditional fine art, but in the world of interaction design, we are primarily guided by where the eye begins reading: in the upper left. This is also informed by a third issue, which is the fact that our eyes respond to basic elements like color, contrast, and movement.

Several guidelines are particular to interaction design. First is a consideration of two views of information: the macroscopic and microscopic views, or the general and specific sets of information. Just as narrative has foreshadowing and imagery has foreshortening, so the image composition of interface design has this collapsing of information sets. It appears everywhere now and is an important part of any web page or operating system interface.

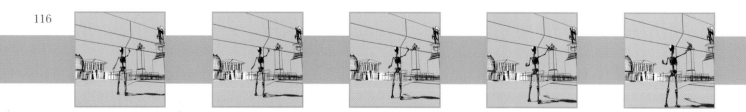

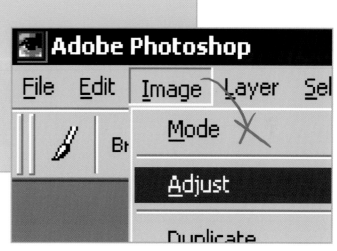

Second is the presentation of subdivisions of information. Graphical cues such as line breaks and boxes around areas of imagery indicate this. Look at the top of any application running on the computer and you see subdivisions of information. This isn't always necessary, but it is useful when there's something specific to be done, such as editing or searching.

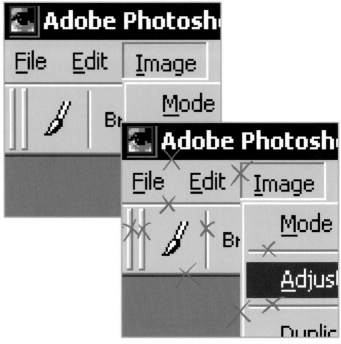

Third is the importance of feedback. This is so that a user knows when he has affected some change. This has to do with what we've termed outside-the-skull interaction and is almost entirely concerned with visual cues that represent change. Depressions, changes of color, movement, or other alterations that seem temporary are useful here.

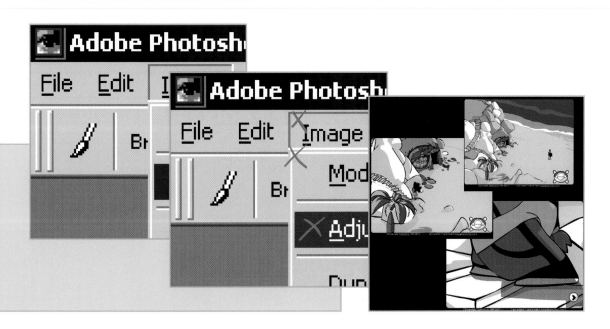

But maybe the most important of this little list is the composition, line of sight, and visual entry point. When a user enters into an interaction—be it a page or a building—it's important to direct her eye to the point of greatest informational depth first. What is the most important element of the interaction? What has the greatest significance to the story? What offers the user the most capacity for change? It is the arrangement of all of the above. This is the composition. Arrangement is a strange thing, culturally speaking. In the case of pages of text, the western eye goes to the upper-left corner first. But when architecture and spatial interfaces are involved, it's important to use other cues such as contrast, color, or placement (more on this in Chapter 3). Making important things large is the other trick when you want to direct a user—it's how the eye works. Things that are closer appear larger. Those are the things that have, for thousands and thousands of years, been what humans have learned to deal with first.

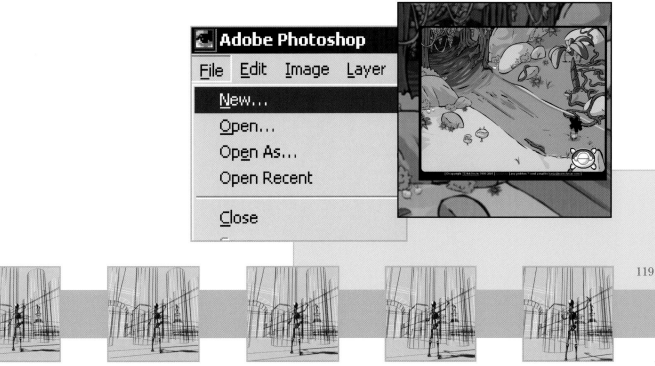

2.4.2 : Designing Image & Icon for Interactivity

Facilitating Interaction

Let's take a look at our four steps of interaction: observation, exploration, modification, and reciprocal change. The visual design of the interaction should not only facilitate, but actually highlight these features. The images should let the reader know where things live and what they do.

First, macroscopic and microscopic views will allow the first step of interaction to occur; presenting macroscopic and microscopic views will allow observation. We are accustomed, in the real world, to telescoping in and out, to adjusting our concentration as we focus on the world around us. By presenting the two views of information (consider these as categories that contain subcategories), observation is accommodated and exploration is encouraged. This assumes that the macroscopic information—or categories—is interesting. If that's the case, then the microscopic information will be inviting. Consider a simple series of icons that each represent subsets of more information:

Second, presenting subdivisions of information allows the second step of interaction, which is exploration. It helps provide a cognitive map to a reader so that he is more inclined to try new things. This process of trying new things helps to build an element of investment in what the reader is doing, and, if all goes well, it provides him with more confidence so that he is able to learn what can and cannot be done.

Third (you should be seeing a pattern emerging), feedback encourages modification. If a reader knows that he has made a change and that there is some residual component to that change, he will more likely than not be at least open to the possibility of making other changes.

So we have an intersection of observation, exploration, modification, and change with: microscopic/macroscopic, subdivisions, feedback, and point of entry.

This last intersection is very general and also significant to interactive narrative. This is the idea that the graphical composition is based on the idea that there is some number of events that needs to be relayed in an order. Composition is the factor that allows a reader to feel as if he or she has changed and been changed. This is a difficult item to understand because graphical composition has traditionally been thought of as a fixed thing. However, tear-off menus are an example of a reconfigurable image composition. Moving through an architectural space is another example of a reconfigurable image composition. A composition can be thought of as a kind of plot. It determines the events of a visual story over a space of time that uses things like foveal vision, peripheral vision, and memory [2.3]. The composition, because it indicates an order, also indicates the beginning of the use-case or interaction flow as well as the beginning of the story.

This intersection of interaction, visual design, and narrative is very important to interactive narrative. This is a sort of recipe for development considerations.

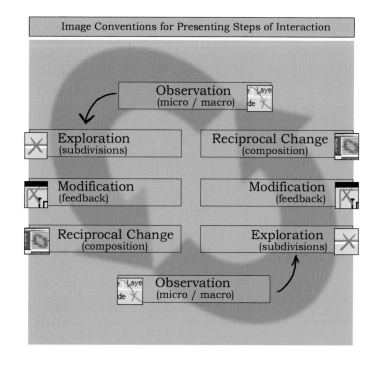

Interactive narrative generally requires multiple forms of interaction; however, the basic approach of allowing observation, exploration, and modification and changing a reader as a result can be broken down into three primary forms of interaction: acquiring information, discovering additional information, and facilitating the distribution of that information among multiple people. These are at least three forms of interaction that are commonly needed in interactive forms of narrative. These categories offer insights into the main forms of interaction that visual narrative requires.

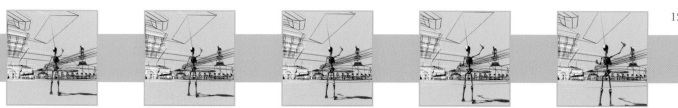

Acquiring Information

One of the things that interaction changes is the way that reading occurs. Readers will have a need to find specific items. They might need to solve a puzzle, read some backstory, or shuffle through an interface so that they can perform a task that they had in mind before they began the process.

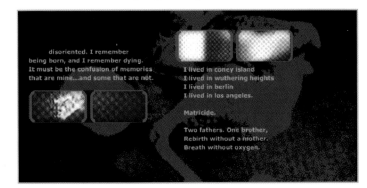

The GUI, at its core, is an image. It is an image that is interactive and adjustable. Its primary goal is to provide readers with the ability to explore and modify.

Another example of an image that allows the acquisition of information is the desktop folder. It's a compressed package that, when opened, expands and spills its contents.

But the folder is just a nonverbal version of the menu text. At the heart of the matter, they're actually the same thing. They share a common feature: They get bigger when they present more information. It's as if they have a kind of magnification characteristic. Their scale is what determines their importance. They get closer, and so they show us more. It's a fundamental principle of interface design—zooming closer to get more information. Although this begs for a 3D metaphor, our inside-the-skull understanding of what happens allows us to gloss over dimensional lapses of the metaphor and find what we're looking for.

Discovering Information

Part of what has made the GUI so successful, however, is the fact that it serves two functions: It provides the ability to acquire information, and it also allows readers the ability to discover and explore. A good design is a good idea that solves multiple problem sets, so this is part of the reason the GUI has continued to evolve without a great deal of fundamental change. It's a bit like an alligator or a shark; ancient but functional.

Two-dimensional interfaces are far simpler than three-dimensional interfaces. In most 2D GUIs, the reader has no need to go around something to explore it. The reader simply pokes it and it pops open.

Redistributing Information

In two-dimensional imagery, the difference between acquiring and discovering imagery is thin: These two functions are served by an expanding interface that can be continually opened for more information. There is, however, a larger difference between these functions and redistributing information. Consequently, the graphic design of these interfaces illustrates these differences. One is information that is related to the application, specifically, and the functions it contains. The other is related to the person on the other end of the line and the back and forth that occurs between the reader and writer.

Consider the simpler ways that you communicate with people from your desktop computer: email, chat, FTP (perhaps simply dragging an icon from one folder into another or perhaps a telnet shell), and in some cases in Europe and Japan, SMS (a mobile technology called Simple Messaging Service). These forms of 2D interface separate function and communication.* The communication is the image's focal point, and the function is the frame.

This is considering 2D interfaces without the help of socially capable interfaces such as VRML (Virtual Reality Modeling Language) that allow readers in a single space to graphically see and interact with each other.

In sum, whether an author of interactive narrative is providing readers with the ability to find, explore, or redistribute information, the fundamentals of image composition all apply. As we take an overview of how authors present stories in a visual framework in the next chapter, we find that the basic methods of presenting stories in a two-dimensional framework are, in many cases, surprisingly similar. Whether the method is a canvas, a television, a movie screen, or a monitor, simple principles of presentation remain the same.

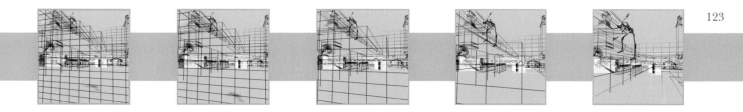

2.5: Examples and Interviews

The following interviews are arranged to provide a perspective on some of what is happening in the world of interactive narrative. These are interviews with developers who are working in the field of interactive narrative. These are largely unedited in the interest of clarity and preserving opinions other than this author's.

2.5.1 - Interview: Scott McCloud

The first interview with Scott McCloud was a relatively general conversation that Scott and I had over the course of a couple of afternoons. Scott is a general theorist and someone who keeps a broad view on the world of visual storytelling, and he was kind enough to outline some of his opinions of the future of narrative and how the Internet will play a role.

2.5.2 - Game: Game Complement to *A.I.* (loosely called *The Beast* or *Cloudmakers*)

The first case study—a project of gothic complexity and modern ambition—interviews some of the creators and players of an interactive narrative that was based around the movie *A.I.*, or *Artificial Intelligence*. This was a game that was produced by Microsoft and included multiple perspectives into a murder mystery. The solution of the mystery required the perspectives of all players to be lens-like, coordinated into a single view. I spoke with Elan Lee, the Producer, Lead Designer, and Director of the game as well as Adrian Hon, a reader of this project who assembled an online community to solve the mystery novel. As Adrian says, "I'm not sure if the game even had a proper name—most people referred to it simply as 'the game.'"

2.5.3 - Television: Liquid Stage

The second case study, *Liquid Stage*, is an interactive television show that was adopted from the United States' Public Broadcasting Service. I interviewed Michael Bovee, the producer of *Liquid Stage*, on how and why the show was developed into an interactive form of narrative. This show was used as a prototype for the American Film Institute's Enhanced Television Workshop.

2.5.4 - Internet: Crutch

The third case study is *Crutch*. This project was designed, written, and animated by the author (who interviews himself in this case study). Based on the Greek Myth of Prometheus, the story uses a combination of 3D and 2D to present a comic narrative of a fellow who gets lost in the desert, falls apart, glues himself back together again, loses his liver, and finally trades his liver in for a Crutch. At least, that's one version of the story.

2.5.5 - Print: Jimmy Corrigan, The Smartest Kid on Earth

Chris Ware's *Jimmy Corrigan* is a comic book that was released over a number of years as a series. When the series was published as a compilation, the comic, in its deep beauty and moving composition, was wrapped with an attractive cover. We take a look at that cover and at a form of printed interactive narrative from a master storyteller in this case study.

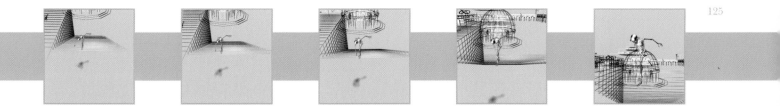

2.5.6 - Internet: Banja

The winner of the 2001 Ars Electronica Golden Nica (Internet category) and the Europrix 2001, *Banja* is a narrative world that readers explore, configure, and build. Olivier Janin, the Concept and Story Writer of the project, was kind enough to give me a tour through their incredible studio and explain how they produce their narratives with their homegrown software packages.

2.5.7 - Internet: The Devil's Tramping Ground

The Devil's Tramping Ground is a short Flash animation that was written, designed, and animated by New York animator Ed Bain. Ed has lived many lives and managed to avoid psychological damage after a harrowing evening in North Carolina. This case study looks at a simple version of a simple narrative that is quickly growing customary on the Internet today.

2.5.8 - Installation: Memex Engine

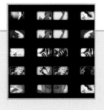

Marc Lafia and several other artists wrote, designed, and animated *Memex Engine*, which was installed at the Zentrum Kunst Medien (ZKM) in Karlsruhe, Germany. The project looks into the modern dialogues of the contemporary art world and uses these tropes to weave a complicated and multi-perspectival structure that can be read from multiple directions to form different conclusions.

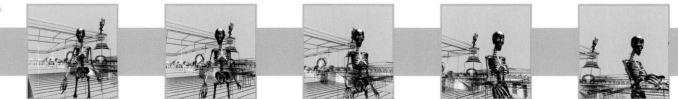

2.5.1 Scott McCloud Interview

http://www.scottmccloud.com/

Scott McCloud is considered by many to be the writer who made the comic narrative form accessible for adults. The author of *Understanding Comics*, Mr. McCloud is currently working on two new books. Although an accomplished illustrator and strong storywriter, Scott's contributions have also been theoretical. His recent opinions on the role of the Internet as it applies to the art of graphic storytelling have caused a flurry of raves, rants, opinions, and subsequent agreements. He lives and works in Los Angeles, California.

MEADOWS: In many ways, comics have gone through the growing pains that interactive narrative will go through. I mean specifically with a redefinition of what makes a story a story. So (to prepare us for these growing pains), where does a sense of story come from? How do we go about writing it?

MCCLOUD: That's a big question. Whatever its core appeal, narrative clearly speaks to something ancient and possibly unchanging in us. I don't know to what degree we live our lives by that roadmap, but we seem to have a need to look at the map again and again to see if the map has changed. Narrative is one of those ways that we can check the road we're on—not only where it's going, but how it's shifted in the last day or in the last year. Our landscape changes. The landscape of our lives changes. Narrative is a map and a diary. Our landmarks don't remain constant.

MEADOWS: So narrative is viewing the landscape of our lives?

MCCLOUD: There is a triangulation between the author and the reader. Anything that is viewed from a variety of vantage points becomes clearer.

MEADOWS: Multiple perspectives, eh?

MCCLOUD: Well, one of the things I've been discovering in my own work as I've tried to help comics to break out of the page is that almost any means of describing narrative that we have uses spatial metaphors. We talk about a story taking an odd turn, circular narratives, or intersecting lives. When allowed to grow to their full shape, comics can actually allow those metaphors to become literal.

MEADOWS: I've noticed this too. What are you imagining?

MCCLOUD: I would like to see the shape of any given work in comics be dictated exclusively by the story and the narrative intent of the author and not by a pre-existing arbitrary or technical requirement which—I think—the shape of the page is.

MEADOWS: ...Or maybe the classic narrative arc, too. Are you asking us to take comics to the monitor?

MCCLOUD: Not the monitor specifically, but to the notion of a limitless space, treating the monitor as a window. But it's the space that we're viewing rather than the monitor. I'm interested in a durable mutation of comics that will scale to accommodate whatever display device we throw at it. Some of the examples are frivolous, but in my latest book I describe some of these ideas; [presenting comics] on a staircase or on a rotated cube. Some of these sound odd, but the point is that each narrative has its own shape. One portion of a story is linear, and that part of the story can be rhythmic and repeating or it can be very shallow and narrow... or it may be very dynamic and angular, maybe best expressed in an explosion of vertical and diagonal shapes. There's no reason the story, if it should take that shape, should worry about bumping up against the edge of the page.

We just need to think of the monitor as a window.

MEADOWS: But what about 2D? There's something very powerful about the use of foveal vision in comics. It forces us into a mode of reading that is a gradual unveiling. Don't you think that there are particular aspects of two-dimensional imagery that are still useful?

MCCLOUD: It's interesting because 3D has two different components when talking about the potential for comics in a digital space. Because the images can still exist in flatland, they don't have to be restricted to the X and the Y, so the assembly of those images can occur in a three-dimensional space.

MEADOWS: And text as well, don't you think?

MCCLOUD: Yeah, and while navigating through *Unreal Tournament* [an online video game] you're in a convincing 3D environment. I think that the existence of first-person shooters, the fact that they're not in a literal 3D space, doesn't diminish the sense that you are at the brink of a true 3D space. We're at a point in history where narrative breaks wide open. Going parallax is not a big deal once you've got the code worked out. There's never been a step as blindingly obvious as that—in all of technical developments. Using 3D is not that difficult. We're not talking about inventing the airplane; we're talking about putting cup holders in minivans.

This is one of my hopes; that what I've described for comics does not shrink in terror from the challenge but could scale quite beautifully in VR [virtual reality]—it could be presented all at once in VR—you could see it all at once and hop from area to area...

[sighs] that works quite well.

MEADOWS: So what happens to the comic art? Different means of implementing a story tend to have an effect on the story itself, doesn't it?

MCCLOUD: Constituent parts of comics don't have to change. Visual devices might go by the wayside, but the power of imagination required to stitch two static images together and find that intermediate movement won't. That will be as relevant as ever when creating comics for that new environment.

I've thought for years that print would become marginalized, but I don't think that any technology becomes extinct. I'm sure someone is still making illuminated manuscripts. In my biz specifically, I think the transition is interesting because those who are working in print do so with a renewed deliberateness, and this latest generation of cartoonists appreciate print because it's not the only game in town. Artists like Chris Ware or Jordan Crane create works of tactile beauty. Because they come from a generation that chooses paper rather than having paper chosen for them.

MEADOWS: So the issue that you're raising isn't one of "This is where it all needs to go" but rather "We could use more options?"

MCCLOUD: I would like to see a vision of comics [that] is strong enough that it will take to new technologies of that sort with zeal.

MEADOWS: You said something earlier about comic style narrative replacing interfaces. Could you say a little more?

MCCLOUD: The thing that strikes me, as I get a bit deeper into games, is the presence of the axis from user-centered to author-centered. The vari-

ability of the proportions that so often get overlooked. We see it as a black and white and gray issue. We see it as the work of the author or the work of the reader and then there's interactivity. But there is a world of gradation in which there are works that include interactivity to varying degrees, and we should get a sense of which partner is leading the dance. It's a matter of proportion. We humans have a propensity to think in binary terms, and a lot of misunderstanding comes from us seeing things as a duality as opposed to a continuum.

MEADOWS: The dance metaphor is great. What is a future you would like to see for interactivity and comics?

MCCLOUD: I would just like it to be at the authors' discretion. I've never found the notion of interactivity the least bit intimidating. In the act of creation, if that creation is entirely self directed, we, as authors, have absolute freedom to allow the user into our world as much or as little as we want, and I think those of our peers who find interactivity a threat to authorial control are missing the point. You can be a gardener and create a garden and the authority of your creation isn't threatened just because visitors can wander through it at their own pace or in whatever direction they may choose.

It reminds me of that adage, "Doctor we've tried nothing and we're all out of ideas!" I think there will always be author-centered works that allow the user to simply sit back and take it all in. I don't think humanity's laziness is going to evaporate overnight.

MEADOWS: I doubt it. Comics seem to be more interactive, as a medium, than pure illustration or pure text. Is this because separate panels and moments in time incite additional energy on the reader's part? Or is it because the image and text are coupled? What's going on here that makes it feel so different from a text-based book?

MCCLOUD: When you're reading a book, there is a continuous form of interactivity—there is a call and response. Comic's form of interactivity is uniquely rhythmic. The author provides that visual input in the panel, and it's up to the reader to provide that imaginative input between the panels. It's a constant call and response. It could be that the pendulum swing between the author and the reader creates a more conspicuous interactivity.

MEADOWS: Do you think imagery is necessary?

MCCLOUD: Time is necessary. We experience interactivity over time and only comics make a map of time. Only comics give us permission to rise above the landscape and look down and see an hour or a week or a year laid out underneath us.

MEADOWS: So you think the time is…

MCCLOUD: Motion pictures would be an extreme example of the reverse where we have an enforced sense of time, and our place in that conveyor belt is forced. The comic is that terminal on the other end of the subway line where all of those movements are laid out all around us and we have license to look at them all at once. And so it's very user-directed, the sense of time.

MEADOWS: Being able to see everything at once. That's a god-like perspective?

MCCLOUD: Comics allow us that perspective. Maybe that's what we comic authors want—we're megalomaniacs.

2.5.2: Case Study One: Game Complement to *A.I.* (loosely called *The Beast* or *Cloudmakers*)

Several months before the movie *A.I.* came out, several websites mysteriously appeared on the Internet. This was a mystery with multiple, apparently unrelated websites:

http://www.donu-tech.com/
http://www.belladerma-srl-it.ro/
http://www.coronersweb.org/eb2183.html
http://www.spcb.org/
http://www.bangaloreworldu-in.co.nz/

The *Cloudmakers* project is an interactive narrative—a mystery—that involved over two million people. These two million people collaborated to solve a mystery that the authors of the game invented as the game was played. The collaboration involved two teams: the authors and the readers.

We interview both in the following case study.

The Cloudmaker Authors:

Elan Lee, the lead designer of *Cloudmakers*, was approached one day in 1999 by a co-worker named Jordan Weisman. Jordan asked Elan to work on a game that would "invade your life with phone and pager." About six months later, Jordan came to him and mentioned that they had permission to do something with the *A.I.* movie and with Warner Brothers. They had an idea for an interactive TV concept, but that idea, for various reasons, never got off the launchpad, so they adapted their idea for the web. On January 4, 2001, Elan, Jordan, Sean Stewart, and Pete Fenlon sat down in the Microsoft offices and started brainstorming. The door didn't open again until January 6, and when they walked out of the conference room, they each had lists of items that needed to be done. It was a simple beginning to a complicated project.

MEADOWS: What integration did this narrative have with the movie?

LEE: It was an interesting situation. There was a lot of secrecy in the movie, and Spielberg was working hard to protect Kubrick's legacy and was really restrictive in what we were allowed to see and what characters we were allowed to use. We were not allowed to affect the story that Kubrick and Spielberg were conveying through the movie, so we decided that if we were going to do this, we would set our story 50 years ahead of the movie's date. In some ways, we were doing an unintentional sequel, I guess.

MEADOWS: Was there an intentional path that you wanted readers to follow?

LEE: We divided the story into six basic arcs, and each one dealt with a different set of characters… and an often entirely unrelated storyline. We chose this construct because one of our main objectives was to push people toward the movie. In order to do that, we had to be diligent in introducing the proper concepts and the themes the movie was going to address. So we chose characters and storylines that each introduced something about the movie, then we built a world around it that allowed us to tie each character's individual story together and have it make

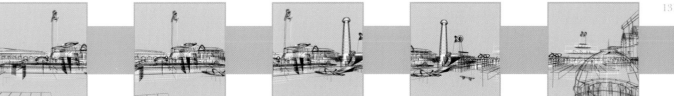

sense for a player that each of these characters could exist in the same world. Because of the hypertext tie-in, we were allowed to flood the users with information. We were able to give them more than a single user was able to comprehend. It was as if we were saying, "This is a whole world. There's no way you can see everything that's in this world, so go find the things that are interesting to you." There was an effect that the players formed groups, and each player became an expert on some area of that world. This facilitated collaborative storytelling because it facilitated the players telling each other the stories.

MEADOWS: How did you orchestrate the production?

LEE: It was chaos all the time! We had a plan, really we did! We had characters that we thought were interesting and a story we thought was compelling and a huge document that listed out everything we'd have to do to get through this on time. After week one, we took all those documents and threw them away! We realized that we were wrong in what the players found interesting, and we rewrote it based on what the players were doing. And then we thought, "We've spent a lot of time on this one part and now [need to] go back and do more work here." Characters were born that way. One of our most popular characters—The Red King, for example, was like this. It was originally written that he had a single line, but he had such a cool graphic that people fell all over it. And as soon as he had the second mention, fan sites were going up and we said, "Okay, fine; time to throw him in."

The answer to this question is that we had no idea! We threw our attention everywhere we could until the players caught on to something; then we pushed that as hard as we could.

MEADOWS: You've got URLs in Britain, New Zealand, the United States, and Romania. How did you set all of this up?

LEE: The cost prohibited the production of all the domains we originally had in mind, but we realized that in order to build a world, it had to be worldly.

MEADOWS: Venus and Evan Chan and a few other characters show up in different photos. Did you have a casting agent acquire these models? How did you handle this photographic portion of the production?

LEE: We decided to treat it like an actual television show, so we hired an entire crew and went to LA for a three-day shoot on location with makeup and wardrobes and the whole bit! This was the only way we could build this large of a body of content. Not only could we not tell them what the project was, but also we couldn't tell them what company it was for! They knew that it was something online, and they knew that their images would be used for "an online marketing campaign," but beyond that we had to keep them in the dark.

MEADOWS: The whole time?

LEE: Well, after it got popular, a second contract was signed. And we had to do more work then, too. We did a total of three shoots, and each one grew progressively more complicated. In the final shoot, we captured a lot of imagery that we never even used for the game.

MEADOWS: What kind of integration took place with the real world?

LEE: The very first thing we did was at a talk at MIT at their Media Lab on [the movie] *A.I.* They wanted to hear about the upcoming movie and we knew there were going to be questions about Jeannine Salla [one of the characters of the narrative]. So we printed out business cards and handed those out pretending that she was on the set. On the biz cards was a puzzle that we wrote in Kannada—a language used in Bangalore. In 5 minutes, they had the puzzle translated! In 15 minutes, they had it solved!! That made us realize that physical puzzles are really good because they got people thinking. So we had weekly email. The game was faxing people and [making] phone calls. These were from numbers that the players could call.

The best forms of integration were with the live parties. We did live events in LA, Chicago, and NY. The anti-robot militia had a rally and invited players. We hired actors at these locations [who] were egging the crowd on and there were puzzles that were set up that encouraged the cities to work together at these physical locations as well as on the Internet. They cracked through every puzzle we created! The players actually got so into it that they followed one of the actors home and kept pressing him for information, so he had to finally break character and tell them to leave him alone.

We tried as much as we could to say, "Yes, this is a game, but we won't admit it."

MEADOWS: How did you know it wasn't too difficult to follow?

LEE: One approach was just testing it out on friends. For extremely hard puzzles, there were a few things we could rely on—if something is easily identifiable as a puzzle, people will treat it as such and they will do exhaustive research until they find at least a method they can use to solve it. We were betting on the fact that the Internet should be used as a massive organic intelligence. Everyone contributes his or her own little bit and you have this machine that is smarter than anything else in history. Puzzles like the Kannada puzzle proved that not only did this work, but we could count on it.

There was one puzzle we set up through Sophia (she was basically a version of the FBI machine carnivore). It tracks you and reads your email and taps your phone line. There's nothing she doesn't know about everyone. We thought, "Let's give the players access to Sophia, but let's do it with a totally blank screen with just two prompts on it. Based on what you type, Sophia will react in a certain way." In prompt one, you put a character's name, and in prompt two an emotion. She then hands back an example—a video clip or image. Each player only gets three guesses per day.

We thought this would be hard and take months.

When they found Sophia, they organized into groups and got a thesaurus, and broke out the entire Sophia database within one hour.

MEADOWS: What is it about this audience? Why are they so good at solving problems?

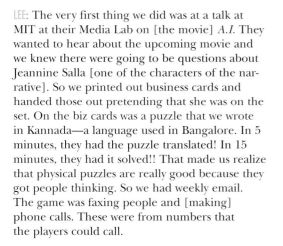

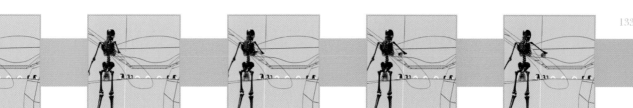

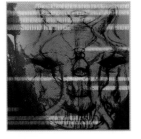

LEE: I'm not sure. In the case of Sophia, there were several hundred really bad ideas. A group of this size has a natural ability to sift ideas. I don't know how it happened, but it happened thousands of times in this game. Sift through the dirt and find the gem.

MEADOWS: How did you know it would draw the attention the project deserved?

LEE: We risked a lot! There's the concept that everyone wants to achieve a level of local fame. It's a human trait. And we knew that this game was providing a way in which each individual person [who] went through it could contribute on some level. These guys all wanted to be able to say "Someone challenged me and I figured it out." We knew that if we could get a core number of people—enough people—and reward them in that fashion, we'd have a winner.

If you attract enough hard-core players [who] are willing to devote the time and energy and research, they're going to go and get their friends and family to play.

MEADOWS: Thirty-eight characters are involved and over half a dozen websites. How many, really?

LEE: Half a dozen core characters, and 25–30 world-building characters, and several hundred peripheral characters. Number of websites? Well, we had about 40 or 45 discreet URLs, but each one hosted a bunch of secret and secondary pages and diaries; this bumped the total up into the hundreds.

MEADOWS: What was the number of groups?

LEE: We did massive amounts of research to encourage those groups to grow as large as they could. There was so much data—we just flooded them—because a single person couldn't know all of this in one head. Biology, luddism, be able to read binary, Morse code, pixel analysis in PhotoShop, speak Kannada. Other players had to have a Japanese i-mode cell phone, had to be running at least six different browsers, and had to be able to complete the second half of any Shakespeare quote we threw at you.

MEADOWS: And the medium of the Internet?

LEE: The medium changes the ability to make it complicated. We said, "Let's make something that is only possible on the Internet and uses the aspects that are unique to the medium."

MEADOWS: Smart approach. Or, well, it's the only approach, isn't it?

LEE: Yeah! It gave us the ability to segment parts of a story into little capsules that people identified as websites and gave us the ability to tie in a means of communication that's specific to those capsules—email and messaging. It was a means to have multiple layers of investigation rewards for each of those capsules. Analyzing source code, looking at the binary elements of everything you're encountering. They have the ability to examine things much closer than with a book.

The other thing, from a puzzle aspect, the Net is powerful because you can provide people with a 100% accurate replica of the thing sitting in your office. I know that if you take pixels 24,24, 25,23 and pass that out, that the precise duplicate ends up in the player's hands.

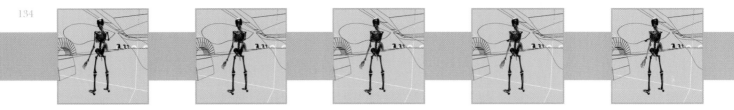

MEADOWS: This borders on a role-playing game. What role did the players have in constructing the story?

LEE: Because we were in essence making a "choose your own adventure" book, we let players alter the course that the story took. At the end of the game, we filmed alternate endings. At the end, players had to vote on whether robots would be allowed to vote. We forced them to think about some serious moral and political issues. We actually conducted it as a real vote.

MEADOWS: And...?

LEE: They voted to free the robots.

MEADOWS: What was the interaction between the authors—you guys—and the readers, or players? Was there an instance when you didn't know what the outcome would be but had to keep writing anyway?

LEE: Oh, definitely. There was one puzzle where there was no answer. We had no idea how it was going to resolve. There was an artificial character that thrived on nightmares and was born in a psychological institute that had become so addicted to nightmares, it was looking for what scared people the most. See, it had to generate more nightmares to feed itself. We opened up the doors to the players and wrote out a distress call: "Help me" came from a character that the players liked who Loki had overwhelmed, but we didn't know what the response would be. We wanted to leave it to the players to come up with something creative. They wanted to find a way to trap Loki and put out bait and destroy him, so they all got together—thousands of people—and they made a dream database and put all of their own nightmares into this database (it was beautiful to see them all work together like that), so we directed Loki toward the site and there he died. We created an animation sequence of Loki living through one line of everyone's nightmare and phrased it in a way that read from everyone's paragraph, but it was a single series of a total, truly nightmarish experience.

MEADOWS: That's a pretty unique form of authorship that gives a lot of control to readers.

LEE: Oh yeah. The players felt totally in control and totally powerful, so the game was changing the story based on their specific writing.

MEADOWS: It sounds like there was a great deal of individual input to generate a larger picture.

LEE: Yeah. One of the concepts that was quite important was the idea that THERE IS NO RIGHT ANSWER. We threw out this question, "Who killed Evan Chan," but the answer to the question totally depends on whom you ask.

Microsoft®

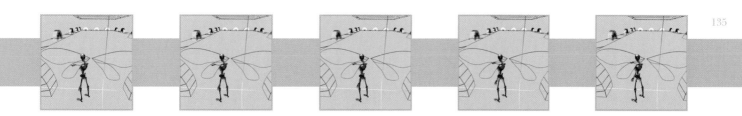

MEADOWS: A perspective-based mystery, eh?

LEE: Right. If you ask friends, they may point to the killer, others may point to the killer's owner, the programmer of the robot, etc. It was very important that no person be able to answer the question with authority; otherwise, the game would end at that point. Everyone had their own perspective on what had happened.
.
MEADOWS: What was the total number of users in this game?

LEE: It's hard to answer—somewhere in the neighborhood of 2.5 million.

MEADOWS: How many people did you expect would play over the course of the entire game?

LEE: Personally, I was hoping for 100,000 users. We hit that number in the first three hours! There's a lot of interest in something new on the Internet, and there's something important about letting each person on an individual basis be the hero to a story. Everyone wants to be a Sherlock Holmes.

The Cloudmaker Readers

In the interest of presenting both sides of this incredibly complicated narrative, I also spoke with Adrian Hon, one of the lead instigators and investigators of Cloudmakers. Adrian, an undergraduate at Cambridge University, first accessed the Internet when he was 11. As one of the early coordinators of the Cloudmakers reading and sleuthing group, he subsequently organized many of the online interactions that went into solving the riddle of the game. This was, essentially, a form of online social organization that facilitated the actual reading of the story. Adrian is also heavily involved with the Mars exploration advocacy movement, being the Chair of Youth Outreach for the Mars Society and the editor of the online magazine *New Mars*.

MEADOWS: How did you folks assemble? What happened? How did the moderators get chosen? What were the primary motivators for people? What did each of you do, and how was that determined?

HON: I think the keyword for all of your questions is self assembly. The Cloudmakers Yahoo Groups mailing list came about from the original discussions of the game on the Ain't It Cool News forums, and were formed by Cabel Sasser; eventually, practically all game-related discussion had moved there within a week or two.

Again, the moderators were simply a group of people within the Cloudmakers who felt that as the mailing list size was growing larger (several hundred at that point), some degree of organization would be required or else discussion and progress within the game would be severely compromised. Some of the more concrete problems we faced included exactly how we could maintain coherent discussion among all list members (solved by instituting the post tags system where all subject lines would be preceded by the identifier META, PUZZLE, SOLUTION, UPDATE, etc).

The moderator's main job was simple enough; they had to moderate discussions on the mailing list and identify good threads and posts that would be "modded" and placed onto a separate lower-volume mailing list that would only contain good speculation and game news.

Some of the moderators were also responsible for creating resources to help game players, e.g. the Guide and the Trail.

MEADOWS: Once you were assembled, how did your individual perspectives—each different—allow you to build a world view? What happened to facilitate that? What were the group dynamics?

HON: If you are referring to the players of the game, then I think that they can be summarized by placing them within two broad spectrums. The first spectrum would have an interest in the puzzles of the game at one end and an interest in the storyline at the other. The second spectrum would consist of how involved they were in the game; how much time they invested in it.

In such a large community as the Cloudmakers, there was a relatively even distribution of people along both spectra—although it may not have seemed like it. There were a few hard-core puzzle solvers whose names you'd begin to recognize, and there were also a few very good storyline speculators (who often provided some of the clues for the puzzles)—these two groups tended to dominate discussions simply because they were the most involved in the game. And, of course, you would also have people who were interested in the storyline and the puzzles.

However, having people specialize in certain areas did help the community as it allowed a good division of resources so there would always be a subcommunity of puzzle solvers working whenever there was an unsolved puzzle—at the

same time the speculators would continue on unabated; and their speculation would rise every time a new piece of information was received (often due to the efforts of the puzzle solvers).

Of course, with such intense members, Cloudmakers was often intimidating to newbies who, I believe, actually fared better than they would in other communities simply due to the existence of the Trail and Guide, which if used in combination, could educate any newcomer right up to the cutting edge of the game (the fact that doing this toward the later stages of the game would have taken a significant amount of time is a bit of a problem, though).

MEADOWS: What made the thing an interesting story?

HON: Some say that the *A.I.* story was interactive. It wasn't, at least not in the traditional terms. The fact is, the players didn't—and weren't—able to influence the main strand of storyline. Whatever we did, events would unfold pretty much as pre-planned by the game creators (who have revealed as much in their IRC chats). Some minor events and end events were player determined (e.g. the vote on the Mann Act at the end of the game), but frankly, even if they wanted to, the creators would not have been able to make a truly interactive story for several reasons:

a) Too much workload—having to rethink the story every time the players did something new

b) Quality of story—the best stories are planned, not written totally on the fly

c) Who is the player, in this situation? The 'Cloudmakers'? How are they supposed to come up with a single decision?

tried to use internet explorer in OS 9 same result tried on 5 other m
finally tried in OS 9 with netscape seemed to work ok? not sure.

id: 6
date: 2001-05-29 23:54:27
name: Geoff
email: geoffh@kcbbs.gen.nz
site: http://www.familiasalla-es.ro
addsite: four women page
os: Mac OS X
browser: Internet Explorer other
addbrowser: mac 5.1
flash: other (specify below)
addflash: how do you find that?
conc: dial-up modem
ram: 192
cpu: 400
detail: Beating heart does not show, never has

id: 7
date: 2001-05-29 23:55:41
name: JayR
email: throwaway4u@yahoo.com
site: http://www.spcb.org

The story was interesting principally because it was well written and had strong themes—family loyalties, jilted lovers, deaths, and so on. The puzzles gave it that extra something that attracted many other game players and gave the players an illusion of influencing the story. If the story wasn't good, no one would have played the game.

MEADOWS: What were you able to add to it?

HON: Not as much as the game creators envisaged, as it happens. They were expecting many more fan-created websites that would sit within the game universe. While there were at least a couple of these, their quality in general wasn't very high. However, if the game had run on a little longer, I'm sure more fan sites would have cropped up. A real problem to this was the fear that if we added to the story in this way, we would be irritating the game creators—muddying the waters of their story universe—and also confusing things for game players who might find it difficult to tell the difference between a "proper" game site and a fan-created site.

Now that we know better, I'm sure that if the game were run again, we'd be seeing many more high-quality game-related websites. We did, in fact, have one good fan site, Shipbrook.com I think, which was the fan-created website of an architecture firm.

Personally, most of my time concerning the game was taken up with maintaining the Guide. It's a very large linear walkthrough for the game, and judging by the emails I've received by readers, it's extremely useful for those who want to get a sense of perspective on the story, for beginners and for those who don't have the time to participate fully in the Cloudmakers mailing list.

I know that many of my readers only play the game through the Guide.

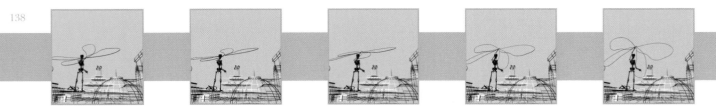

2.5.3: Case Study Two: Liquid Stage / Bovee Productions

http://www.afionline.org/etv/

Liquid Stage is an interactive television prototype that was built at the American Film Institute's 2000 Enhanced Television Workshop. It was one of many excellent projects that emerged from this collaboration. The ETV workshop is hosted at the American Film Institute and funded by multiple corporate sponsors. Its intent is to bring together developers, theorists, industry experts, and designers to develop possibilities of the future of enhanced television.

I met Michael Bovee, the project director of *Liquid Stage* at this workshop. Michael is a long-time television and video producer who's kept a strong penchant for working on projects that are outside the mainstream. He lives and works in San Diego.

Liquid Stage started as a documentary on PBS that aired for several seasons before Michael decided to take it to a new level and add interaction to it. The project was a challenge because the storyline wasn't designed as an inherently interactive piece. This presents problems in any project. Despite this challenge, Michael and his group of designers (of which this author helped with the graphic and interaction design of the project) worked to put together a piece that, finally, won a couple of awards and made something of a splash in the design world.

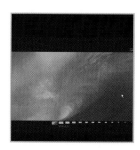

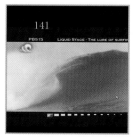

MEADOWS: What is your vision? How do you conceptualize things?

BOVEE: We had a certain linear experience that was in a two-dimensional world of film, and we were asking ourselves, "If we move into an interactive realm, what do we want to do?" We wanted to increase the experience of the *Liquid Stage* experience. We wanted to extend the experience of surfing so that it really was more free flowing and more surfing-like. We wanted users to be able to guide their own surfboard rather than us guiding them both in the design and the interaction.

MEADOWS: How did you approach this kind of a project? What knowledge did you need to have? What was the most important?

BOVEE: You need the whole team. You need someone [who] knows the material and someone that understands all of the narrative aspects of the material.

You need a graphic designer and also an interaction designer—someone [who] understands the power of interactivity and can break down into several different people. You might have an interaction producer, an interaction designer, and a graphic designer, and then under that a programmer. Someone needs to be there to come up with interactive content that fits the subject matter. And then the interaction designer and graphic designer come up with a way to make that work with the real estate and imagery that works with that space. And then the programmer

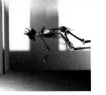

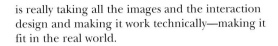

is really taking all the images and the interaction design and making it work technically—making it fit in the real world.

The interaction designer is working with strategy and blocks and lines, and the graphic designer extends this functionality and basic layout into a compelling form.

MEADOWS: How did you decide which platform to use?

BOVEE: It depends on the highest distribution. For us, it had to be easily programmable because we didn't have a lot money to spend. We could make it specific because the first version was a prototype; so then we looked at how it was going to be used.

MEADOWS: And, while I know the answer to some degree, can you tell me who was involved?

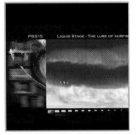

BOVEE: Right. Well, here:
Michael Bovee—producer and director
Robert Greaves—writer and co-producer, subject matter expert
Mark Stephen Meadows / Chris Carcher—interaction and graphic design
Carolyn May / Chris Swain / Dale Herigstad—mentors
Interactive programmer—Neil Tippler (from Upsidedowndog Productions)

MEADOWS: How was the story organized and written?

BOVEE: The original film was kind of a snowball. We started out by doing a small documentary on Wind-and-Sea and the history of surfing in San Diego. This then exploded into a national piece, and so we, in a sense, developed the story based on the chronological history and the legends of surfing. From the very conception up to now, the underlying theme of the film was that commercialism had changed the essence of surfing into something that maybe didn't honor the origins of surfing and giving people a choice—would you rather get paid to go surfing or maintain the essence of the sport?

MEADOWS: If you were to diagram the story, what would it look like?

BOVEE: The original diagram was a wave—if you took a horizontal line and then took a wave form that went down and then back up, and the frequency of that wave could change based on the interactivity. You're always crossing the main narrative line—that minimum horizontal line. That was what I was trying to design. I didn't want it to be a feeling of taking a lefthand turn, and then always having to choose right or left, and then having to return to the starting point. I wanted it to always, in a sense, reflect the motion of surfing. You're always moving forward, but you have options within the main narrative that will always allow you to return to the main line and follow that motion. Or you could experience "Surf Koans"—comments from the show that we thought were little nodes of surf wisdom... These played along with music from the show—almost like you're treading water. You're not stopped. There's still a certain amount of audiovisual experience. But you have the option to go back to the main narrative.

2.5.4: Case Study Three: Crutch

http://www.boar.com/crutch/

MEADOWS: So what's the history with *Crutch*?

MEADOWS: Well, while I've participated in the design of several of the projects in this book, *Crutch*, which I began in 1996, was probably my first serious attempt at building a story structure that was both nonlinear and interactive. It seems to have been pretty succesful since hundreds of people still read it each month and it's part of at least a half-dozen university-level courses around the world. I'm still pretty proud of it, as you can tell.

MEADOWS: Uhm, okay. So why three characters? What did this lend to the structure of the story?

MEADOWS: It's based on the myth of Prometheus, and so, partly because of that, the story is about three characters named Crutch, Io, and Buzerd. Each character has a separate story loop, but each of these stories intersects each other. So while the three stories themselves can be read as individual narratives, each character in the story also has some interaction with the other two. These interactions between the characters provide "bridges" between the loops, allowing for different plot lines. It also provides three different perspectives on the same story. Consequently, there isn't a single protagonist as much as there is a single environment with the same number of events. Does that make sense?

MEADOWS: Sure, but what's the relationship between Crutch and Prometheus? Didn't Prometheus get punished for giving fire to man and threatening the gods?

MEADOWS: Yeah. He introduced technology. I guess you know a little about this...

MEADOWS: Sure, we have more or less the same perspective on this story here...

MEADOWS: Maybe. Anyway, because this is a parable, I had to rely pretty heavily on metaphors. For example, the interactions between the three main characters orbit around two objects: a crutch and a liver. The Crutch was intended as a metaphor of technology, while the liver as a metaphor of the body, the one being traded for the other. The character of Crutch was designed with the metaphor of the crutch in mind—splintered, brown, angular and jaunty—which lent itself to the display technology that was being used at the time (a splintered and jaunty 3D rendering technology named VRML). But basically, it's a commentary on technology and how it weakens us, I guess.

MEADOWS: Well, that was quite clever of you.

MEADOWS: Are you being sarcastic?

MEADOWS: Maybe.

MEADOWS: Well, anyway, I was trying to write a narrative that had three totally different views on the same story by representing different perspectives of both the emotional and visual type. I think you talk about this in your book. There's actually a scene that shares two cameras in the io / buzerd interaction. I'm actually using the same geometry for both stories because it gets inlined by the browser when...

MEADOWS: <Interrupting> Wait a minute... So you want to tell a single story with three different stories? Isn't that a bit schizophrenic?

MEADOWS: Yeah, I guess. It was sort of a bother to write, but in the end, if a story doesn't have a little madness it's, well, a bore to read.

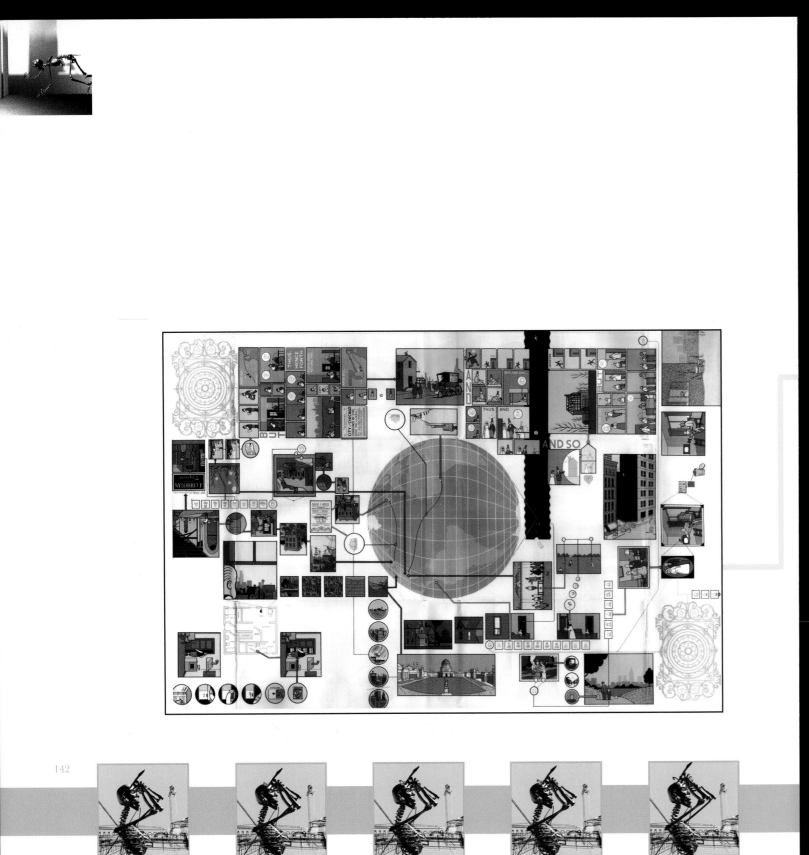

2.5.5: Case Study Four: Jimmy Corrigan

Chris Ware, a writer and illustrator from Chicago, Illinois, has been working on *Jimmy Corrigan, The Smartest Kid on Earth* for the better part of a decade. Beginning as a series of small comics of odd sizes, these beautifully crafted and incredibly detailed narratives cover a range of topics from the sad to the strange to the nostalgic. Though the subject matter is often autobiographical, the fictionalized account of Jimmy Corrigan was framed with experimental forms of graphic stories. The interplay between the detailed imagery and the insightful narrative is interesting to watch because it is a story that changes form as you read it.

This is no longer an experiment for Ware—it's a printed form of interactive narrative that allows a reader to travel from one point in the narrative to another by following lines that, rather than framing imagery, associate it. It makes for some interesting possibilities in the world of comics as McCloud describes them. The stories that Ware presents give a telescoping time and provide a worldview that is historic and informative. The compositions guide readers through a tale that serves as a counterpoint and supplementary reference to a more linear-based plot that is in the interior book.

What's nice to see is that this format he is using incorporates existing formats of comic narrative. The lines that guide the eye generally have more to do with a change of scale (in both space and time) than a momentary shift we generally see in comic cels. In some cases, these are simply associations or identifications. In other cases, they link together separate portions of the plot that Ware has already presented in his book. The different stories all relate, but they can be chosen in different orders, read in different directions, and the order that they're read in give different emotional responses to a story that is held within them (remember, this is, after all, just the cover of the book).

Ware is stretching the traditional approaches to print narrative. He's made something that relies more on the reader's perception than the author's presentation.

http://www.banja.com/

Banja is an "interactive cartoon." Of the projects featured in this book, this is the one that can be most appropriately named "State of the Art."

Each year, top international recognition in digital art is awarded by the Prix Ars Electronica. Based in Austria, the competition is juried by a visionary group of researchers, industry forerunners, academicians, curators, and artists. Olivier Janin, *Banja's* Concept and Story Writer, lives and works in Lille, France.

Olivier and his company, Team cHmAn, won the Ars Electronica Golden Nica and the Europrix 2001. *Banja* is the company's focus. It is one of the deepest interactive narratives that exist on the Internet today. Readers are able to configure the environment, interact with other characters, and explore different environments. Janin explains that there are also, in each monthly episode, "problems" that the readers need to solve. This is in many ways a safe approach to an interactive narrative because it puts readers in the position of being investigators of a mystery genre rather than watchers. A small woolly mammoth is often missing, a character has moved some piece of furniture, etc. These small items that represent change in the world are the plot elements that drive readers to explore further.

Updates are sent to subscribers when a new issue is released:

```
> ====What's Happening ?=============

> The aims of the Patchouli family have now become quite clear: they have come
to
> Itland to search for a treasure that would be buried in the seabed. Their
> quest is based on a holographic treasure map, a legacy of an ancestor. But
> the hologram machine is broken, and the gorgeous Wampa is asking for help to
> repair it.
>
> Marguerite, the dino-cow is a new friend for Banja. This unique specimen of
> the Jurassic era that strolls about the isle. She is a sensitive creature,
> and now she seems to have lost a friend of hers...
```

Banja also has small games, chat centers, discussion forums, and other items that are paving a new road for Internet usage. It's an approach worth studying. But *Banja* also has an incredibly strong production capability in part because they've had to produce their own toolsets for the production. "Epi-Generator" is a GUI interface that they have developed that allows for their writers, producers, and designers to actually generate interactive narratives from pre-existing assets. It is composed of two primary pieces. There is a piece that any film director would recognize. It allows for scene composition, camera cuts, backdrop choice, character

positioning, and dialogue scripting. Then there is another piece that allows for the interaction design: conversational character scripting (they have dozens and dozens of NPC Ais that are used in the narrative), buttons, onMouseOvers, narrative questions, etc. Tools like Epi-Generator will surely become more prevalent as the art form ripens. It's a reasonable solution to a complicated problem.

At a conference one day while Janin was speaking, an audience member asked, "What is your business plan?" Janin, surprised at the question, answered, "We're doing it. Our business is to do what we love!" This, more than anything else, will be the key to their success.

Their office of nearly 40 people is a collaborating collage of comics, graffiti, computers, sketches, screens, and music. Their culture is hive-like, borrowing from around the globe, opting, changing, and inventing. It's the basis of their approach: synthesis and adaptation. It's a hyper-modern speedtank of programmers, writers, and artists.

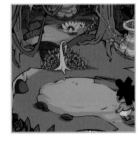

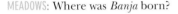

MEADOWS: Where was *Banja* born?

JANIN: The first drawing of *Banja* was made by Tony in May 1998, when Seb spoke about the idea. [The] first standalone game *Banja Free Style Dub* was made in the summer of 1998. The concept was written in January 1999 and then the animation and graphic style was defined by March 1999 (3D cartoon rendering into 2D back-grounds), and the moving engine was developed in the fall of 1999.

MEADOWS: How did you come up with the story?

JANIN: There is a general story which has been written before we start production. Then for each episode, we build a scenario that must fulfill two aims at the same time: The episode must evolve according to the general storyline, and players must be able to understand the episode as an independent story.

MEADOWS: How is the writing integrated with the interaction and the networking?

JANIN: Sometimes writing a scenario gets very close to coding a program: Each action has specific conditions, and from those conditions, we can derive several different actions. Generally, the style of the scenario is not very pleasant to read, as it's mostly a working tool. For every scene, the screenplay is described technically, including collision areas, roll-over hints, visual indications, etc.

MEADOWS: Interesting. It sounds as if there is very little difference between coding and writing for you guys. How could the story be represented visually? Can it be diagramed?

JANIN: The general story could be diagrammed as a succession of different phases and events, evolving toward a definite goal. Each episode represents a single phase in the evolution. Besides, we have our own diagram to represent the evolution of an episode through time and space. Our scheme is a segmentation of every action through the different periods of the episode as well as a balanced distribution of the events in the various scenes.

MEADOWS: How do you decide when you have enough interactivity?

BAIN: I didn't want people to linger particularly long. I wanted them to feel like they were moving from place to place—as if they were being led. I don't know… one of the screens is just a note that appears next to the fire. That's the only thing they can do. But it felt right. There's a flow… and it's a difficult thing as an artist. You don't have control over how people will perceive it. This gets into the technical issues.. it's always a concern if the monitor is too bright, for example. As far as the structure of it, it feels like any art form.

MEADOWS: Do you think there is a dramatic arc? What's the story structure look like?

BAIN: It's pretty linear because the interaction is part of the story.

MEADOWS: How is the writing integrated with the interaction and the networking?

BAIN: This piece was kind of organic. The first thing I created was the forest, then the fire, then I knew I wanted to bring the camera closer. Then closer again. So these felt like the appropriate amount of steps. From there, it becomes a hodge-podge of memories from my childhood. A man named Tom Savini used to live in the neighborhood that adjoined mine, and on the weekends, he would pull out a film projector and hang a sheet between the trees and show horror movies to the children.. and that feeling of seeing those spooky images of the sheet hanging between the trees and these old Lon Chaney movies. It was an image I needed to include in the piece. It was an odd thing to work on for me.

The site has no publicity. It's just word of mouth. A more gothic crowd seems to be drawn to it, but my friend's wife—it frightens her!

It really does.

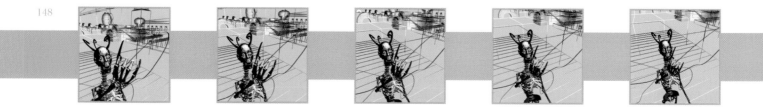

2.5.8: Case Study Seven: Memex Engine

http://memexengine.com/

Marc Lafia received his MFA degree in film practice and theory at UCLA, where he "got inside questions of montage and image" and began to explore the limits of visual narrative at an early stage in his career. This led him to develop experimental forms of video that included music, and eventually, he found himself working with Madonna, Michael Jackson, Billy Idol, and others. As digital media continued to evolve, he realized that there was a great deal of overlap with his training. As Marc puts it, "CD-ROMS and the web—in having computation, hypertext, and network—give us a very rich grammar to explore a number of issues from narrative to database to interaction to social aspects." Marc's emphasis over the years has been on information design and information systems.

In addition to exhibiting work internationally as an artist, Marc is a visiting curator in new media at the Institute of Contemporary Art in Boston and consultant to several museums, including the Museum of Modern Art in New York.

Marc is founder and information architect of artandculture.com, launched in

December 1999. Marc lives and works in San Francisco.

LAFIA: I'd like to show you Ambient Machines at http://ambientmachines.com/.

MEADOWS: Do you think there's a narrative in here?

LAFIA: This is a language of texture. It doesn't translate into words—it's more poetic. You don't need to start at a beginning. If you look at artandculture.com, you start inside a conversation. You're inside the event of conversations being made. Everything has its own relationship with the visitors of the site. When you come to visit the site, the world shifts to accommodate you. It's your world that's based on your context and the things that relate to you.

MEADOWS: So it's really as interactive as you could make it.

LAFIA: Yes. Godard says, "Yes, there's a beginning,

a middle, and an end, but not in that order." And this notion is much more evident in a hypertextual and computational world. In fact, what is fascinating is that the network and computation have been perfomative of contemporary critical theory in terms of the notion of 'difference,' 'the death of the author' intertextuality—all of it. Remember every form constrains meaning as much as it allows meaning to speak. So how narrative operates is as much the story as anything else. So ambient machines is about the authoring procedures of the machine, not so much the output of texts, even though there are saved there hundreds of short films that people have made from around the world. These participants being authors—what it suggests is that the underlying materials that make up the clips are infinitely malleable and that the author now sets up a set of parameters, a set of procedures, a set of instructions, and then lets things happen. So, now on to the Memex.

MEADOWS: The Memex is complicated because

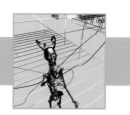

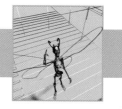

there are complicated dialogues happening. Can you give us an overview on the project? Something short?

LAFIA: The memexengine refers back to Vannevar Bush (a scientist with the United States government). One of the problems he wrestled with is how to deal with vast amounts of information and make a machine that could annotate and interrelate varied text and varied subject matter in a way that it was always relational. It was a knowledge machine that allows one to add on and aggregate and annotate one's own personal engagement with their own knowledge and others. Clearly the web, both because of computation and hypertext, is that very thing. It's the ultimate archive that through the browser one has an optic to which to bring those various kinds of information and records into their purview. What the Memex Engine—in this project—represents is this polyoptic register through which (and in which) one engages the network. In that space, one's agency and identity and even, in the narrative, who's speaking—because it is removed—we can never be certain of and we can construct varied identities. It uses the traditional genre of a mystery and the tropes of gaming to engage the reader. It's an information crime in the landscape of high technology in the space of the network.

MEADOWS: Whew.

LAFIA: In a sense, the metatext is a reading of the network. It encapsulates and informs the web. It puts on the network. That is the conceit of the project. It has a humor about this as well.

MEADOWS: Well, that's lucky. So how was this project written?

LAFIA: There were multiple creators in this project, including yourself, which was what this project was about, also. Normally in a production, there is a disparity of roles, but I started with a novel. I started with a story and then found you and

wanted to put this work in the space of the web and make it performative and find a way to parse out the various stories and then take the plot and turn those into small games or small activity sets and engage the machine by becoming complicit with the tools and environments. This experience was intended to perform the memex. A lot of the production—the images and text fold into each other. Collage and cut-up that formats them and composes them—we wanted them to be seamless and become part of the whole.

MEADOWS: Besides you and me, who was involved?

LAFIA: Gabriella Marks, Josh Draper, and Darin Fong.

MEADOWS: This project has always seemed, to me, hard to access and complicated. What's the basic structure of the story?

LAFIA: It is by virtue of the point of entry to it—it's six clicks until the system is totally open to the reader. The best way to do that is to show you the various registers. The project starts at a beginning and I don't think that was a good choice. You get to this first page—this is the narrative track that engages the user at the start, saying, "This is the Memex." But right away, I am trying to implicate the reader by asking them to make a choice and suggesting that this choice, one of five images to be selected, is the beginning of a psychological profiling of them. Once inside, I suggest that there are different motives and needs from different perspectives of different narrators as the reader discovers the chronological register.

There are seven registers, each one a chronology with the five characters speaking their tale. That means that there are at least fifteen plots. The memex screens—of which there are 12—narrate to you the story. Given your Psych Profile, you have a distinct memex. The engines are the tools that can scan and make a match for people, the

avatar engine, the mapping tool, the tool that allows you to randomly access the whole story.

MEADOWS: So what kind of interaction is this?

LAFIA: A performative one. You make stories. You perform it. You engage it.

MEADOWS: What is a specific example of this?

LAFIA: Well, any path you take—any set of clicks—is the tactile register of being inside the memex. Just like in *Doom*, you go through levels [and] have an arsenal—here you have an informational arsenal. You build an avatar, move through various story registers, etc. You are able to change the sequences of parts of the narrative, scroll the map and move the interface, change the size and scale of any of the image assets, and run them in a sequence so it plays back for you.

This is not just multi-perspective storytelling. This is engaging and performing story in which there is consequence as a player. It's between a multi-linear story and a video game.

So it's a task-oriented plot that you actively engage and participate in by forming an allegiance with one of the narrators of the story. You use the toolset to engage the story formally instead of just narrationally. All of it to give sense of this idea of a very robust polyoptic information apparatus while in turn writing over or through story a lot of contemporary art practice. That's the content proper of the story, but unless you read visually and/or closely, you'll never get that nor need you.

MEADOWS: How did the fact that this is on the Internet affect its development?

LAFIA: Unlike a film, the network demanded that the user engage the tool as opposed to read the story; they had to perform the crime or the investigation or the sabotage. And your skill at engaging with the tool makes the story and makes you understand the sense of it by the fact that you interact with it. The interaction is, as we know, various hurdles—plug-ins, email, DLLs, etc. As you take that further, your skill as a navigator, as someone that can engage the tools and master them (or not), allows you to succeed at comprehending or experiencing the story. In the end, you experience what Vannevar Bush meant by the power of what this machine could be.

MEADOWS: What role does the individual perspective have?

LAFIA: People would see the story differently depending on the way they read it. Some people read for story and some people read for the shape, the form of the thing, and see that as story, and some simply see a set of procedures, which is as much what this work is about as well. I wanted people to experience the texture of this kind of an interface and experience as much as follow it through stories. It's graphically very saturated and sumptuous, and to move around the various images and activity sets was important. If we'd stripped almost all the words out it—IT would have read more like a comic. Some people might read it visually and some might read it textually. But, of course, it's all these things.

The audience was never calculated. It was our enthusiasm that motivated us to do this, so we weren't so concerned about it. But we were always aware that there was a reader and that they would make the event.

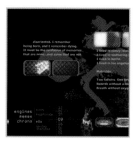

Three: The Third Dimension

Place
& Space

3.1: Introduction

*We must remember that everything depends
on how we use the material, not on the material itself.... We must be as familiar with the
functions of our buildings as with our materials. We must learn what a building can be,
what it should be, and also what it must not
be.... And just as we acquaint ourselves with
materials, just as we must understand functions, so we must become familiar with the
psychological and spiritual factors of our day.
No cultural activity is possible otherwise; for
we are dependent on the spirit of our time.*

— Mies van der Rohe

Narrative and architecture have been woven
together for millennia. Religious architecture contains processional passages that tell us about events
that have passed, or will come to pass. The footprint
of many European churches is a cross—an image that
itself represents a story. Political ceremonies such as
inaugurations and persecutions often take place
somewhere that emphasizes the importance of the
ceremony. Architecture that is intended to convey a
processional passage through a building—a prescribed route or course of action—has been a peren-
nial favorite for millennia.

The ancient Greeks built the Acropolis with a specific intent; to present a view of the world, from the
Acropolis—that inspired their religion and confirmed
their hold on the territory. The Acropolis, on top of a
hill above Athens, tells a story about Athenian
supremacy. There were three primary temples here,
and two of them were for Athena, the town's matron
deity. As visitors approached an opening gate, they
entered from a compressed entrance into an open
courtyard with the space framing the entrance of
the Parthenon.

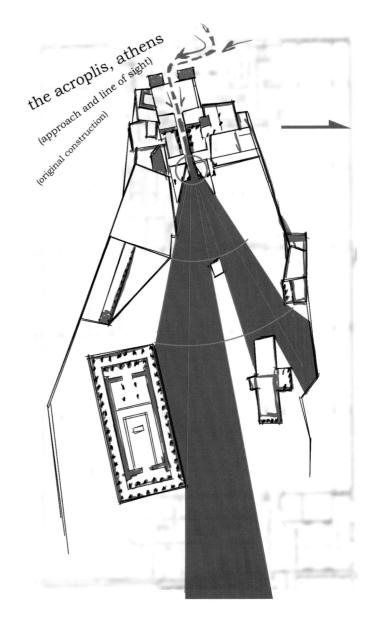

the acroplis, athens
(approach and line of sight)
(original construction)

This classic approach to architecture—a processional course of compression and expansion—is still used today. Compression in architecture is much like the functions of suspense and tension in classic narrative. But the narrative on the Acropolis was power, freedom, and a sense of proximity to a god that watched over the city. The processional visit to the Acropolis delivered this inspiration and narrative form, this string of events and subsequent thoughts, to its visitors.

These days our interests are as different as our techniques are unsubtle.

But the basic idea of using architecture to present opinion, narrate events, and provide perspective endures. Histories are probably the simplest of architectural narratives because, like a television documentary such as *Liquid Stage* [2.5.3], the issues are clear and the story is simple. It does not require a great deal of metaphorical interpretation and investment on the part of the viewer because, ostensibly, what's being reported is "fact." It's an informative story rather than an interpretation.

But many forms of information can be interpreted. This is where narrative has the greatest possibilities.

Consider the Holocaust Memorial in Washington DC, commissioned in 1980 by President Jimmy Carter. In 1999, this building, costing U.S. $195m, was the third most visited tourist stop in Washington DC. Replete with photographs, videos, postcards, ammunition, and boxcars, the building tells a very specific story: the extermination of a population.

The Holocaust Memorial takes this interpretation of history and looks at it under a strong interpretational lamp, depicting narrative in a very spatial sense. The metaphor of the building is one of a concentration camp. This is a narrative technique that delivers both an inside-the-skull and outside-the-skull representation of the story.

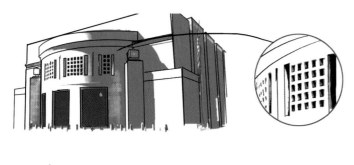

After descending the stairs to the third floor, museum visitors approach a huge steel and wood railroad car (this car is on loan from the Polish government as it is understood that it delivered prisoners to the death camps). The metaphor builds a redundant environment of style, but the function of the building and the railroad car also serve functions as the frame and the image itself.

These tools build a narrative that is unquestionably clear to the viewer, bringing us as close to the story as we can get. But it also helps to build a suspension of disbelief and transports visitors back to the days of the war. Even the entrance to Hitler's "office" is equally narrated. The visitor's approach across the open hall, the imposing desk, the acoustic snapping of the feet on a cold, smooth floor all give cues to the visitor of, as architect James Ingo Freed says of his intentions,

"a feeling of a procession. Of choices: either/or. Selections. The long lulls and sudden bumps forward, the steps to death."

What he is describing is a narrative. An interactive form of a narrative that is based in architecture.

3.2: Perspective

Computed perspectives can displace us further. They can take us beyond the boundaries of the real world and insert our disembodied viewing presences into modeled, fictional worlds—three-dimensional worlds that once, might have been, will be, or are projected forward by designers, imagined by film directors, sought by visionaries, proffered by disimulators.

—William J. Mitchell

Giotto's ideas of perspective suggest that a viewer must be in a particular place at a particular time for an idea to be properly conveyed. It was a form of representation that bridged the foreground to the background and the context of the environment to the decisions, opinions, or understandings of someone in that environment. It was a fundamentally architectural mindset. It was a fundamentally architectural perspective. But he was a narrative painter.

Many graphical conventions that employ perspective also have narrative equivalents. Consider as an example the relationship and similarities between foreshortening and foreshadowing. Both of these conventions give a protracted and condensed sense of what is ahead. They are both a telescoping of information. Foreshortening says "Here is what is ahead in space" and foreshadowing says "Here is what is ahead in time."

Conversely, most written narrative conventions that employ perspective have graphical equivalents as well. Examples include the first- and second-person representations of characters, or "breaking the fourth wall" in theatre and cinema.

Consider the members of an audience. We're at a play, Shakespeare again, maybe *Romeo and Juliet.* These audience members sit in the theater and look forward. They can't move very much. They're sitting at a distance, each facing the same direction, looking into a dollhouse or menagerie. The audience is in a removed point of view. The playwright is aware of this and so he or she develops soliloquies or monologues in an effort to indicate the individuals' perspectives, thereby shrinking that inconvenient distance between the speaker and the listener. It's a tradition older than the language you're reading right now. Cinema—the art of the motion picture—started to change this by packaging the audience into a tiny box called a movie camera. Suddenly the audience was able to swing up into the face of the character in question.

We suddenly reduced the distance and changed the point of view, or perspective, from one that was staid, distant, and removed to one that was saturated with motion and right in the face of the protagonist, antagonist, or environment. The dollhouse, or menagerie, came closer to being the real thing.

This all had to do with the position of the camera in relation to the characters and the events of the story. The camera is an interpretation of space, but of three-dimensional space. This is just as a page is an interpretation of two-dimensional space. Nowadays we might think of space as a dataset. If we consider standard Cartesian coordinates such as X, Y, Z, and Rotations, we can think of a camera as an interpretation of information. With these thoughts in mind, the camera becomes a kind of tool for interface design. Not only is it useful for interpreting three-dimensional data, it's also useful for telling stories. The camera in a three-dimensional dataspace is a great device, therefore, for interactive forms of narrative. It follows to consider that interactive narrative forms will inherit the rules of cinema—the cuts, pans, and crossovers as well as the actors, contracts, and paparazzi.*

These six items will all be quite different in the coming years. The stars of the future are beginning to show their shape, and they still appear human. Consider AnaNova, Lara Croft, or the grandfather of Idoru Stars, Max Headroom.

3.2.1: The Position of the Camera

Options are what allow us to make decisions and act, but they are always part of a larger context. Context provides the raw material for decision making and, by extension, for interaction. As we've illustrated, perspective provides the foundation for understanding and providing context. Finally, context and understanding allow decisions to be made by readers. This is why perspective is so important to interactive narrative. The perspective that a person has not only frames the context, but actually generates it, and, as we saw at the chapel in Assisi, determines the meaning received. This is what we're calling the Perspectivist Approach.

This isn't a long jump to make. We all know that the physical location we are in impacts our decisions. This is something architects since Vitruvius have known. But it's not only buildings that rely on a sense of narrative. Amusement parks, movie theatres, town squares, shopping malls, and even streets and civic zoning plans all have elements of narrative. If not narrative itself.

In most buildings, there is an intended starting place called an "Entrance," there are compressed and expanded elements of the space, etc. There is a series of events that is scripted over a period of time, and this is inundated with opinion and perspective. The opinions of the founders of Denver's Wal-Mart differ from the opinions of the founders of Athen's Acropolis, and the architecture reflects this. The more consciously constructed the architecture is, the more these opinions come to the forefront of a visitor's perception.

With any form of narrative, the particular view of the narrator or character is important in determining what the reader learns, sees, and understands. This influences what he or she does. Most stories these days—tales told in television, movies, books, websites and magazines—are third person. This allows the reader a sense of visualizing what's happening, but it's told from the point of view of an outside, often dispassionate, observer.

First-person and second-person voice is used by many writers to insert the reader into the body of the protagonist, pressing the reader's face against the mask the protagonist looks through, and forcing the reader to peer out of the eyes of that character into their world. It's an effective means of immersion.

In the story of the minotaur's labyrinth, first person can be used to tell the tale; "I walked through the mist, leaving the string behind me as I turned corner after corner, my hair on end, each strand unable to help my over-taxed eyes and ears."

In most gaming conventions, especially multi-user role-playing games that require a high level of immersion and a strong suspension of disbelief, the second person is used; "You walk through the mist, leaving the string behind as you turn corner after corner, your hair on end, each strand unable to help your over-taxed eyes and ears."

First-person narrative isn't used so often these days because narrative has traditionally relied on the third-person's influence (the narrator's) to convey the story of the character. This is simply because we're emerging from an oral tradition and transitioning into a more image-driven basis of interaction.

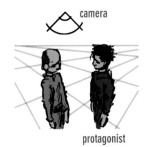

Second-person perspective—the least-used point of view in traditional forms of text-based narrative—pulls the reader back a bit so that he or she is capable of seeing things from a slightly elevated perspective. The effect that this has is, of course, to keep some amount of distance between the reader and the protagonist, both emotional and dimensional, but it also has the obvious effect of giving information to the reader that the protagonist might not have. It is, in effect, a conceptual camera zoom; "You walk through the misty halls of the labyrinth thinking that the string you are trailing will lead you out, when you realize—too late—that it's leading the minotaur directly to you." Same scene, different cut. Same cause, different effect. Same motions, different emotions.

Brenda Laurel, in her book *Computers as Theater*, points to the importance of first-person perspective:

> *"First-person sensory qualities are as important as the sense of agency in creating satisfying human-computer experiences. Quite simply, the experience of first-person participation tends to be related to the number, variety, and integration of sensory modalities involved in the representation. The underlying principle here is mimetic; that is, a human-computer experience is more nearly "first-person" when the activity it represents unfolds in the appropriate sensory modalities. The intuitive correctness of this notion is witnessed by the directions of technical evolution in the areas of simulators and games—toward higher-resolution graphics and faster animation, greater sound capabilities, motion platforms, and mimetic input devices like force-feedback controllers."*

Before we go on, it's worth noting that the word "mimetic" or "mimesis" is a word that Aristotle used frequently in his discussions of art. It's the imitation, mimicking, or representation of things like portraits, poems, and prose. Dr. Laurel is discussing outside-the-skull interaction and how it informs what goes on inside. She's talking about the form of representation used by the writer, and the concomitant perception by the reader.

But when it comes to things that require some level of mimesis, both the representation and the perception need to be taken into account. As far as interactive narrative is concerned, what is going on inside our heads is as important as what is happening outside. In addition, sometimes it's important to switch from one to another. This is why literature has these narrative forms of perspective. First-, second-, and third-person perspectives allow shifting modalities inside the skull. They provides a shift of interaction, emotional investment, and, as the good Dr. Laurel indicates, mimesis.

As noted, perspective is odd because it's something that exists both visually and cognitively (or "dimensionally" and "emotionally" as we've been using the terms). It exists in the form of a first- and second-person perspective in literature and has visual equivalents in painting, architecture, and interface design.

Understanding these issues helps graphic designers, interaction designers, and writers convey the appropriate level of removal from a scene so that the audience is zoomed back to the appropriate distance. Sometimes it's appropriate to be "close" to something, both dimensionally and emotionally, and other times farther back.

This "Zoom"—this visual cue of emotional proximity—is another part of the language of interactivity and narrative that has been inherited from the history of animation, film, and theater.

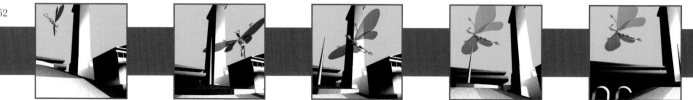

The Audience View

It's like a wedding cake. Imagine a tiny box without a top or front. It is a meter tall. In that box stand two tiny figures of a woman and a man. They're getting ready to kiss.

Would you feel more of what was happening if you were there, standing next to them, a breath away, or would you feel more if you were sitting in front of the box, looking in? What about overhead? Directly below a glass floor?

Let's look first at the Theatric Camera—that perspective that every member of a theater audience shares. This is the one that doesn't move and sits outside the scene of action. The scene, like a dollhouse, is spread in front of you. You have a continual overview of the actions, but you are mentally rotoscoping in, closer to the action, considering the consequences, and feeling the emotions of the actors as they whisper or talk or shout or sing from the center of the stage, stomping on the boards, throwing their cloaks, and slowly losing the dryness of the powder on their foreheads.

The design of the theater was intended to offer maximum freedom—but to the playwright, not the audience. The audience is in a fixed position. It is not interactive. The theater is a place where the audience is chained to their seats, immobilized with a single camera at a single angle on a single scene. There were no jump-cuts, and there were no zooms other than those that happened inside the skulls of the audience. It was a kind of tyranny of perspective. It's clear to see why this theatric environment for telling stories is losing its wind.

Consider, by contrast, the time when the moving image appeared on the scene. It introduced a sense of the first-person and the immediate, lifting the audience, as a body, into the stage itself, spinning and panning, and snapping from face to face, generating more information, and increasing both the perceptions and the understandings of the audience by this one move. But it also gave the authors the latitude to edit, alter, and repair powders that were belying the actors under their masks.

The tail-end of the 1800s generated a marketing hype of Hollywood proportion for something called a "kinetoscope"—an invention that Thomas Edison developed—that showed moving pictures. But this technology wasn't the real power of telling the story. Edison continued development of the projection systems until, by puncturing technical (as well as moral) boundaries, they started producing their own films as a means of showing what was possible. In 1896, the Edison Company produced a short film of two people kissing. It was titled *The Kiss Between May Irwin and John C. Rice* and got scathing reviews for its scandalous subject matter. *The New York Times* (quoting *The Chap Book*) on January 15 of that year, wrote,

Note the focus on size. Was it size or was it simply that the camera was closer, thereby making the viewer closer? Individual perspective seems to change physical size. This is one of perspective's defining characteristics. Could it be that when we are closer, we feel a bit more in touch with the activity of the narrative? We seem to have grown accustomed to sticking our noses close to—if not in—the business of our actors.

A designer who is developing perspective in 3D space is wise to consider the language of procession, architecture, film, theater, video, and cinema… he or she is advised to think about the position of a person and the view that the position affords them. This is an important part of the design of interactive narrative.

But we can combine these techniques, too. First-person perspective can be overlapped with third person, and second person can even again overlap these—that is, if it's a narrative form that allows for that kind of interaction.

The Sega gaming platform stitches together first-person and second-person cameras. The game player can toggle between these and use them to their advantage to see around corners, anticipate enemy moves, or recontextualize the game on a visual level. This has emotional implications for the player.

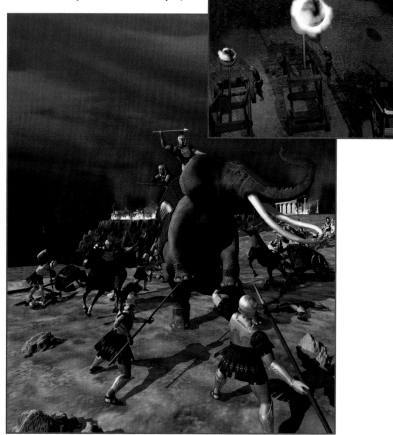

The essential distinction between theater and movies dwells in the camera. The location and movement of a video camera is what separates movies from theatre. This is because it provides both dimensional and emotional perspectives. It affects the viewers understanding of the space in question.

This is useful to narrative because when something is closer to the eye, it's closer to the heart.

This isn't the place to detail film techniques, but there is something to note: the affect on readers and the type of information that is presented in these two art forms of theater and motion picture. Theatric Camera provides an overview that introduces an amount of impersonality and removal from the activities of the scene. It's ancient. The cinematic camera of movies provides a more immediate, gripping, and personal perspective. It's at least modern (if not contemporary). These statements can be turned against themselves with specific examples because, as we know, an entire play at the theater could be filmed from a single seat in the audience and shown to the movie-going crowd. So a Cinematic Camera can also show overviews (but people won't pay to see too many of them).

The third-person perspective has a few different variations in literature, but in most forms of contemporary narrative, it's not yet as refined. Interactive narrative is a very young art. These days, third person amounts to that objective and cold point of view that provides mastery and control. Imagine the driver of a car: Just as a driver who looks away from the road and down at the dashboard shifts gears into a different concentration mode, that same shift in reference is used in these narratives as well. We're used to it, and, in fact, we now expect it.

Starcraft Brood War and the *Sims Cottage* (two admittedly different games for respectively different audiences) give us different flavors of the same classic recipe. Subdivisions of information, color-coded icons, and sub-frame text insertion make these interfaces suspiciously similar. Almost always, the HUD is shoved up against the bottom of the screen. For those of us who are native readers of Germanic or Romantic languages, this feels natural because we read from top-left to lower-right. Meanwhile, there are four primary sets of information: information that relates to time, information that relates to space, metaphor and narrative context, and a set of information that provides the ability to switch from microscopic to macroscopic.

These narratives rely mostly on third-person perspective. These are narrative forms that keep the reader in a chilly, removed, and elevated gods-eye perspective. The reader is never engaging on the same emotional level, but rather floating, solidly, far above in the firmament, passing edicts and bids down to the characters who carry out the action.

These techniques of design and presentation are the inheritance of interactive narrative, the work and toolsets of the other techniques that have come before. These forms of perspective will continue to evolve until they have found their proper place in the work environment and art form that's emerging.

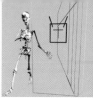

3.2.2: The Benefits of Place & Space

Computer-generated dimensional imagery offers some handy means of representing perspective that flat imagery does not. Movement and the interaction that happens in "Real Time" is significant and should not be glossed over, but the fact that such things as atmospheric perspective (something that da Vinci noticed one day in the hills and named "Chiaroscuro") and aerial perspective are far more clear in three-dimensional data formats. Not surprisingly, they offer themselves as conventions used in narrative. What is mysterious if not the atmospheric obscuration of mists and fog?*

The terms for mist and mystery both come from the same IndoEuropean root of "neigh" meaning, roughly, "what is hard to see?"

Technologies that rely on dimensional imagery are improving. Movie companies, such as Industrial Light and Magic, and video game companies, such as Sega and Id, are continually inventing, investing, or buying new 3D rendering technologies. Why is it that these gaming and movie fanatics aren't satisfied with their 2D imagery just as they are satisfied with the pixel density or tungsten values of their desktop monitor? Why is it these two communities that deal so exclusively in narrative are always pushing these developments? Because they understand the implicit capabilities that motion and dimension offer to narrative. Because we live in a 3D world. It's an issue of metaphor.

Let's return to Dr. Laurel's notion discussed previously: "A human-computer experience is more nearly 'first-person' when the activity it represents unfolds in the appropriate sensory modalities." This is to say that a suspension of disbelief will be more easily incited when someone feels like he is really there because he is provided with both inside-the-skull and outside-the-skull interaction. And this is a simple thing to do with a dimensional graphic that is using an architectural metaphor.

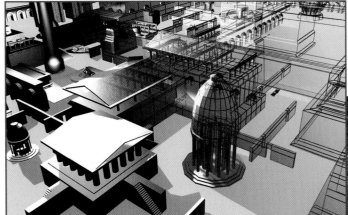

Dimensional imagery is most effective because it provides perspective, but it also provides at least three capabilities.

First, quantitatively, it is capable of representing cubed information. Part of the reason why the GUI became so valuable was because it represented squared information rather than linear information (as in the "command line"). The GUI took the one dimensionality of the command line and extended it to the metaphor of the desktop. Dimensional information has the potential to offer denser information sets than flat imagery. Just as the desktop metaphor is able to contain one-dimensional text and writing, three-dimensional imagery is able to contain two-dimensional desktop and GUI metaphors (and by extension, writing and text). As of today, there is precious little development happening in this space because there are few designers who understand how to incorporate these issues into a navigable interface, much less a narrative. We overcame these issues once (in other words, we now have functional desktop metaphors and 2D GUIs), and it seems it is a matter of time until we do the same with a wider range of 3D metaphors.

The cubed, 3D evolution of the Desktop Metaphor won't be, let's hope, cubicles.

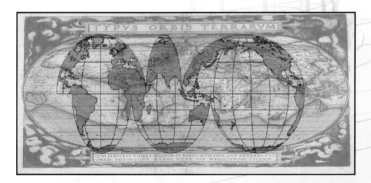

Second, dimensional imagery allows juxtaposed information sets, such as text, audio, animation, picture, and object, to be presented next to each other, and that helps learning (educators have known the value of these non-verbal texts, set side by side, for some years, now). This is something that text simply does not do. Flat imagery is able to pull this off, but there are often limitations that prevent large datasets from being seen in accurate context, such as being able to get an overview of a building or city.

Third—and this is to address what Laurel says—we're already familiar with dimensional imagery. We move around in space, we reach under and over and step behind and walk through. This is great for building a mimetic sense of narrative; the reader already knows something about how to use it. Compared to a command-line representation, 3D representation can be far more intuitive for a reader to use. Books on shelves are 3D representations. Escalators and city streets are, as well.

But the most successful 3D interfaces rely on some sense of narrative. This is part of the reason, to back up the problem, why video games have come to rely on them so much. Plus they seem sexy, and no one clearly states why. The benefits seem apparent to people who have solved this set of problems and have a specific need for them, but their "market penetration" remains a bit flaccid. At least for now.

In 1968, Ivan Sutherland, one of the early explorers of 3D graphics, invented the Head Mounted Display. He used two small conference reflector-type computer displays—CRTs—and a location sensor. That sensor gave input on the position of the CRTs and put it on his head. This was a new form of monitor that allowed for traversal of dimensional graphics. It was also a sort of virtual decapitation.

But not everyone is going to go to these rarified depths to develop new interfaces for interaction. The HMD, now more than three decades old, still remains an implementation that's a part of the now-antiquated future.

It's important to consider the meaning and the metaphor of the narrative before considering the display technology. The specifics of the display need to be considered as part of the design, and the metaphor may even inform the display. This approach to design is the difference between the architect and the construction crew.

3.3: Narrative

Now we're at the threshold of the next revolution in user-computer interaction: a technology which will take the user through the screen into the world inside the computer—a world in which the user can interact with three-dimensional objects whose fidelity will grow as computing power increases and display technology progresses. The world inside the computer can be whatever the designer makes it; entirely new experiences and modes of interaction can be explored and as designers and users explore this strange new world, they will be jointly defining the next generation of user interaction with computers.

—John Walker

3.3.1: Principles of Narrative in Place & Space

In the world of buildings—the indigenous environment of modern mankind—the role of the architect is similar to the role of a narrator. Many buildings, such as churches, courthouses, and office buildings, clearly indicate an approach up the stairs of the building, prior to entry. This is designed to tell the person that he is entering a place that is important. They frame a beginning, middle, and end by utilizing scale and material. Tall columns, large double doors, and stairs are key ingredients. Homes, too, often use small hand-woven items like a welcome mat or a wooden porch rather than impressive colonnades. Buildings have beginnings and they have endings, but this is not to say that all buildings exhibit Mr. Freytag's narrative arc with a denouement near the exit sign.

The architect's role, like the narrator's, is to frame the beginnings, middles, and endings of a passage through a building in such a way that the building serves its function first. As American architect Louis Sullivan said in 1896, "Form follows function." But the architect's role—especially when presenting multiple options to a visitor—becomes almost identical to the role of an author of interactive narrative because options need to be presented that allow interactivity and frame the decision-making process. Christopher Alexander, from his important book *A Pattern Language*, writes:

"When a person arrives in a complex of offices or services or workshops, or in a group of related houses, there is a good chance he will experience confusion unless the whole collection is laid out before him, so that he can see the entrance of the place where he is going."

It's evident how the creators of Banja* [2.5.6] have integrated this idea into a graphical interface that's only a small part of their larger narrative. This presentation of the "whole collection" being laid out before the reader is an important element to this interface.

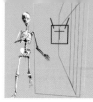

We often speak of narrative in spatial terms: suspense, tension, compression, exploration, discovery, a "turn of events," or a "twist in the plot." Suspense, in particular, is interesting: the hanging of an item over an empty space. It's easy to see how these translate to architectural terms when you consider a horror movie and the elongated passages a protagonist travels through before he or she gets attacked by the boogeyman.

What's important is to note that there are narrative tools that architects use that would be a rewarding study to not only interface and graphic designers, but to narrative designers as well. Tension / relaxation and compression / expansion are part of architectural design just as they are part of narrative design.

The narrator's job, like the architect's, is to organize information in a way that builds context, symbology, metaphor, and meaning. One of architecture's primary goals is to appropriately subdivide space. This process of subdivision is not only for social interaction, but, like punctuation in a sentence, it is also a means of framing concentration and the presentation of information. The basic approach to narrative is the same.

3.3.2: Designing Place & Space for Narrative

Only about 160 years ago, in the rolling hills of eastern Kansas, battles were fought under a hot sun. They were Cowboys and Indians. Or, more accurately, Dragoons and Osage.

The U.S. National Park Service has altered, as they have many historical districts and buildings, the Fort Scott military installation that was originally built in the 1840s. The narrative presented is historic and so some of the problems of narrative presentation are solved. The specifics of the information become easier to articulate because there is little interpretation—of either the author or the viewer. The opinion of the author is the opinion of history (since history is written by winners, as we're told).

Several key elements of this architecture provide an excellent lesson for multiple forms of narrative. First, there are overviews that are presented. On the assumption that someone is looking for something in particular, or, more likely, on the assumption that people may get lost, a macroscopic plan is provided near the entrance.

This macroscopic view gives both the dimensional and the emotional perspectives; it not only shows a visitor where he is standing, but it shows him what he needs to understand about where he is standing. This is a framing of the space and the time of the narrative that helps, by introduction, to prepare the visitor. It sets their expectations and provides context.

After leaving through an obviously organized entry point (all paths lead up into this beginning building), the open courtyard serves as a simple and effective interface to the rest of the space. Placards are scattered about. Paths lead up to buildings. Doors are left open so that these entrances may be easily seen.

As a visitor walks about the park, different spaces contain different sets of information. These are narrative points of perspective. Some rooms are reconstructed and intentionally left to look unintentional—as if someone has just left the room seconds before you arrived. There are no signs.

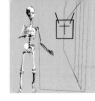

Other areas appear to be only signs, such as display cases that take you out of the sense of immersion and inform you on a more direct level, by tutelage.

And still others are a combination of these two information sets, presenting the historic information that is not obvious with a sign that rests on the wall next to the objects under scrutiny. This is the most effective, most flexible, and most efficient design because it allows multiple viewing modes without removing the visitor's choices.

Each of these elements provides vantage points and perspective, and because there is a beginning, middle, and end, it takes on a narrative form. The opinions and perspectives are slight and muted. Because it's a historic presentation, artistic license is nearly revoked.

These tools of storytelling can be applied to other tasks. The way the narrative is built is applicable to a wider range of material than historic education. The methods of combining the space of the multiple buildings, the place of the courtyard, the images and icons on the walls, the explanatory text, and the general procession through the narrative builds an educational and interesting story. This makes it a template example for other forms of narrative. The interactive interfaces of the place are what make it such.

Here's an example of one. Her name is Kelly Collins. She represents the highest form of interaction that is available with current technology.

3.4: Interaction

… several spectrums of interactivity focus on how much control the audience has over the outcome or the rate, sequence, or type of action, and how much feedback exists in the interface.

—Nathan Shedroff

3.4.1: Principles of Interaction in Place & Space: Separating and Joining

Walls frame worldviews.

Architecture contains elements of interaction and may be said to be interactive because, if designed for such, it allows visitors to participate in the key steps of interaction: Observation, Exploration, Modification, and Reciprocal Change. Rate, sequence, and type of action are all determined by the visitor, not by the architect, so forms of interactivity have flexibility in their implementation. Elevators, stairs, hallways, windows, doors, large rooms, and small alcoves each provide interaction of some sort. Each of these environments may also include forms of interaction that are more than dimensional, such as interactive widgets, nested stories, or even nested buildings. In the worlds of virtual architecture, the possibilities are limited only by the author's imagination (and not, contrary to popular opinion, the technology).

The acts of observation and exploration are certainly there; we tend to do some exploration when we enter a new building. We are able to modify it to some degree by opening doors and altering the arrangements of individual rooms or desks. And we are changed by it—if nothing else than by where we stand.

But an empty building is a corpse. The interaction that's implicit in architecture is not generally the richest when it is considered an interaction with the object or space of the building. The building is only a frame for most of what happens there. It's the people who make a space or place interesting.

The process of subdividing space—framing the interaction among the people in that space—is a primary goal of architecture. A skilled architect builds places that allow people to choose how they want to interact with each other; Intimately on small benches or in private places, publicly on daises or podiums, professionally, instructionally, romantically, etc. This happens to more than the individuals. This kind of design takes place on a civic level as well. A village square, for example, is a kind of civic meeting room in that it allows large groups to gather to discuss, present, or rearrange themselves for whatever meeting is taking place at that time.

Most meeting places—such as gardens, piazzas, squares, etc—are defined by boundaries. For cities, these are lines of buildings, but in an individual building, it's a simpler version of the same thing: a wall. From an architectural standpoint (not a sculptural one), the wall is the thing that defines civic, social, and personal forms of interaction.

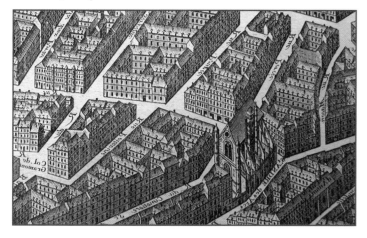

From the civic standpoint, we can consider a plaza a civic kind of room. Walls are there to separate people and divide interaction among people, but walls are also the point at which individual self expression occurs. Interior walls are the point where people hang their pictures, prop their bookshelves, and make whatever personal changes to a room they want. We learn a lot about a person based on the walls of their home. Walls are used to frame different modes of concentration and interaction. Christopher Alexander says, "The identity of a house comes from its walls." Not only that, but:

> "Adjust the walls, openings, and windows in each
> indoor space until you reach the right balance between
> open, flowing space, and closed cell-like space. Do not
> take it for granted that each space is a room; nor, on
> the other hand, that all spaces must flow into each
> other. The right balance will always lie between these
> extremes: no one room entirely enclosed; and no space
> totally connected to another. Use combinations of
> columns, half-open walls, porches, indoor windows,
> sliding doors, low sills, french doors, sitting walls, and
> so on, to hit the right balance."

These are valuable clues for designers of interactive narrative. And, of course, when we walk through a building (or "Navigate," as it's unfortunately called in contemporary 3D interface design), the interaction between the architect and the visitor of the building is most apparent. It's a kind of choreography. This is a particular kind of interaction that is most similar to interactive narrative as we're considering it here—a time-based representation of action in which a reader can affect, choose, or change the series of events. This interaction of the architect and the visitor is similar to the interaction of the author and the reader.

As Marcos Novak [3.5.1] approaches it, walls can be thought of in ways that don't necessarily have anything to do with gravity or its demands:

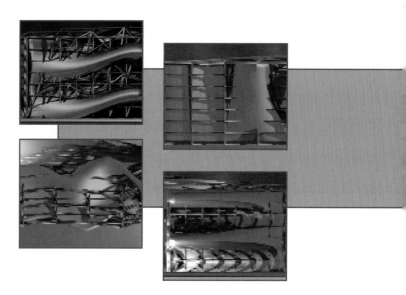

Walls, as we see in the above floorplans, divide, but they also cover. Without covering, nothing can be found, so it's evident that the use of walls can be a means of building mystery, exploration, and discovery. Discovery requires obfuscation. The process of finding is itself interactive, and childhood games are premised on this activity.

175

It's the same basic action that many storytellers are trying to incite—a process of fascination, captivation, investment, and interest.

In short, use your walls as a writer uses punctuation, indentation, paragraph returns, or words themselves. Use walls to separate parts of the story and interaction. Use walls as an interface designer uses decisions. Use walls as a graphic designer uses composition.

Conversely, in all forms of interaction, the association of information is important so that people understand the relationships of different sets. If someone doesn't understand that the buttons on a coke machine are buttons, he will have a hard time getting a coke. A designer can use metaphor and other forms of introducing redundancy, but the most effective means of dealing with specifics of association is a simple visual cue.

Visual cues are used to associate parts. Where walls divide parts, visual cues connect them. This gives us those important functions that most tools provide: separate and join. But as far as interactive narrative is concerned, this is the added ingredient that lets a reader know where to travel or what to do next. This might be an animation, a character, a sign (such as "Exit") or something as gauche as a series of footsteps on the pathway in front of the reader. Visual cues are critical for narrative because without them, the interactivity is simply exploration rather than narrative.

But walls and visual cues go together like tape and scissors. They can be used together to guide and inform readers and can work as complementary. Like sentence structure in traditional forms of narrative, walls and other visual forms of separation and association can be used to encourage, discourage, inform, or befuddle readers. The goal is to help readers uncover the story and explore the world.

3.4.2: Designing Place & Space for Interactivity

The way a space is divided is what determines its method of presenting information. It can also be said that the method of presenting information and orchestrating human interaction is at the heart of telling a story (these days we call it a character-driven plot). We have covered some of these items in Part 02 [2.4.2]. I cite this because, despite the inside-the-skull understandings of three-dimensional space, it is, after all, still being presented on a screen, and so many of these principles still apply.

Acquiring and discovering information and then facilitating the redistribution of that information are at least three forms of interaction that are needed in most forms of interactive narrative. These categories are chosen to offer examples of the main forms of interaction that architectural narrative will require. Interfaces for interactive narratives will generally allow readers of the narrative to understand the story and then collect information, browse for information, and share it with others.*

Acquiring Information

A reader will generally have a need to search for information. This is a primary function of the Internet, books, conversation, and many forms of interactive reading. Some architectural spaces are more suited to acquiring information than others. Consider rooms with smaller rooms branching off of them. Each smaller room represents a group. Or, better yet, a single room that subdivides. Libraries offer multiple examples in that there are large clusters that are categorized into subclusters for efficient searching. The key visual characteristic is the branch, or the subdivision.

According to our principles of interaction, there would also be the ability to change these architectural forms of moving information (and to be changed by them), but in the interest of keeping the focus of this work general, I will leave that deeper study for another place.

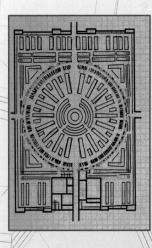

Discovering Information

Looking for something that you don't yet know about—browsing or discovering—is a different process and requires different presentation than acquiring information. The basic idea is seen in many European open-air markets in which a pathway is framed by options or shops that are grouped according to categories such as meat, cheese, fruit, etc. In contemporary American markets, such as malls, the simple pathway has been altered to form a circulation—in some cases to tyrannical degrees. The visitor needs to walk around or past or through other shops in order to get to the next floor or exit. Open air markets are a bit more interactive and give visitors more control.

Redistributing Information

Social space is used to distribute information between people. In the case of our recipe here, it will be narrative information that's found or discovered. Sometimes the redistribution is from one person to many (as an amphitheater) other times from many to many (as a bank or BBS provides) but, mostly, from one person to another (as a park bench). Forms of virtual architecture are curious because they extend these possibilities a bit; the telephone, an early cyberspace, allows one-to-one over remote distances. Many MUDs (Multi-User Domains or Multi-User Dungeons) have a "shout" function or a "broadcast" function that can allow many-to-many communication. But visually speaking, the trick to building these forms of architectural interface is one of visual composition; draw the viewer's eye to the point where the information is coming from.

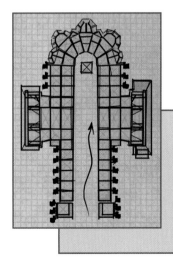

179

3.5: Examples and Interviews

The only thing to do with good advice is to pass it on. It is never of any use to oneself.

—Oscar Wilde

The following interviews are presented to offer some alternative perspectives into the methods, means, and madness of building interactive narrative—specifically in 3D. As with the examples and interviews of Part 02, these interviews are edited only to the degree that makes them readable (some of the people interviewed are not native English speakers). I have chosen a range of people from theorists to developers in hopes of capturing some of the specifics of a field of general study. I was not able to accommodate all of the projects and people who are doing incredible and innovative work—this is merely a sample of an emerging industry.

These people work outside normal civilization; the stage for these stars are the rocky cliffs of development. Because I know most of these people as personal friends and work associates, I can also point out that these rough environments of grueling development are their indigenous turf. They prefer the wild.

In the eyes of these people, if it works, it's obsolete.

3.5.2 - Theater: La Noche de Santa Inés

In Caracas in the early 1990s, a theater project was installed in the collapsed basement of the President's mansion. It allowed audience members to walk from one room to another and speak with the cast. Though not a digital project, all the elements of a good interactive narrative are present. Anita Pantin, the producer and director of the show, assembled a group of local writers/actors and, based on a pre-existing Japanese play, developed an experimental theater production named La Noche de Santa Inés.

3.5.3 - Video Game: Deus Ex 2

Deus Ex 2 is the follow-up to the immensely successful video game, *Deus Ex*. After having won an award from the British Academy of Film and Television Arts, Harvey Smith of Austin, Texas led the design of the next version of the game. He discusses some of his thoughts on how the game is built and what goes into the design process. A long-time game player and designer, his perspectives on interactive narrative outline some of what the futures of interactive narrative might bring.

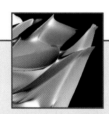

3.5.1 - Interview: Marcos Novak

Marcos Novak, one of the early homesteaders of virtual reality, is an architect who makes buildings that float. They're often generated from music. Marcos algorithmically analyzes music and then uses that analysis to generate geometry. That geometry is intended to be understood as a building. Marcos discusses his artistic and theoretical approaches to his work and underlines some important points on architectural narrative.

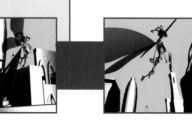

3.5.4 - Installation: Is God Flat / Is The Devil Round / What About Me

Maurice Benayoun is a Parisian artist who works with interactive 3D graphics. His projects, spanning 12 years of development and with a concentration in procedural modeling techniques, have gained him an international reputation. Maurice reviews some of his work and looks into how databases can be not only visualized for narrative purposes, but use feedback from readers to generate new narrative structures.

3.5.5 - Internet: Ultima Online

Raph Koster, the lead designer of *Ultima Online*, who is currently designing Sony Station's *Star Wars Galaxies* online game, has been "making games for as long as I can remember." He started with a Sears Pong console and an 8-bit Atari. Armed with these dull weapons, by the time he was in high school, he and his friends had formed a computer game company. They sold a game that was wrapped in a sandwich bag. They sold one. But it sold. The years passed and now Raph's ideas on the interaction between the author and the reader are helping define the art of interactive narratives today—in particular, his distinction between "Impositional" and "Expressional" forms of interaction.

3.5.6 - Mobile Phones: Top Agent

Mobile technology in the United States is still prenatal. However, in Finland, it has reached a toddling state that allows us to see some of its potential. Although this case study is not about 3D graphics, it is about 3D interaction because, in juxtaposition to what Marcos Novak is doing, it inverts the world of virtual reality into something that has been termed "Ubiquitous Computing." *Top Agent* is a narrative game that was developed by Orchimedia, a Finnish development agency, for a hybridized television, Internet, and mobile platform. It continues to be one of Finland's most frequently used mobile games.

3.5.7 - Development Tools: Virtools

In development, the loftiest of theories is carried by crude metal. The development team at Virtools has managed to distill multiple design philosophies into practical applications for development of interactive narrative. This is no simple task when you consider that this toolset allows teams of people to work on the same project at the same time. As Ludovic Duchâteau says, "The central nervous system of interactivity lies in the ability to program potentiality."

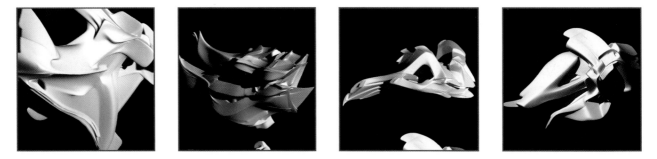

3.5.1: Marcos Novak Interview
http://www.centrifuge.org/marcos/

Marcos Novak is one of, if not the, inventor of virtual architecture. An internationally renowned artist, educator, theoretician, and programmer, he pioneered the invention and exploration of environments that may define what future generations see in the wires. His work has taken many directions over the years, generally developing methods and means of algorithmic generation. The architecture that he generates is often coupled with music. Using musical notation as a kind of DNA he translates chords and keys into polygons and walls.

MEADOWS: How do you build a narrative in an environment that retains an individual perspective? How can virtual architecture accomplish this?

NOVAK: The single most important feature is perspective. Ever since the invention of perspective, all the different forms of expression have dictated the position of the viewer so the author of the work places the person in the space but does not allow them any freedom. So when you look at a painting, you see depth, but the position is dictated by the painter. You can find the very same thing in literature and dance and history and all of the arts.

The single exception is architecture in which a construct is made [that] may have narrative intent, but no guarantees that someone will follow it. There's a lot more freedom in architecture. People are always changing buildings. Religions change, slaughterhouses become libraries, schools turn into apartments, etc. So the relationship [between the architect and the visitor] is one of suggestion—it's a coloration or a flavor of the building that suggests what it does—but within which anything can happen.

It's a task of density and intensification that we're facing in doing this stuff. But what the architectural analogy brings to this is that while the outcome can't be dictated, the process of authoring it has to have a certain depth of coherence. Anything can happen anywhere. Everything is optional.

Well, that indicates a kind of vector. We're moving from a specific to a general relocation. When this happens, the viewpoint becomes unhinged. The perspective still works, but the freedom is the thing that makes the difference.

Once that freedom is established, then you need to think what the consequences [of designing an environment] are. This is where everything becomes unhinged. The whole apparatus—the entire design—becomes conditional on the attitude and condition of the viewer.

The future of cinema is world making. The author no longer constructs a single narrative and no longer constructs a multiple choice tree structure but constructs a continuum—a matrix of possibilities—the generalization of the viewpoint implies you need to think about what you're making.

MEADOWS: So this represents a new kind of plot line?

NOVAK: It's not a plot line but a stochastic density of events through which any trajectory will project a plotline. The Holy Grail is how to do that in a continuous way. It's fairly easy to enumerate this in a discreet way. That's not cracking the problems.

MEADOWS: Can you give me an example of this?

NOVAK: Here I am on the freeway. The general plot is that I'm going to SIG-GRAPH, and if I swerve and hit one of these cones on the road, that affects the plot. But the option is always available.

MEADOWS: Is it possible to offer multiple plots in architectural spaces?

NOVAK: Definitely. There's an economy to observing a movie or reading a book or taking in any kind of expressive artwork. It's going to take a certain amount of your life for that experience and in choosing to read that or see it I'm foregoing whatever else I might have been doing. I might rather sit in the sun, or make love, or have a picnic, or pet my cat. The only economic reason I would

do that is because the book or story will provide you with an intensified experience of life. So there's a trade-off. We know how to do that with linear pieces of music or writing. We're just finding out how to do that in interactive spaces.

MEADOWS: You're saying that time's an implicit part of narrative?

NOVAK: Yes. No matter how spatial something is, it's going to carry a timeline in the fact that someone is going to experience it. But time now, instead of being an axis, is a trajectory that someone carries with them. You don't know how long someone will spend in the narrative of a building or where they will go, so you have to put enough episodes in such a way that someone will bump into them.

MEADOWS: Gustav Freytag's triangle diagram charts plot as a function of time. How would plot change if the time that someone is spending is up to them and not the architect-narrator?

NOVAK: They bring their own time and so it's not entirely guaranteed

that they would traverse the triangle. The axes are elastic, and so we don't quite know. But you can make the space such that it will end at any moment and make a bigger or smaller [Freytag] triangle at any time. Or another model would be a train station model. If I'm on a train, I can get off or I can wait for the next station. The resolution comes in increments. Or I can always jump off the train.

To me architecture is very much like music. Not only in its formal structure that contains rhythm proportion and harmony, but also like a piece of music, architecture can be soothing, aggravating, too loud, too soft. Architecture affects us at that very primary level, on the whole. You pick certain forms and you pick certain colors, and they tell as much of the story.

MEADOWS: Let's talk about the language of specifically virtual spaces for a few minutes. Suspense—actual suspension—seems to be a function of narrative and architecture. Your structures seem to be in a strange sort of suspense, hanging as they do in the middle of nowhere. What's going on?

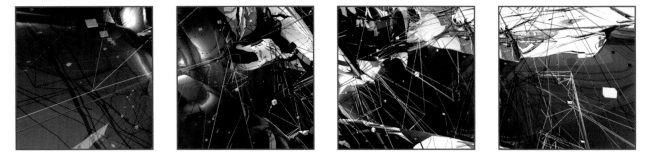

This seminal piece from John Cage's career was 4:33 of actively listening to the environment where traditional music would normally be heard. The difference is that the listener is listening to the ambient environment, not constructed music.

NOVAK: The suspense, as it occurs in narrative, is something created by a structure of expectation. You're led to the edge of something and don't know when it will transpire. That sets up the suspense.

Are you familiar with John Cage's piece "4:33"?*

Well, it took him a couple of years to write the piece, and he actually wrote it and it caused him all sorts of trouble and he lost friends over it. But I remember going through something very similar when I started making virtual spaces through algorithmic composition, and had to claim those pieces as part of architecture. It's one thing to have your building leak, it's another to have it floating in the air. So there's this point of taking a deep breath and proposing that this is part of it [architectural study] and [seeing] if I survive the castigations.

Another level was when I finally took the horizon plane and tilted it and disengaged the architecture and started composing in three-space. It's a moment in architecture—a threshold gets crossed—when you say architecture must fly.

MEADOWS: So it was just that the rules of architecture weren't serving your values any more?

NOVAK: When people like you and I come in and propose these crazy ideas, it isn't because its gratuitous! It's because we perceive either intuitively or consciously that the previous set of rules [is] failing. The previous rules simply can't address a new set of possibilities.

So with music, if you think of the score or the staff as a grid, the interval that it proposes in time and in pitch is coarse. What I mean is that the step size between notes is rather big. In digital format, the sampling rate breaks the second down to 44,000. Then, in terms of distinctions of loudness, where the traditional notation goes from "Pianissimo to Fortissimo," digital has tens of thousands of distinctions. So this is a system that no longer supports the rules.

MEADOWS: What about the rulesets that we use to define metaphors? For example, let's look at the railroad car that sits in the Holocaust

Memorial in Washington, D.C. That car is not only a metaphor that defines the space; it's also an actual functioning part of the environment, but what makes it so powerful is the fact that it's the real car that was actually carting real people around to real death camps.

NOVAK: Those tangible things that are nameable belong to the symbolic and the discreet. Someone could bring those very same things and put them in a Costco warehouse and cancel their power. The symbolic can only guarantee half the communication—if that. What artists add is the concern for the other half, all the continuous things… the lighting and distance and placement… the balancing act.

There are two acts that we engage in: discreet and symbolic acts. The first one is discreet. This is counting. The other, which is balancing, is symbolic. We have an easier time with counting because we can explain it so much easier. The things that we call powerful are in the balancing.

MEADOWS: So you mean that the things that we call beautiful are actually a balancing act? How "suspenseful" of you!

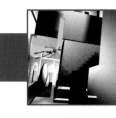

   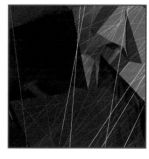

NOVAK: Well, intonation, lighting, distance, articulation, modulation… these things that we do that are in the realm of balancing and sometimes the symbolic. So when Shakespeare says

"Full fathom five
they father live"

you could take the words or letters and rearrange them or you could try to paraphrase that statement into something that says the same thing. Which is to say, here is a symbolic expression that strikes a balance that we find powerful. That balance is what we call poetry.

MEADOWS: But what about representing this? How is it communicated in architectural narrative? Is it possible that we have more than first-, second-, and third-person perspectives in virtual space? Is there a kind of social perspective that also exists, or would this be considered something like third person? What about the raw data?
Is that zero-person?

NOVAK: Peter Greenaway tries that with time codes. There is a sort of distributed viewpoint that we get… something big I've been developing for years is following through on this notion of "trans" to its conclusion. There's a whole host of

other ways of seeing things that has been opened.
I can pack a lot of information into a small spot, but our experience with the world is that we have ancillary and peripheral information we bring it. Imagine a book that has a soundtrack…

MEADOWS: We did that at [Xerox] PARC. Maribeth Back, a member of the RED group, developed an interactivebook that you could sit down at and as you moved your hand over the pages of the book, different soundtracks would occur— galloping horses, wind in the trees, etc. But it always matched what you were reading. It was amazing.

NOVAK: Okay, imagine this. Imagine a book that watches your eye as you read it, and as you scan through a sentence, it rewrites the entire book as you read. So the act of reading becomes an act of rewriting.

MEADOWS: A literary Heisenberg? A situation in which your seeing it affects the object itself?

NOVAK: Something like that. This is an entirely new viewpoint in which the book is watching the reader. So you have the structure of all of the possible viewpoints we know through literature and then we have this new kind that we've never had the means to expect before.

This is a curious thing. It's a very dialectic mode. I'm having a conversation with you, and your model of the conversation is shifting. You're generating a counter-structure or reciprocal POV at any moment.

MEADOWS: I've talked with quite a few developers [who] are really honing in on the algorithmic generation of spaces. They're determined that the only way to make a space really interactive is to get away from scripting scenes and do on-the-fly and procedural development.

NOVAK: That's an example of a book responding. But the next phase is that it's not just the book but also the world. The whole world has eyes… the idea that space is intelligent. It's no longer innocent. Every point in space is watching you.

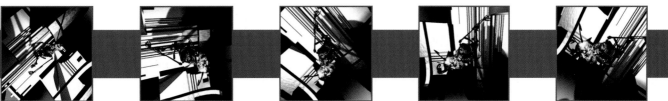

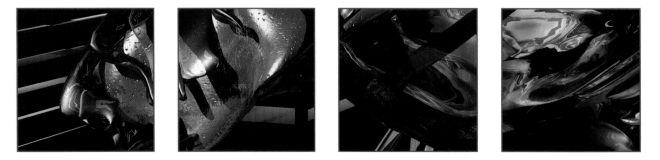

So then every element of the environment of the space is actually rewriting itself as a function of your presence.

So if I'm the subject, I have XYZ/ROT but also my emotional state—happy, distracted, etc. What I'm describing is this dialogue between [the notion that] every point of space is its own as well as the viewer's. Say the subject is a series of sliders as on a [sound] mixer, and every point in space is a set of similar sliders. As one moves through the space, all of these are changing at the same time in relation to each other—every point in space is changing along all these parameters.

One thing that comes out of this is another preoccupation—an idea that narrative forms move into world making. There's a question implicit in what I say. "What constitutes a world?" In its simplest formulation, I know that the world exists because it disagrees with me.

MEADOWS: Philip K. Dick said one time that "Reality is that which won't go away." So you're saying

that if the world agrees with you then it's not a world?

NOVAK: If it agreed with me, then it would be under my control. The fact that the world has its own agenda that I can't alter. I can negotiate with it—such as get an umbrella—but I can't control it. So in terms of how to do this, you realize it has to have its own motivations. I always give it an element of autonomy versus the viewer. Many games don't have that. The agents are still substitute subjects.

MEADOWS: As far as narrative goes, what benefits do we get from 3D that we don't get from 2D?

NOVAK: You get an entirely different phenomenology. As soon as you enter it [you realize] the fact that one thing can obscure another and you can move around something and it can get in the way. If you have perspective, you get the diminution of objects at a distance; you might also get atmospheric effects, and lighting. These are all things that don't apply to 2D worlds. Each of these things is a problem or an opportunity.

For most people it's a problem, and I think this is why it's such a difficulty to get people to deal with the third dimension when the 2D world is already clear. But these things are meaningful. The world rearranges its meaning along these features. They articulate things you couldn't say otherwise.

If you're reading a story and you're getting foreshadowed hints, you're building various outcomes of the story as you're reading it—and they are in a fog. You're structuring a story that is architectural, and these things should be thought of as moving and changing.

"Liquid architecture" applies to more than just architecture. When you're working with these machines, everything that was a constant becomes a variable. And the environments are liquid and changing.

It's changing according to your reading.

3.5.2: Case Study One: La Noche de Santa Inés

When Anita Pantin, a native Venezuelan, was thirteen years old she was living in Rome. She had started her career there as a painter, but, wanting a "less solitary pursuit," shifted to theater and started doing lighting design. Her work took her to Paris, Montreal, and New York where she worked as a set and lighting designer. Then, not content to settle down, Anita turned to opera where, among other projects, she produced *Madame Butterfly* in Caracas (1985) and Tosca (1986). In the late 1990s she had begun to work with alternative production methods that included computer-assisted screen production in Boston and Montreal. Anita currently lives in Texas.

But despite the size and technology of her productions, one project in particular was intimate and interactive. It was done in the collapsed basement of the Venezuelan President's house called Villa Santa Inés. The play was based on a Japanese play named *Kesa And Morito*, written by Akutagawa Ryunosuke (1892–1927, cf. Rashomon). Anita adapted the story to celebrate the writers of Caracas by presenting them as actors in her play. This was done through audience participation in which each actor, or writer, was available to present his own perspective of the story.

MEADOWS: Can you give me an overview of what happened during the show?

PANTIN: Well, the whole space was so big, so dark, and so humid! I always like things that are humid. It was a sense of mystery, and it was very dark. People would come in, and we would just do the play there. It was great. The people were moving all around in the building and there was light and there was sound, but the audience was never sitting down. So the design was difficult.

MEADOWS: How did this affect the way the audience viewed the play?

PANTIN: The floor at that time was only earth. The building had lost its floor, so they had to walk on this uneven thing that they could not see because it was very dark. Some of the women had on high heels!

They would walk in and listen to one of the writers and then if [the audience member] left somewhere, there was something to see in another room. One monologue was too long and so people got uncomfortable. We would move people. For example, there was an action with the lights and so then they would listen from somewhere else in the basement—they would hear a horrible scream and the lights where [the audience member] was were dimmed and turned off, but turned on elsewhere at the same time. So they could go to discover a door there and walk to that door. They saw the light and would go there to see a new act—in this case, a dining room in the middle of this dark space and this writer that they … some of them know him—it was a famous writer—sitting in this dining room with a dead woman in his lap with a big cut in her throat. And so they would stop there to see what was happening… I think that the light would lead the people.

   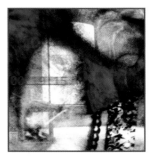

MEADOWS: So how did the audience change what was happening?

PANTIN: Well, they had to be there for the action to happen! Some of the actors were intermingled with the audience, and so the actors would interact with them if they asked questions or said something.

MEADOWS: Was it impromptu or pre-scripted?

PANTIN: It was mostly scripted, but we didn't know what was going to happen. The places where the audience was going to be placed… they were free to be where they wanted, but they tended to stay close together because it was dark and spooky. Hee!

I remember spending a day, the whole day long, walking through the ruins of ancient buildings in Rome. As a small girl, this was so much more magical to me. This was what made this project dear to me. Of course, Rome is so much more architectural with these columns. But it had that same beauty. Walking through Rome was much better than Disney World…this nar-

rative of walking through the ruins—as a small girl this was so much more magical to me.

The building was so dark and abandoned that it was like a … in the bottom of the building there was a little creek that made a gurgling sound.

MEADOWS: Did people have to step around that?

PANTIN: No, they didn't go so far. One of the actors there were the rats! It was so fun. So I was wondering what would happen if a rat passed through the audience. One did, but no one noticed.

MEADOWS: Unappreciated talent. Too bad. What did the actors do?

PANTIN: I have to tell you—the idea was that there were famous writers reading a horror story that they wrote or that they liked from another writer…I chose this interesting story by this Japanese author [who] was leading this story, so inside that story, the writers would read their own story. In the Japanese story, it

was too [much] monologue so I started with some people [who] were digging a grave. I started from the death of one of the characters and then it was the character [who] was writing the story from inside of his own casket. It was the story of one of the writers. For example, the audience was all around this dining table and suddenly there was this dead woman. And so the writer placed her on the table and intermingled with the audience. So he was standing there with the audience. But then this dead woman came to life and said her monologue. So they forgot about him standing there in the audience—so he faded and disappeared. But from the audience appeared two tall guys who were actors—they took him to jail in the basement and the audience followed the whole action. Suddenly, they walked with them and moved with them.

MEADOWS: If someone spoke to an actor, how did the actor respond?

PANTIN: It was strange because if some were not actors but writers… if they were to talk to them then the actor—or writer—would reply, but it was odd because the actor or writer would have to conduct an improvisation with the audience. I think that they were … I was worried about this, and so I

See <http://www.aozora.gr.jp/sakka_akutagawa_ka.html> for original text in Japanese.

said "If you are a policeman, you treat the audience as a policeman." There was very little rehearsal.

MEADOWS: How was the story organized and written? There's a lot of architecture that...

PANTIN: At the beginning when the writers were sitting down, there were slides and pictures of people in prison. The roof had collapsed, allowing visitors to see the.. how do you put it.. to see into the room above and the moon shone in. But in other places, the basement was very low and close. There were some holes in the walls, and so one of the writers used that and stuck his head through to talk to the audience from the other room.

We started with this Japanese story— that was the lead—but I changed it a great deal. The original story was written for theater and so we changed the action of the actors. *Kesa And Morito* by Akutagawa who also wrote *Rashomon.**

MEADOWS: How did you change the actors' roles?

PANTIN: It started with an introduction of the writers, and we presented them as criminals. But when the audience came

to the basement, they [saw] the writers, who then read their stories, so then the scream introduced the next act. The woman [who] screamed was dressed in this bright red dress who then presents her monologue of one of the actors from the original story—of Kesa— and then we altered it again from there. The leading story was the only one that was acted without improvisation.

It wasn't linear at all. It was very modern and nonlinear.

MEADOWS: Are you familiar with *Tamara*?*

PANTIN: Yes, I heard about it.

MEADOWS: How would you compare these?

PANTIN: I haven't seen it, but mine was much smaller and humble and was intent on celebrating writers. The Venezuela National Arts Commission asked me to celebrate this "day of the writers," so it was really focused on the writers and it was a small production. We also had more sound effects and music in our theatre.

I had seen, many years ago now, a show called *El Grand Circo Del Sur* by Rudolpho Santana—this was something like 10 years before. It was a very good piece. They had actor-viewer interaction there as well. It happened just in front of me and I could touch the head of the actors and I was so .. it was terrible! It was in a huge building... I remember that this actor was being tortured, and I put my hand on his head and consoled him and he looked at me and thanked me for my kindness. It was horrible! This was one of the best pieces I have ever seen and so, of course I was influenced.

My show was very simple and we kept it very small.

MEADOWS: So, as far as the narrative was concerned, what was most important for you in your show?

PANTIN: That people get a nonlinear reading. There are other authors [who] do this. Hypertext theater, hypertext writing, etc. This is the way that it's done visually. If you are mainly visual, you are mainly non-linear. All last year, I was working on many, many projects with video

Conceived by Richard Rose and John Krizanc, *Tamara* was an interactive dinner theater that debuted in Toronto in 1981 and then ran for ten years in Los Angeles. Like Ms. Pantin's work, the play was performed in a building in which actors and audience engaged in dialogue.

189

and animation but the only way that I can present these ideas is in a way that is said by the images, not by the story.

MEADOWS: Yeah, I know the feeling. It seems to me as if there's some linearity to images, but not so much as text, certainly. What is the relationship between an image and a story?

PANTIN: For me, it has to be an image that adds to the story. It is never illustrated, and the image by itself has to have its own power. It would be… if you take one of my works that image has to be able to stand by itself, but my interest is in incorporating the text, the image, and the music. The three of them together make something new because they each do something different.

All of my work in theater has been to give more power to the image. I don't like theater that is just

illustrating a text. I can appreciate the stage and costumes and the videos in a show that are well done, but I am not interested in illustrating a text. I wanted the independence of using the images by themselves.

That's part of the reason why it has to be nonlinear.

MEADOWS: What is the value of nonlinear?

PANTIN: It's the only way I can do things. It's the way that I think.

A day after our interview, I received an email from Ms. Pantin. She added:

```
> The actress's name is Morela
> Monagas, she did Kesa. The actor's
> name Javier Paredes. He did Morito
> (he said the monologue), and
> the writer Ednodio Quintero was
> also Morito, the one sitting on
> the dining table with the dead
> woman in his lap.

> Other writers were Wilfredo
> Machado and Gabriel Gimenez
> Eman. Sound, Edgard Moreno.
```

190

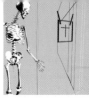

3.5.3: Case Study Two: Deus Ex 2

http://www.deusex.com/

Borrowed from "Deus Ex Machina" a Latin phrase that literally means "God from the machine," this is a term that refers to the resolution of a plot by some highly improbable chance or coincidence—i.e., the hand of God. Greek dramatists are known to have taken the dodgy solution of having a god hoisted, literally by a crane, onto the stage to rescue the protagonist from an impossibly complicated situation.

IonStorm, the company that designs and produces *Deus Ex* and *Deus Ex 2* is a small firm of two 20-person teams of concentrated game designers and supporting staff.

I met with Harvey Smith, Project Director/Lead Designer for *Deus Ex 2*.

MEADOWS: Can you tell me about the design process of *Deus Ex 2*? How did you come up with the ideas behind it? I'm referring to the metaphors, the plot, the backstory, the characters, etc.

SMITH: Fictionally speaking, Sheldon Pacotti, Warren Spector, the mission design team, and two contract writers all worked together to flesh out the world of *Deus Ex*. It was quite the collaborative effort. Sometimes, for instance, one of us would create a character in broad strokes (with intentions of plugging her into a mission/map somewhere), later a writer would create the 'voice' for this character, and later still a group of us (in brainstorming) would plan out an optional death or major scene for the character. It was frustrating at times, but amazing once complete.

Early on, Warren had the major points of a story worked out. We ended up using this for a starting point, but then diverging so that the game could come to its more natural, organic conclusion, based on the collaboration of the team. There was some resistance to this—fiction in games is problematic that way: People become slaves to the tyranny of the story. It's better to put every idea through the wringer, to let nothing stand as sacred or in intellectual/creative isolation.

MEADOWS: How do you and Warren work off of each other? What is the actual process here?

SMITH: I came to hate prescripted fiction during *Deus Ex 1*. I came to see it as something so structured as to be at odds with the player creating his own narrative experience as he plays. Warren and I came at the game from different angles. This is just my own take, but I see it like this: Warren is a writer-game designer (who is also the best, [most] informed producer in the business). I am a game designer-writer (who started as a game tester). We both represented the values we hold most dear and of course those values overlap quite a bit. Through this friction, we created something better, I believe, than we could have done individually. As to the actual process, it was a back-and-forth thing: I'd meet with Chris Norden and Warren, work out some ideas (including

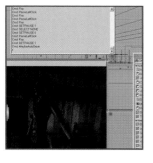

technological dictates from Chris, high-level concept direction from Warren, all mixed with the game design aesthetic that each of us carried), then I'd go off and work with other groups on the team, the other disciplines like art and design. The same viral exchange would happen with these groups too—we'd all talk about ideas, add in our own flavors, then I'd meet with others. After a while, everyone began to allow the ideas to melt and flow, becoming an alchemical mixture that we had all created.

MEADOWS: Can you tell me a little about your schedules and your budgets? What's the production process like?

SMITH: This took two and a half years to create a series of missions. This was with 20 people, and it cost over five million dollars. Because of the degree of detail, everything had to be touched by hand. This is a lot of work.

Eidos is the publisher. They have faith that Warren Spector has put together a good team. Our focus is "Immersive Simulations"—we hire people [who] like those games. Then we do pre-production and discuss the story, the setting, the characters, what tools the player has, what capabilities and rules, and the technical implementation. We try to get everyone involved. We try to keep all intra-team disciplines talking to each other.

MEADOWS: How does that happen?

SMITH: Usually, a producer and a director will facilitate the conversation. Then we have the director, the producer, and discipline leads all sit down and hash it out.

MEADOWS: And the specifics of production? What kind of production tools do you use?

SMITH: Budgets and schedules are managed with Microsoft Project and Microsoft Excel, and the associate producers oversee the individual representatives of the team.

MEADOWS: Okay. Now when everyone is "hashing it out," are you also working off of a prescripted narrative structure?

SMITH: Generally, no. The story is not generally diagrammed because the flow of the narrative is too organic. Generally, we work out a series of "Abstract Alternatives."

MEADOWS: So how does that affect game play? Is it weighted more, for example, to solitary game play or more for multiple person game play?

SMITH: Some games are focused on either a single player or multiple players. When the game was shipped, it was a single-player game, but after a while, we started to get a multi-player demand from the players. We went ahead and allowed this—we released some modules—but we found that it wasn't very cost-effective, for one, and for another, we found that the story and gameplay were not cleanly adaptable. So eventually our interest in MU died down. There's a spectrum between multi-player and single-player. *Everquest* is one extreme. *Deus Ex* is another.

MEADOWS: Which do you prefer? Single-player, I'd assume?

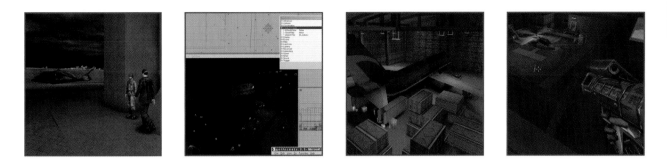

SMITH: Mostly, yes. The pace of a game is determined by the number of people. With more people, the game goes faster and there's less emphasis on the intentions of any one player. Consequently, the environments that are created by these groups are super simple. The ultimate single-player game is found in Neal Stephenson's book, *The Diamond Age*. This novel features a game (in the form of a book) that is a trainer and a therapist. It focuses all of the attention on the single person using it, adapting to the self expression of that person.

MEADOWS: How, then, do multi-player games work?

SMITH: People are fascinated by themselves. Yet, people also like to reach out to one another. But there's a balance that's needed. This is important to games that have multiple players. Look at virtual goldfish bowls or the Tomagochi. It responds to you. It's something that disagrees with you. Doug Church, who worked on *Underworld* and several other projects, said something one time along the lines of "The purpose of AI is not to be more intelligent than the player, but to make the player feel more intelligent than the AI."

MEADOWS: If a chariot were to arrive with the ultimate technology sent from the God of AI, what would you want to see?

SMITH: We—all of us here—would have the same answer: Eliminate the team. We would all get rid of each other. Well, mostly. But really what we need right now is deep simulation. We need it so that everything gets simulated—and not just the environment. A game character or NPC, for example, can't get angry. If we had something like this, things would start to change. Exclusively single- or multi-player games are going away. The goal is to make multi-player irrelevant. Multi-player is just a phase, or a fad. As soon as virtual actors are as complicated and unpredictable as the people [who] are playing … THIS is when things will get interesting.

MEADOWS: So how would this affect narrative flow? If you have a hundred people doing something or one person doing something, it seems that the shape of the narrative will be affected.

SMITH: Definitely. We have spent a lot of time looking at different forms of narrative and asking ourselves if a basketball game has a narrative. Getting developers to acknowledge a dramatic arc is hard. Video games, for example, are more interesting if the player drives them. The author might feel otherwise, but the author has to relinquish control so that the player can engage in things that might seem trivial.

As an example, when we were testing *Deus Ex*, we had this one tester who kept throwing the boxes on the dock into the water. She didn't want to get on the boat that was idling at the end of the dock. She threw boxes into the water, and threw a barrel into the water and swam under the dock and followed the rat that ran by. But this was fine; she was in a particular area of the game in which she had that interaction as her given right. At other times, she's on a sled through the narrative. We call this a "string of pearls." These moments in the narrative are bottlenecks where there's no interaction. If there was no bottleneck, it would become a

total action game and the narrative would disappear. At periodic points, you have bottlenecks.

In *Diablo* and *Thief*, for example, the story and the gameplay are on different tracks. In *Deus Ex*, we've tried to link them. There are multiple levels of interaction from no freedom to a simple branching structure. But then, on the far end, we need more simulation. The *Sims*, for example, are great because they provide an overlap of narrative.

When we do our testing, we generally try to get someone to play the game and someone else to watch. This allows us to determine if it's as meaningful to an observer as it is to a player.

MEADOWS: And...?

SMITH: Perversely, I feel like we've met our studio's goals if the player is really engaged and the observer is bored. Traditional approaches to drama would create a game that is just as interesting for the observer as it is for the player. Progressive approaches to drama create a game

that is fascinating for the player (since she is creating her own narrative, which is then personally meaningful to her), yet boring for the observer (since nothing particularly theatrical is occurring). The test playing around with crates and rats on the dock in *Deus Ex* is a good example: people observing her wanted to see something cinematic; while she was enjoying her own agency. This is one of our criteria for the game. Simulation facilitates more player expression, allowing players to experiment with a very granular range of outcomes. More detailed simulation (and the emergent behavior that springs from the interaction of multiple systems) will be increasingly important in the future. It's only a matter of time until everyone is approaching games in this way.

MEADOWS: What makes someone interested in the narrative line?

SMITH: It might be control or agency. It might be the ability to experiment with things. This is the reason designers are really smart to turn the creation over to the player. But

it's a trade-off. Elements of *Deus Ex* were closed. In a conversation, for example, there's only three branches. A door, though, is open because you can destroy it in many different ways. Using physics and simulation is what it's all about. We have in the game these grenades that can be attached to the wall. They obey certain laws in the environment. We never thought that this would happen, but during testing one day, we found out that this guy had gathered together a bunch of these bombs and stuck them on the wall so that he was actually able to use them to climb the statue of liberty. He sent screen grabs around. We couldn't believe it. It was great. This was a kind of 'metagame'—an exploration of the rules of the game.

Really, simulation is what it's all about. Algorithmically or procedurally generated environments are the only thing that will save the game industry.

It just has to be more flexible.

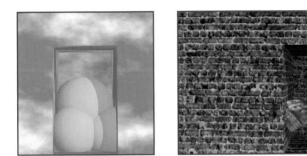

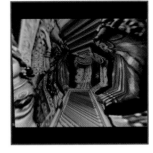

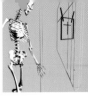

3.5.4: Case Study Three: Is God Flat / Is The Devil Round / And What About Me

http://www.benayoun.com/

Maurice Benayoun has been building and exploring virtual worlds for over 12 years. With a wide repertoire of work including *The Tunnel Under the Atlantic, Is God Flat?, Is the Devil Round?*, and *And What About Me?*, his works have gained international accolades. In 1987, Maurice cofounded Z-A Production where he works as Art Director, overseeing concept, design, and production. He teaches at the National School of Fine Arts in Paris, France. Eleven years and as many projects later, he won the Ars Electronica Golden Nica (Linz, Austria) for his work *World Skin* in 1998.

Maurice considers his artwork to be a representation of another world that we are building in which the architecture becomes a memory of our activities. One of his goals is to produce work that is continually changing to "seduce and feed the eyes of the audience as if it were a prime-time program."

MEADOWS: Do you think designing for interactivity might take something away from the author?

BENAYOUN: For a certain kind of work. But when you say "designing for interaction" I have a problem with that. The term "design" is too formal for me and is associated with "trying to find a nice shape," but the problem is not only a problem with design. It is more about original concept. I think that interactivity brings something to art that is, in a certain way, closer to our experience of the real world. Interactivity and virtu-

ality are components of the real world that we can represent in the computers. The difference between our experiences in the real and the virtual is not a difference that has to do with materials, but it is because in the virtual world there is a human intention. In the real world, there might not be. You don't have to build the space— actually, you just decide on the rules of the space. You decide on the logic of this world. The reason I was talking about God is not that I am interested in the religious equa-

tion. So when you are building a virtual world, you are doing the work of a "Demiurge"—so you are the god-figure here—and I thought it was interesting to think about this in relationship to playing a god and then you think, "Why do we have a god? Why do we need a god?" Maybe because we need to understand how the world works?

MEADOWS: So these are the rules? These rules of the space then define the metaphor?

BENAYOUN: Yes. What I do not want to do is build a complicated architectural environment. I prefer to build a world where the logic of this world is the message. So the authorship—the work of the author in this kind of work—is to build the meaning by organizing and structuring the rules and the laws.

MEADOWS: So as far as algorithmic generation of environments is concerned, the ruleset that we choose is the definition of the metaphor?

BENAYOUN: Yes, of course. But it is easier to explain that with an

example. Imagine that—instead of digging into the material and generating it as we are in my projects—instead imagine that we are just visiting a regular building. So maybe we meet someone and the meaning would come from that. This would be the ruleset. In this case, as in *Is God Flat*, the building of the walls are a result of the way you move. Then the walls are talking about your experience. And whatever you do, the result will be a labyrinth. It is considered a trace or your track, but it's still a labyrinth. It is your own labyrinth that you build.

MEADOWS: How did you develop the project?

BENAYOUN: I'm not developing and programming by myself—I am coming from the art field. So I worked with Patrick Bouchaud, who is a very good engineer from SGI. We spent a long time working on that and finding a solution for this real-time dynamic modeling. It's not very common. Everybody knows how to build a database and move through it, but the representation of this interaction is very difficult. Very often, people are talking about simulation—you build some-

thing and then you move inside. This is not the real kind of simulation. I'm working on dynamically modeled environments. So the way to work was that I described a thing—a concept—and I did the 3D model as an example. So I was using SoftImage and doing the animation of it and then Patrick did the implementation from that mockup.

MEADOWS: How do you use your database to tell a story?

BENAYOUN: What do you mean?

MEADOWS: How can you use Oracle8 or SQL (or whatever it is you use) to tell a story? That seems to be what you're doing here. You have "the devil" responding to people as they move through the environment and, additionally, you're generating data. So, you've got some kind of database around here somewhere…

BENAYOUN: There is software we call The Z-A Profiler. This compiles a list of statistics based on what someone is doing in the space.

MEADOWS: What is it used for?

BENAYOUN: When you are moving around inside of this space, you can choose from these different pictures around you. Digging through images then… [Maurice demonstrates the interface by "drilling" his way through a 3D interface] You probably want me to explain this since you're writing.

MEADOWS: Yes, that would be great. But I can include screenshots, too.

BENAYOUN: Okay. When you are moving inside of the pictures, you are looking at some and avoiding others. All of these things are taken into account by the database—speed orientation, size, position of the screen, etc. They are all considered and analyzed, and then we create a dynamic profile of the user. This is an automatic profiling system. Your profile is renewed in 30 seconds, but you also have long-term profiling that remains, and so when you are making decisions and using this kind of software, it knows you in a deeper way after a few days or after a few months.

MEADOWS: It gets better with use.

BENAYOUN: Yes. So the way that it works is

only to compare the profile of the pictures to your profile at this time. And so we are trying to find the appropriate interaction between them. For example, if I move away from water imagery and move more toward rocks, I am generating my profile in the database. And then, if I see a building here, I can turn left and go to a more historical building. [Maurice continues driving through a landscape of images] Here is some history, architecture, water, people, relaxing. These are the things I like. And so your profile can change a lot in just a short time. There. Now look at my profile—"You like water, sun, and exotic architecture."[Maurice then conducts a second example with slightly different behavior.] Now, after we have done this again, we get the overall views of "human, city, romance, and adventure" listed here. The results that you get back are very accurate.

MEADOWS: That's assuming the user's interpretation of those images is the same as the author's. Now, this takes information on a user and sends back an analysis of their behavior. It is, essentially, output based on a user's input. Can this be reversed? How can it be used to give information to the user that is not a list of analyses?

BENAYOUN: Yes, it can be made… This is what we did with the *Is The Devil Round?* This is what is behind the moving spheres—analyzing your interest. This was my first experience with some basic agent technology.

The devil was the second stage of this [project] for us. I'm more interested in this—our reference is the real world. And what do we expect from a virtual world if we don't want something that is only a copy of the real world? We want this world to be able to give us a more intense, faster experience. If I'm looking in a catalog of landscapes and travel, what I'm doing is…trying to find the page that seduces me. I try to organize the information by exploring the book. So we have to propose something that works this way. That means that the user has to organize a personal path. But when we are using a book, the order of the pictures has been organized with a structure that is hopefully relevant for everybody—but maybe this is not relevant for us. Maybe we want something with a certain kind of light. But there is no book that is

organized like this. You, Mark, are looking for an apartment right now. You might want one that has nice light. But apartment catalogs are never organized by "nice light coming from the flat and going out the other wind," but it's possible. If you are using a dynamic structure for your database and can analyze what is interesting for each user in this case, it is possible to reorganize the information.

MEADOWS: So we can make stories more interesting than before?

BENAYOUN: It's a very difficult problem. You can't say that you are going to do a more interesting story—narrative has to do something different. It has to take interest not in the way to organize the events in time and space as in the traditional story line, but we have to think in terms of a different form of living. We are not supposed to be one of the heroes. We are just ourselves. That is the difference. We are ourselves.

I think it will be intense and sometimes stronger because what will happen will happen to us. We can have this experience in front of a movie, but with interactive forms of narrative, we can decide on the amount of time we spend in front of it. And we can have a narrative structure that is reorganized according to how we reacted before.

197

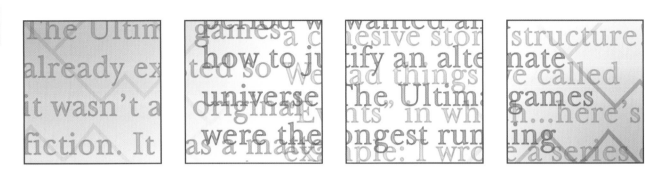

3.5.5: Case Study Four: Ultima Online

http://www.uo.com/

Raph Koster, the lead designer of *Ultima Online* who is currently designing Sony Station's *Star Wars Galaxies* online game, has been making games for as long as he can remember.

He started with a Sears Pong console and an 8-bit Atari. Equipped with these tools, by the time he was in high school, he and his friends had formed a computer game company. They sold a game that was wrapped in a sandwich bag. One. But it sold.

Like most serious game designers, the popular line of games issued by a company named TSR heavily influenced Raph. Through junior high and high school, Raph rabidly played *Dungeons & Dragons* and *Star Frontiers*. He and his friends would develop their own pen and paper role-playing games, and this eventually turned into a *Dungeons & Dragons* campaign that lasted for "a good number of years." Toward the end of this period of their lives, they eventually moved away from the rules and dice, turning the game into a freeform role-play narrative.

There had been several attempts at graphical MUDs, such as LucasFilm's *Habitat*, but these didn't really offer more than preliminary promise. By 1995, there was something in the air and suddenly multiple graphical MUDs started to appear. *Worlds Away*, *Dragon Spires*, and *Meridian 59* (which Raph claims as "the first real graphical MUD") were first-person perspective games that used roughly *Doom*-caliber graphics. But there was nothing with any real impact. Until *Ultima Online* was launched.

MEADOWS: How was the story organized and written?

KOSTER: The *Ultima* games already existed, so it wasn't an original fiction. It was a matter of hooking these pieces together, and we needed to pick and choose which time period we wanted and how to justify an alternate universe. The *Ultima* games were the longest-running series of computer RPGs, started in 1991. These games are about ethics. Instead of slaying monsters, you had to behave in a particular way and be a good guy—you had to give money to the NPCs that rewarded the players. A complicated series of systems developed around this. We had to find a way to combine games that were heavily narrative "hero's-journey" type games with heavily simulated multi-user environment games. Then we had to splice these two together.

Fortunately, the *Ultima* mythos made it easy for us to generate parallel worlds. Which was good because we had to launch multiple worlds because the user base was so large!

We were able to split the narrative line at *Ultima 3* while still having many of the things that players found familiar from the standalone games. So it worked out alright.

MEADOWS: Can the game be diagrammed? With a dramatic arc?

KOSTER: Ha! There was no interest in keeping a cohesive story structure! We had things we called "Events" in which game administrators...Here's an example: I wrote a series of riddles in verse that we scattered all over the game, and I wrote fragments of short stories that

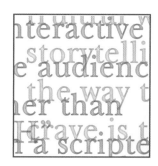

we published on the website and we would come into the game and act out "Events" over a global channel. If they were paying attention to the website and they were online as the event was happening, they could see the story going by and they could participate by solving riddles and locating the clues. This was difficult to do, and almost every time we did it, people solved it remarkably quickly or would change the outcome of the game.

MEADOWS: So how would they change the game? Can you give me an example?

KOSTER: This is a good one. This was during beta testing, before we'd even really gotten started. Lord British, one of the key characters, appeared with all his counselors and his jester up on the parapet of the castle, above the crowd. One of the people in the crowd—one of the players [who] was there at the event—cast a magic spell that caused a fire on the parapet and Lord British accidentally walked into it—and he died! It was outrageous! This was huge news inside of the game, but it was such a surprise that it turned into "THEY KILLED LORD BRITISH" in the industry news. So it was a harbinger of things to come as to how quickly the expressive

freedom we gave to players mucked with the story!

And that has been the ongoing challenge ever since. To this day, any online game that tries to run events finds that people will always do the unexpected. It's not a surprise. In any form of interactive storytelling, the audience will derail rather than cooperate with a scripted plot.

The point to online games is to surrender control, but players really crave narrative.

MEADOWS: So if the players crave this thing that they keep messing up, what's the solution?

KOSTER: Well, there's Imposition and there's Expression. We [designers and authors] can choose to be Expressive in one way, but that often means that we won't be as Impositional as a result. See, online games tend to fall over on the Expression scale—a traditional role-playing game is Impositional—it says you are this person, then they reward you very specifically and they put you in a specific place. In

an online game, you can roam and decide who you are, and we might tell you how to behave, but not that much. So it's a big difference.

The *Sims* is a very expressional game, for example.

Online games are constantly balanced on the line between these two, which makes them very different from desktop games. The most fruitful way to do storytelling online in the way that players crave is to hold a mirror up to their activities and do what I call post-facto storytelling.

We talk about a-priori storytelling, which is telling the story before the events of the game happen. And then we also talk about post-facto storytelling, in which the events of the story unfold as the game is played. Post-facto is what we do in real life when we mythologize and do memoirs, biographies, or history.

It's the shaping of events that did not have a narrative arc into something that satisfies a story.

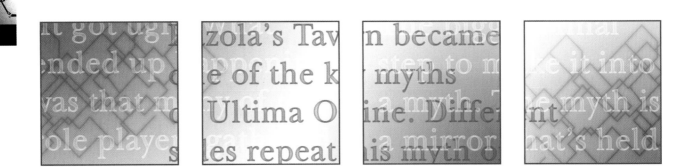

MEADOWS: Then what makes for a satisfying story?

KOSTER: Players still want a traditional arc. They want the same thing that the other media have, but online environments are without ending and there is no temporal and somatic bound. There's a classic example from *Ultima Online*.

There was this place called Kazola's tavern—a player-run bar that was out in the woods in a wild area—and for some reason, it was very popular. It was a very pacifist community. They just liked to hang out and talk. It got a lot of recognition and so one of the game administrators noticed it and, as per game policy, he "Blessed" it. He designated it as important to the game. Which instantly made it the most valuable piece of real estate in the game. This attracted the less pacifistic crowd who came over, started killing people, and tried to take over the tavern. They came in and circled the tavern, and there were fights and everything. It got ugly. What ended up happening was that many of the role players gathered together to fight off the

bad guys. They stood out front and defended the place. And they made it! This story of Kazola's Tavern became one of the key myths of *Ultima Online*. Different sides repeat this myth of what happened in different ways. The pacifists tell their side, and the more unruly biker-band types tell their side of it. Good myths lend themselves to interpretation. But this took nine months to go by, and no one, as they were experiencing it, thought it had any kind of dramatic arc whatsoever. It's only on looking back on it that we shaped it into a story.

MEADOWS: So while it happened it was a narrative, but the thing that made it a myth was the interpretation and the opinions of the people involved? Is that it?

KOSTER: Yes, definitely. It was a kind of mirror they made for themselves.

MEADOWS: What can be done to help shape interaction into a myth or a story?

KOSTER: First is to make sure the players have real emotional engagement. This is important. Second,

the environment has to offer scope for actions that are significant enough to affect changes. The biggest final step to make it into a myth. The myth is a mirror that's held up to it.

You have to give the players "Affordance"—a term I've recently heard used. "Affordance" defines what scope players have to make changes and do things. These games offer a lot of that kind of thing.

Everquest, for example, has a lot of static content and narratives that are built into the game. When you walk to a certain location on the map and say a particular word to a particular person, they will give you the same response all the time and do something like prescribe a task. This is a classic modus operandi, and it's a very impositional narrative. It tends to be unforgiving, and players recognize that it's static or at least cyclic real quickly. They get frustrated that they're not affecting real change in the environment.

It carries them along, but most narratives that people get interested in are about changing the state of something.

People tend not to like narratives where things...well...don't change.

3.5.6: Case Study Five: Top Agent

http://www.orchimedia.com/

While it is not, graphically, a 3D project it seems appropriate to include an example of an old form of dimensional interface: "the real world." Mark Weiser, formerly Chief Technology Officer of Xerox-PARC, understood this basic idea approximately a decade ago and named it "ubiquitous computing"—a term that might be considered the opposite of virtual reality.*

As Weiser defined it, "Ubiquitous computing is the method of enhancing computer use by making many computers available throughout the physical environment, but making them effectively invisible to the user."

Mobile technologies—and the ways they integrate with the real world—hold a potential that seems likely to be explored deeply in the coming decade. Currently, these are brittle technologies that offer thin datastreams and graphics that might look familiar to someone who still owns a 1980's Commodore 64. In North America, mobile technology hardly works. It's almost as common for calls to be dropped as it is for them to be connected.

Things are different in Finland (in more ways than one).

In Helsinki, near the center of town, in a small but fastidious office in a quiet alley, a company that is only a couple of years old forges hot iron out of thin air. Orchimedia (possibly the most talented and knowledgeable design and development company of mobile technology on the planet) has been developing interactive narratives since they founded their company. *Top Agent* is a game that is played by multiple players over SMS services on mobile telephones and hand-held computers. As if this weren't enough, the game is also integrated into television and website media.

Although virtual reality removes the reader from the physical world and replaces it, "ubiquitous computing" integrates computers into it and causes it to become aware of us. In some ways, these two approaches to "Simulated Environments" can be thought of as opposites or complements, depending on the applications.

The element that is interesting about mobile forms of narrative is the interplay it has with the real-world architecture that surrounds it. Consider, for example, a multiplayer game in which an opponent, if they are in the same room (at, say, a dinner party or dance club), will be notified because his phone recognizes that yours is in range. *Top Agent* offers a few insights into this form of mobile narrative and some of the curves on the road ahead.

The following are contributions by Mitja Kurki (Lead Game Developer) and Marko Laukasto (Orchimedia's Head of Project Management).

MEADOWS: Mitja, what is your background? How did you end up here?

KURKI: I have always been really fanatic about all kinds of games. Especially, I loved all video game consoles. In the era of 8-bit Nintendo, I had completed about 90% of all games published to it in Finland, so it was more serious to me than just a hobby. :)

Also, I loved to play "pen & pencil" role-playing games mostly as a dungeon master (the storyteller) because I love to use my imagination to create new worlds. After high school, I was also interested in the technical side of things and I took a course in an adult educational center of Kuopio and gradu-

ated to be "net application expert" if I translate it freely. I coded a couple of applications and small games as a hobby, and then I went to the University of Kuopio to study computing science. Around the same time, I happened to browse to Orchimedia's website and because the company seemed to be really interesting, I decided to apply for a job, and I got hired. First, I started as a regular programmer, but because my supervisors thought I was an innovative person, I became Lead Game Developer. I'm now working here full time, but I'm also a university student and slowly progressing in my studies.

MEADOWS: How did you come up with the idea for this story?

KURKI: First idea when we started to think about [it] was to create a mobile game where players would really get to interact and get involved in the action but still maintain the game to be easy to play. We started to think what kind of a story would interest the target audience [who] are people aged from young to young adults with mobile phones, and after thinking about various stories, we ended up with [an] agent story. We still had to solve the "easy to play" problem, and we solved it with multiple choice situations.

MEADOWS: How many people are using *Top Agent*, total?

KURKI: Around 7,000 – 8,000 in Finland at the moment but Top Agent is starting in Singapore and later, I believe, around the world.

MEADOWS: Technology and design have always shared a compromising dialogue that also creates many new ideas. What influences did the technology have on the design?

LAUKASTO: This is a good question in SMS game design. At the moment, there's one big restriction in SMS technology, and that is max. 160 characters in a

message. When we started to make the storyline for the first episode of *Top Agent*, we really hit the reality that 160 isn't so much to tell a story. Nevertheless, we got used to this problem as we learned to use every character available. We used compressed sentences and we just said what was needed to tell the story and more importantly to create emotions. Everything we said had to give wings to the imagination as much as possible. Furthermore, we realized the importance of creating a feeling of the reality for the game. We had to build up a real agent world to really summon the game alive. We also learned that we must emphasize the meaning of the web for getting more information about the game play. Anyway, this task was hard to schedule beforehand, and perhaps it's needless to say we, exceeded our estimations.

Generally, other aspects of the SMS technology came pretty easily for us since we had executed successfully a couple of other SMS projects previously. Schedule for these tasks went right on target and thus it took a lot of pressure out from the project group. In the end we just had to make sure that [t]he storyline [was] good, playability [was] there, and so on.

Worth[y] of mention is a testing phase we had to arrange before the launch. After we had put everything together, we wanted to be extra sure that everything was working since there was TV (TiLT Game Show) involved in Finland. We tested out that the storyline is working, playability was good, web has got a real value for the game and the game looks visually great.

All in all, [the] project was a success since we accomplished all of our main objectives; [the] project was completed in time, we created the first SMS agent adventure game with a realistic world and characters, the game was nicely visualized and narrated both in TV and web, and most of all, people liked it!

KURKI: When we wrote the first script, we realized that we had written it in a too traditional way. By that I mean that we spent too much of those precious 160 characters to describe various things: emotions, surroundings, etc. The main plot behind the script remained, but then we had to start the really tiring process of squeez-

ing the story into messages of 160 characters.

MEADOWS: How did this affect the financial model of the story?

KURKI: We could have used multiple messages to tell everything we wanted, but because every sent message costs money, it wouldn't have been financially affordable.

MEADOWS: How do the website and the mobile technologies integrate?

KURKI: It was one of the main design decision[s] to integrate [the] website tightly into the mobile game in order to enrich the game world. All the characters in the game have bios in there, and also organizations and criminals are present. [The] main integrator between mobile and web is the A-Com, where players receive data from various sources: messages from headquarters, threats from criminals, and so on. This data is personal for all players, and when players reach certain points in the game, they receive [a] message containing [the] letters WWW in their mobile phone, and that means that A-Com

has been updated. Basically, this A-Com serves as a way to tell lots of things without having to worry about message lengths.

MEADOWS: What role do images have in the game?

KURKI: Images had a great role in the game in both the website as well as in TV shows. Images were a great way to visualize characters players encounter and places they visit.

MEADOWS: What role does the individual's perspective play? In other words, are there points at which different readers of the story get different stories?

KURKI: Individual perspectives affected the story: It most often pays to solve [a] situation using intelligence rather than strength. In the first part of topagent [sic] we wanted to keep things relatively simple.

So the destination of all the players are the same, but there are different ways to get there. In coming parts we are going to change that.

MEADOWS: What keeps people interested? What do you think is most interesting about this?

KURKI: I think [it] is the possibility to interact and really "be the agent" solving crimes and mysteries. Player plays the role of an agent who has emotional bonds to other characters in the game, which connects [the] player and the game world emotionally together. Of course, it needs a great plot in order to be really interesting to play.

The new technology just allows the game to be played anywhere at anytime.

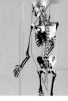

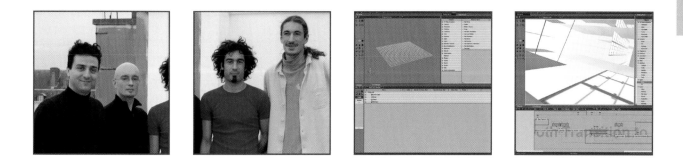

3.5.7: Case Study Six: Virtools Development Toolset

http://www.virtools.com/

Virtools, a company located in the center of Paris, grew from the desire to design a toolset for managing both three-dimensional graphics and interactivity. Employing some of the most gifted designers, programmers, and artists in France, the company combines these talents in solving a difficult problem: how to provide authors with a toolset to build interactive narratives. But the creation of a toolset for industry use can present a problem for artistic development because industry use is constrained by real-world problems such as time, budget, and personnel management—something with which many artists don't contend.

Founded in 1993 by Bertrand Duplat and Bertrand de la Chapelle, along with developers Nicolas Galinotti and Romain Sididris, Virtools has grown to more than 30 people and works at the intersection of real-time 3D and interactive technologies.

In 1997, Ludovic Duchâteau joined the founders to help develop the Virtools Dev toolset, powered by a unique Behavioral Engine. As an artist trained at major French schools including the Ecole Estienne for design and graphic arts, as well as the Ecole Duperré and Ecole Olivier de Serre for applied arts, Ludovic's focus at Virtools has been on product design and interface concepts. As such, his perspectives on the technical development process have had a strong influence on Virtools' approach.

MEADOWS: What were some of the main questions you looked at while developing this interface?

DUCHÂTEAU: Aside from the GUI, when we designed the toolset, we were looking for ways to give authors more power and room to maneuver in creating interactive fiction, video games, and interactive artistic projects.

Our situation was comparable to that of the early days of cinema—a time when only technical masters of the medium could envision the final creation. In our case, you needed to master the language of computer programming, just as in the early years of cinema you needed to master the techniques of chemistry and the mechanisms of

camera optics before shooting the slightest film.

When we began designing the toolset, the technical skills necessary to create interactive narrative were so complex they often left little room for experimentation with the actual narrative structures. What's more, it cost a great deal to put together a team that would (re)lay technical foundations (3D, sound and event-based engines) each and every time a new game or interactive work was produced. That burden definitely kept risk taking to a strict minimum as far as forging innovative narrative structures and themes was concerned. Programmers not only had to develop the interactive content modules, but also the technical framework on which the content rested. Creative exploration was often secondary to the technical exploration that could guarantee optimal performance, and only very good programmers were able to handle both loads at once. Some of the pioneers of video games are a good illustration: The most revolutionary, innovative games were almost always created by programmers whose technical mastery was significant enough

205

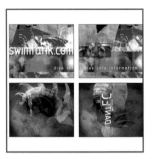

to let them take risks and develop new directions for the story, theme, or narrative treatment. To create an important game or a work of interactive fiction, you inevitably had to be a programmer, and a very high-level programmer at that! So there weren't any "standard" tools available for creating interactive projects, no "plug-and-play" solutions. We felt that providing an accessible authoring tool might help reduce costs, and thus give people outside of programming circles a chance to take significant narrative risks. Parallels might be drawn [to] different areas of the visual arts like painting, with the invention of oils, then acrylics, then paints sold in ready-to-mix tubes...

The challenge was overwhelming but incredibly exciting. The first question we asked ourselves in creating the toolset was, "How might authors approach and understand narrative structures that are fundamentally nonlinear?"

The nature of interactivity lies in the "potential" that exists—what can (but doesn't always) happen. Rather than writing a sequence of linear events, authors set out to create a world of potentialities, a realm of probabilities that may not necessarily be deterministic. This type of organization is based on artistic premises we are only now beginning to grasp, and such a narrative structure must be resolved differently than purely linear structures.

We translated that into technical terms, keeping in mind that the central nervous system of interactivity lies in the ability to program potentiality and apply it to actors in an interactive narrative. Our question took on a new light: "How might authors inscribe/describe powerful interactivity, without doing any actual programming?"

We had two ways of conceptually tackling this problem: we could either design a toolset that would enable any kind of programming, fully recognizing that the product might be difficult to handle at first, but would guarantee that authors could create exactly what they wanted; or we could design a toolset that would allow authors to tell one kind of story very easily and free them from technical issues, fully recognizing that the product might turn out to be a template to let authors tell a single type of story—the one we had chosen.

In reality, the question simply became, "How might authors develop their interactive narratives without having to learn programming languages, so they can concentrate solely on their storytelling?"

MEADOWS: How were these questions resolved?

DUCHÂTEAU: With great difficulty :) First, we had to take the burden off of authors and their technical workspace by managing as many tedious and repetitive tasks as possible with a state-of-the-art 3D engine, sound engine, and behavioral engine to handle events. And as a software publisher, Virtools would provide updates to give users access to the latest technical options.

With these important technical issues resolved, we had to create real added value for authors and developers by focusing on the artistic and narrative issues. We then had to envision a programming language that would be straightforward, modular, and powerful.

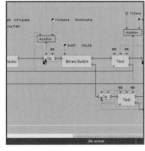

But at the same time, it had to be accessible to non-programmers. It had to be an authoring language that would allow authors to "see" what they were doing as they sketched and composed interactivity.

We opted for a low-level language as the basic programming layer to give authors as much freedom and control as possible. The key was to leave all the doors wide open so that language could be easily expanded into something much more high-level if needed. In other words, we fused low-level and high-level to create a something new.

So the conceptual layer of the toolset moves from micro-orders like "rotate around your axis," to high-level events that authors manage like a choreographer would. This seamless process translates into a graphical representation for assembling the different micro-orders used to create complex interactivity. Our language was based on the simple concept of behaviors. According to our definition, behaviors were the basic capabilities given to objects and media (2D, 3D, audio, characters…). Any combination of behaviors would create interactivity. Behind the scenes, the behavioral engine would manage interactions between the behaviors of various objects, or between objects and the interactor. Though this involved hardcore C++ programming, we made sure authors would only be handling the aspects relevant to interactivity.

In the Virtools Dev GUI, you compose your interactivity by hooking up chains of Lego-like "behavioral building blocks." We currently have over 400 of these "building blocks," so authors can

manage the 3D space, media, and object events, as well as interactive sound, animated characters, control devices, collisions, lights, cameras, materials, special effects...
This is very low-level design, meaning authors work with the most basic elements. But that's also what ensures the flexibility, modularity, and compatibility as building blocks are added and improved. Users can create their own behavior graphs by encapsulating several behaviors and leaving only the parameters visible for adjustment. That was one answer for authors, to give them streamlined control over how their narratives and interactivity work, and the possibility to make realtime adjustments without touching the scripts.
We also wanted authors to be able to save a series of behaviors created for a specific context. When you solve a problem and tweak interactivity, you want to have the option of saving that solution and applying it elsewhere in the same project or in future projects.

When you separate scripts and their parameter adjustments, you also make it possible for several people to work simultaneously on the same

interactive projects. Interactivity becomes an "asset" like any other, which brings down cost, speeds up production. In theory, the result is that more time and energy can be spent on the story and thus, the narrative structures that emerge are more innovative.

We intended the software's learning curve to be exponential. To ensure that any author can tell any story the way he sees fit, we chose a difficult initial progression that would guarantee the toolset's flexibility.

By and large, I'd say the toolset is entirely focused on content. Nothing gets in the author's way. This rigor, verging on asceticism, sometimes wears a harsh face—a lot like what an author sees when looking in the mirror of his own work.

MEADOWS: What influence has your art background—or the history of art itself—had on the development of this toolset? Specifically painting?

DUCHÂTEAU: The main motivating factor was that I was in urgent need of a toolset to make my own work. :)

207

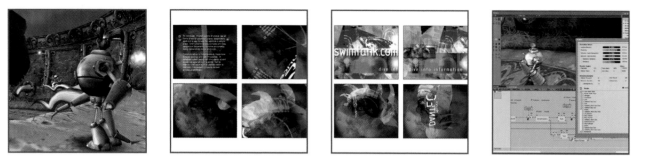

When I met the founders of Virtools, I was struggling with traditional programming and looking for solutions to let me build my interactive 3D projects. But the thought of having to delegate work to a programmer—or anyone else for that matter—went, and still goes, against my overriding desire to control the different artistic vectors that come into play.

I was keenly aware of the difficulties facing an author with no programming skills, of trying to grasp interactive design from a technical point of view. So I had ideas about what might potentially ease the process, allowing authors to work with the highest level of autonomy and the least possible compromise in quality.

My experience with 3D and 2D software, and fundamentally modular tools like paints, pigments, brushes or methods like collage, fed my desire for a tool that would make itself transparent, to become literally an extension of the author's thoughts during the creative process.

Dance, music, text, and film played a vital role in the development of the toolset. Above all, the extraordinary richness of the visual arts and "aesthetics" (referring here to representations of a worldview) acted as a driving force.

But painting was an especially fertile source of inspiration, given the tremendous number of directions that have been explored throughout history, as people searched for the best ways to describe emotions, sentiments, impressions, stories, and daily life experiences.

Throughout the entire time we were designing Virtools Dev, we constantly kept our eye on visual references from all different periods: from the Lascaux cave paintings to Middle Age icons and Chinese art forms, up to the most experimental and conceptual art movements.

MEADOWS: What do you know as a painter that you might not know as a programmer? And vice versa?

DUCHÂTEAU: Honestly, I can't say: I'm neither a painter nor a programmer. I don't tackle things as if I'm coming from a specific background. I grew up with computers, television, telephone, science in accessible forms, but also with art history, dance, music... In that sense, going head-to-head with a computer isn't like facing the conceptual unknown—even if programming techniques are still strange animals to me. :-)

I mostly feel like an artist who wants to work with the tools of his time and use the whole range of his experience and the media around him. My technical knowledge—or actually its limits—covers only specific problems. Still, my knowledge of the history of art remains indisputably better than my knowledge of the history of programming languages.

My greatest fortune (and brightest move) was not to have been scared off by this design adventure.

MEADOWS: Why is it that 3D represents such possibility for interaction?

DUCHÂTEAU: If we consider the fact that we have to see the things we can interact with, then 3D representations are unquestionably essential. They come

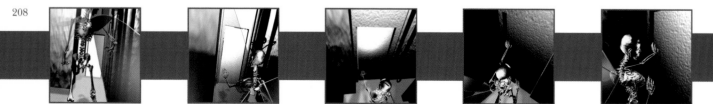

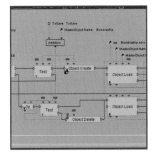 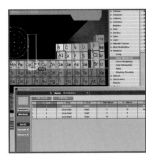  

very close to our actual visual perception and may even amplify our ability to perceive potential interactions with objects, architecture, and characters.

When I refer to 3D, I'm not focusing on what is traditionally called 3D. I'm thinking of 3D as an extra dimension that adds to the already rich symbolism of 2D representations. 3D narrative fiction is in no way explicitly bound to 3D media. The real importance lies in the strength and relevance of the interactivity.

We obviously have to keep in mind that this 3D we're discussing is most often viewed on the flat surface of a screen. There is much left to invent if we hope to get closer to reality—that is, if we believe the quest for reality makes sense…

Aside from its ability to stick more closely to perceived reality, 3D also offers the possibility of hierarchically organizing objects in a physical, tangible way, according to how we place them spatially. Sixteenth-century painting was especially good at capitalizing on this capacity, newly recognized at the time, to (re)invent perspective.

3D makes the shift from being a symbol of reality to being a representation of reality—and reality is an amazing source of inspirations for all possible interactions! :)

MEADOWS: What would you say are the key elements of art that [have] an interactive component to it?

DUCHÂTEAU: Very difficult question since I think there are as many types of interactivity as there are genres of art works.

Everything hinges on the kind of interactivity the author wants to create. His needs won't be the same when producing a hyperrealistic historical multiplayer game or an interactive installation requiring great intimacy between the system and the user.

Often the key to interactivity will be the reaction to the spectator/player's physical actions. Sometimes the most important aspect is the way in which the narration so perfectly mirrors the spectator's mental logic.

If I had to find a common ground or a key element common to interactive works of art, I would say it's the comprehension—the conceptual grasp—of how the work evolves spatially and temporally, even if that knowledge is often made intentionally difficult to access. …So the author then holds the key to his own control, if there is, indeed, a key to interactivity.

Ultimately, our goal was to allow maximum experimentation and iterative loops for inventive interactivity, while also providing a common language so multiple members of development teams could work together on complex productions.

Four: Development & Practice

4.1: Introduction

If the wind will not serve, take to the oars.

—Roman Proverb

At the end of the day, as with many "creative" projects and forms of "content," the success of the project isn't measured by numbers but by communication and emotional result. Finally, interactive narrative, like any other form of narrative, is something that will fall within subjective purview and emotional borders. This is to say, like graphic design or music composition, interactive narrative is something that will resonate with a reader only if that reader has established some relationship with the narrative. This is the responsibility of the author first and the reader second.

This isn't a new relationship. Some kinds of music, such as classical forms that Bach composed, certainly have formula and structure that can be clearly communicated once understood. However, it's the specific implementation and whether it moves the listener that is the final factor of its success. This is not only harder to understand and communicate, but for some people, it's impossible to do in the first place.

Action is the highest form of thought. This is to say that we really understand something only when we've done it. It's one thing to espouse that interactive narrative is a new art form or that it has new capabilities or that it even exists in the first place, but it's certainly a different issue to build it.

4.2: Design Considerations—The Technical Perspective

As we learn to replace trees of prebuilt explicitly listed courses of action with procedural rules-based systems, we can imagine ceding far more control to players. Once procedural tools can model a town council (or whatever), which reacts dynamically to events in the world, then designers don't have to second guess every move a player might make, and instead can write high-level reactions, goals, and behaviors that player actions will drive. But designers have to let go of detailed control of every action, and figure out how to get the most out of the procedural tools computers are good at.

—Doug Church

For someone like a painter or architect, technique has more to do with efficiency and effectiveness than it does with durability. Questions swarm the constraints of the design. Is it networked or does it run locally? How much processor speed does it use? Who are the readers and what do they know? To complicate matters, the process of the development and the conceptual design intersect and often conflict.

This is the thorny space of System Design.

4.2.1: Designing the System

In Austin, Texas, the designers, writers, and developers of IonStorm work toward the second release of their BAFTA (British Academy of Film and Television Arts) award-winning game *Deus Ex2*. At IonStorm, these designers use a process that is relatively straightforward and familiar to the schools of game design, software design, and cinematic writing. They start large. They begin the project with early meetings. These meetings include the individuals who have the most experience, passion, and investment in the game and start with widest perspective: the global view.

Then they narrow that perspective. When they start a new project, they hold a preproduction meeting and discuss the story, the setting, the characters, and what tools, or capabilities, the reader will have in the game. This is a useful approach because they're not putting the story ahead of the interaction design or vice versa. They look over the technical implementation. They try to get everyone involved. They try to get both sides of the collective brain—the creative and the technical—talking to each other.

This is what, in 1.5.3, we've previously termed a Nodal story structure and something Smith calls "string of pearls" story structure.

The project begins with a director, a producer, and "discipline leads"—the folks who keep an eye on a practice area such as graphic design or networking—and as the project continues, they snowball more people in as needed. This ensures that the design is straightforward in the beginning, the concentration is focused, and the budget is small. While doing this early conceptualization, they don't need to be building diagrams of use-case or narrative flow. As with any writing, the process is a distillation. It's a refinement of the details of the total concept and the imaginative exercises—the visual process—of understanding those details. What is different about the way that they write for interactive narrative is that in these early meetings, they are developing a world view, so the refinement of the details isn't linear because the way the story is told isn't linear. Checklists and databases need to be kept, but this maintenance isn't an issue of writing a narrative art; it's an issue of producing a world-view perspective.

It's night at the dock and a boat sits in the water. It's a relatively industrial environment, and the authors and designers of the story want readers to have room to explore, but finally, the authors want the readers, for the sake of the story and of the gameplay, to get in the boat and drive away. The authors begin this development by looking at what might be done on a real dock, and how to attract attention to the boat for most everyone who passes through this node of interaction.

The end result is a narrative line that allows some looking around and exploration, then a relatively fixed and linear passage to a new node of interaction.* Readers need guidance at occasional points to keep the narrative line intact, and, as we've seen, these moments of constraint help guide any interaction. Stoplights do the same job. Interaction requires constraint just as narrative requires imagination. If there were no bottleneck, it would become total action and the narrative would run the risk of disappearing.

A goal for IonStorm is to see that the pacing and timing of the game are driven by the player, not the author. As Raph Koster terms it, this is an "expressive" approach. It's more interesting for the player if this is the case. While the author or designer might feel otherwise, Smith notes that "designers are smart to turn over the creation to the player."

But finding the right balance is important. As any software developer, they check their work as they go. For IonStorm, there are two real tests to their success.

The first test is the user testing. In one instance, a woman was starting the game and rather than take the anticipated route of getting off the dock onto the boat and driving the boat to the nearby city, she instead stayed on the dock and began to experiment with objects there. She threw a barrel into the water. She stood on the barrel. She got back on the dock. She shot the barrel. The barrel exploded.

She jumped in the water and swam under the dock. She got back onto the dock. She followed a rat. At first, this caused some concern among the interaction designers who were watching over her shoulder because they assumed that the cues they had given her to follow (such as the nearby, idling boat at the end of the pier) were missed and, subsequently, her experience was boring. On the contrary, she loved the exploration. Her time in this node of interaction simply allowed her the chance to build a different experience for herself.

The second test is the story testing. IonStorm asks a second person to watch the game as it's being played by the first person. This observer, removed from the interaction, if still engaged in the experience is a sensitive weathervane to the movements of the narrative. If the observer's attention is still on the game without having the experience of control and exploration, IonStorm knows they've got a solid narrative structure.

A Good Design

A good design is one that solves more than one problem with a single solution.

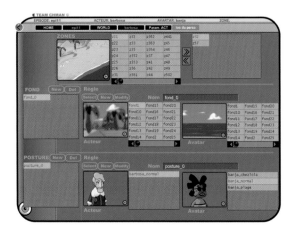

In contemporary narrative, when so many forms of design have been woven together, a narrative designer has to weave at multiple looms. The best interactive narrative designers need at least cursory familiarity with interface design, graphic design, interaction design, and information design. Let's not forget story structure, graphic composition, animation, camera cuts, lighting effects, and the knowledge of the thread of technology used to weave these together. Most designers who are involved in interactive narrative have backgrounds that cover at least three or four of these disciplines. It seems to be a characteristic of digital designers; they work in multiple arenas.

But the process of design can be murky, especially when stirring in so many different ingredients. Fortunately, interactive narrative can be developed by following formula that, like any discipline, can be spelled out and, if followed, will at least frame the appropriate questions, if not answer them.

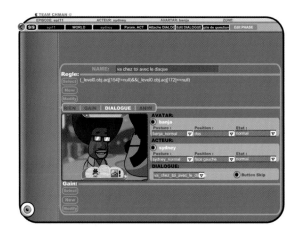

As Team ChMan organizes for another of their monthly episodes of Banja, they have to consider more than a single form of design. Starting from the bottom, they have a team of programmers who have developed a proprietary authoring and editing platform named "Epi_Editor." This is software that allows a meta-form of editing, integrating characters, camera cuts, background scenes, dialogue, and even the iconographic interface that runs along the bottom of the screen as nonplayer characters speak with the reader. These pieces of the design, each one a part of another form of design (illustration, dialogue, color, sound, etc) are all integrated, just as the design of a classic form of narrative, but, in many cases, with far more complexity.

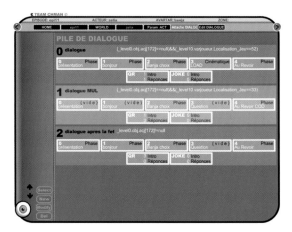

Define the Requirements

The larger a project is, the more requirements it has. Any time multiple millions of dollars are put together, everyone who is working on the project is excited. And then they receive a list of requirements, and morale takes a sharp nosedive. But the requirements—at least for the engineers and designers—serve as a design constraint, forcing some decisions and informing others. But everyone needs to know what the project requirements are at the early stages, so a tradition has developed in most software development areas that has been named a "Software Requirements Document," or "SRD" as it's called at Oracle, Microsoft, and AOL, large companies that have long histories of staunch requirements.

Generally, a well-built SRD will contain items that are useful to interactive narrative design. The effort of an SRD is largely administrative, but it's a worthwhile exercise for a serious project. A table of contents might include, for example, the items in the table at the right.

The Software Requirements Document will be different for different projects, but the basic premise is the same: Define the requirements. This allows the group of designers and engineers working on the project to know what the goal is. If "quality" can be defined as "adherence to the requirements," then you need to get those requirements on paper so everyone knows what's "good enough."

This is important because any design project is never, really, finished; it's abandoned.

Document Ownership (author, editor, etc)
Table of Contents
Introduction
User and Target Segments
Development Approach
- Technology Development Method (do we build, buy, or rent)
- Market Analysis (who's the customer and why)
- Competitor Analysis (who's the competitor and why)
- Software Features (what the software does)
- Business Objectives   (how money is made doing this)
Design Approach -
Use-Case and Workflow (what information is used)
- User Interface and Interaction Design   (how people use it)
- Visual Design (what the information looks like)
Examples and Scenarios (specific citations)

Build the Production Metrics

Any project that may include a large number of people requires measurement of some form if not only for the determination of financial success, for the determination of whether or not the assets (images, text, audio, video, or other content being integrated) and materials for the project have all been completed. Production metrics include several flavors of accounting, but they generally measure what assets are due, when they are due, and how many there are. Generally, this is the role of a project manager.

Production metrics tell the team what is due when and how many of it are going to be made. The more accurately this can be identified at the outset of the project, the more smoothly the project will run. You need to determine what the production metrics are for a narrative production as if it were being done for a website design, television production, or mobile technology system. The same principles apply.

Determining the Reader

In order to ensure some level of success when the project arrives in the market it's worth knowing a few things before you begin: Who are the readers of the specific project and what are their experiences, abilities, needs, and concerns?

Who Is the Reader?

Determining the reader is the first step. What are their likes, dislikes, attitudes, budgets? How do they spend their time? What magazines do they read? Where do they go on the weekend? What music do they listen to? What television shows do they watch? How old are they? Where do they live? What, in essence, do they like?

It wouldn't make sense to design a predictable and business-oriented narrative for a slash-and-stash gaming crowd. Likewise, at least a cursory knowledge of the level of technical expertise is needed before launching a design campaign for a machine that only 5 percent of the potential population may use (be it the top five percent with gigabytes of RAM or the bottom five percent with hand-held calculators).

How Many Readers Are There?

The more you know your reader, the better your job as a writer will be.

Determining single or multiple readers—and if multiple, how many—is the next step. First, there should generally be some initial consideration of whether the project is intended as being primarily networked or primarily standalone. *Deus Ex* was developed as a game that was intended to be played as a solitary experience, and then it was taken online because there were a wide number of capabilities that would map well to multiplayer use. Or so they thought. Once they got the game online, the developers anticipated a large number of visitors and were disappointed when their party never really got swinging. *Everquest*, on the other hand, is designed specifically as being a large-scale multiplayer game. If you try to play it alone, it quickly becomes evident that the party worth visiting is the online environment. So the form of interaction among people over a network is an important element in the design.

The quantity and frequency of the networked traffic should be known. RespondTV—an interactive television company based in San Francisco—developed backend servers for millions of simultaneous visitors. Knowing that they had to develop software that accommodated four or five million simultaneous users, obviously, guided their approach to their development.

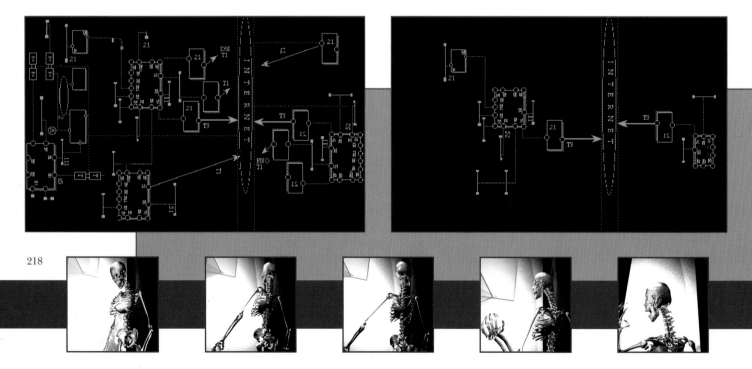

There are two factors that are being discussed in the previous paragraphs: the number of people who are using the physical hardware and the number of people who are using the networked machine. Alen Wexelblat, a long-time VR researcher, developer, and theorist, listed, in 1993 seven items to be considered when designing networked environments. The relevance of the list persists:

· How much data will be used at the same time?
· Who will have control over the output and the input and for how long?
· How will users communicate with one another?
· How will users know what other users are doing when?
· What parts of the system will users see at any one time?
· How will users know what other users are seeing?
· How does what others see affect them?

Design Constraints and Balancing Trade-Offs

Multiple readers interacting with shifting conditions gets complicated.

Design constraints guide decisions. One thing to note is that there are two sorts of constraints that we've looked at in this book. The first was interaction constraint on the reader; the second is design constraint on the author. Our first example of a design constraint is intended to frame interaction capabilities of the reader and the second is there as a means of development for the author. It's a kind of buttress. In architecture, one design constraint is the footprint of the building. In movie production it's the dimensions of the screen.

Design constraints serve as a means of starting the project and actually inform the design. When Michelangelo said, "My lines follow the lines that led them there," what he meant was that as soon as he puts down one line it constrains and informs the ones that follow it.

There are three primary design constraints we'll consider here. There's possibly thousands of design constraints that are worth considering, but these three in particular will remain issues, regardless of technical improvements in the coming decades:
1. Responsiveness vs. Resolution
2. Optimization vs. Ubiquity
3. Customization vs. Design

The first two are technical, and the third is artistic.

The first question is probably the most significant. The term, "latency" is another way to look at this problem. Here's the problem: Two users are in the same room and one leaves the room at 12:00. This input is sent to the server and takes one minute to get there, hitting the server at 12:01. The other users in the room will see the door close at 12:02 since it takes one more minute for the output to get to them. Meanwhile, another person in the room decides to leave at 12:01. What happens? Do they have to open the door in front of them? Or is the door already open? How can they tell?

1. Responsiveness vs. Resolution

I was in a video game parlor with a 14-year old and her mother. The video games were in the foyer of a multiplex movie theater. We were taking a quick survey of the available game options. For the 14-year old, it was no question: the game to be played was the game with the best graphics. After the three of us left the movie (it involved a large reptile wrecking things) I stood outside and listened to some of the departing comments. "Neat CG, but the plot was a mess." "Loved the image of…" and then as the crowd was thinning I heard "Sheesh, that was stupid." And the response of "Yeah, but it looked cool."

It can't be left unsaid that movies, television shows, magazines, websites, and video games have all sold marvelously and won small mountains of rewards because of their looks alone. But beauty isn't screen deep. The image is critical, but the interactive responsiveness is also important. Sometimes you will have to choose one over the other because processing speeds are insufficient, network lagtimes are too slow, and so on.

Frederick P. Brooks, Jr., an early pioneer of virtual reality, sees real-time motion and high-quality imagery as a trade-off that will always exist in specific forms of interaction design. His vote is to prioritize them so that objects always move realistically at the expense of everything else. He also mentions that jumps in objects need to be avoided at all costs. This, of course, applies anywhere there is a hit on the rendering calculations of the display device, be it a cell phone, a television, a desktop computer, or Dick Tracy's two-way wrist radio.

Emphasizing movement makes sense when you consider that the human race has been hunting live animals for many millennia and our bifocal eyes have evolved to first isolate movement, then contrast, then color. This can well be reflected in graphic design with the priority placed on movement—the characteristic to which we're most sensitive. But responsiveness isn't simply the way things appear to move. When we move something else, we expect to see a change, and if that change doesn't happen when we expect it, we feel like we're involved with something that is broken, vacuumed of life, and stripped of change.

To determine where to put responsiveness and where to put resolution, ask yourself the following;

Q: Where will people need to do the most interaction (is it with objects or the plot of the story)?

Q: What is background and what is foreground (with objects and the plot of the story)?

Q: Where is the focus of the reader's attention?

Q: What movement is absolutely necessary?

2. Optimization vs. Ubiquity

The web has been successful because so many people can both author and read. This is also the reason why it's such a bother to use. Not all authors will work with the same goals in mind and, despite ISO standardizations, not all readers will view content through the same lens.

It's a simple idea, this notion of the ubiquity, lowest common denominators, and simple subtractions, but it's just not the way the real world works. Author once and view everywhere is not a reality for serious development, so a choice has to be made. It's generally a ratio: The ubiquity is inversely proportional to the optimization. The higher the level of specification (speed, color, timing, behaviors, network latency, etc), the smaller the audience.

It ends up being an issue of quality versus quantity. There is a rather brutal approach to solving this sticky problem (it's a method that works well in many cases); and that's the financial answer. If the money is coming from a large, undedicated crowd, then ubiquity is the best solution. If a high level of loyalty, interest, and quality is needed, then optimization is the best solution. This might also be something to consider from a perspective of personal pride and prejudice; some artists don't care about accessibility any more than they care about money. Here are some questions to help:

Q: What functionality can be rewritten for different technologies at what cost?

Q: How many people need to see this work as it was intended so that the production costs of the project are covered?

Q: Are there small features that could be modified or excised altogether to make the project available to a larger readership?

3. Customization vs. Design

As we've already seen, reader participation is critical. Providing readers with the ability to change the story causes an increased interest. Likewise, powerful visual design is critical. But these two are often in opposition to each other. Allowing readers to change the design will generally wreck it. If you don't believe me, hand your favorite photograph to the first stranger you meet, hand them a ballpoint pen, and ask him or her to make the photo better.

Despite democratic ideals, people are trained to be designers, musicians, chefs, and architects. And some are more talented, skilled, and educated than others. Our society of specialized labor doesn't let architects in the kitchen any more than we allow chefs to mix concrete. And, despite aristocratic ideals, interactive systems are structured such that the more people use them, the better they get (such as the web, which has been named fundamentally democratic).

So the initial phases of design need to weigh these conflicting issues. It amounts to determining what changes readers are allowed to make so that they feel invested, interested, and have the chance to make change. Or whether you put your designers in charge, knowing that the beauty and function of an environment outweighs the first-person participation of an individual reader.

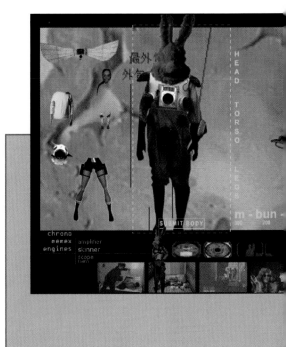

One way to solve this problem is to consider where the opinion of the narration lies and decide what affect allowing a user to interact with this opinion will have. Let's consider this as asking whether the element to be altered by the reader is a component of form or function. In the case of interface design, form includes the color, size, and location of a button. In the case of character design, it includes the color, accessories, and body shape of the character. These are all components of form rather than function, so it's a safe bet that in a narrative where readers can change the specifics of plot, these are acceptable plugs for interaction.

As Harvey Smith of IonStorm puts it, "Designers are smart to turn over the creation to the player." The answer also rests in whether the interaction is inside or outside the skull. If it's inside, then the users should be given a large share of customization and bullocks to the design. If otherwise, trim down the customization features and beef up the visual design.

Q: What parts of the design frame the metaphor?
Q: What parts frame the interaction?
Q: What part of the narrative opinion cannot be changed?
Q: What are the worst changes a reader should be allowed to make?
Q: What changes that they make will increase their interest most?

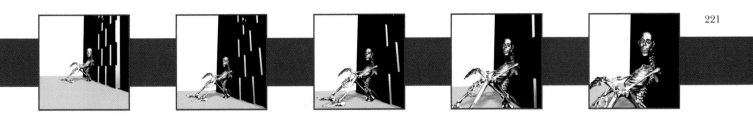

The Importance of Metaphor

The quality of a good metaphor is determined by its predictability and its internal consistency. Because it's a relationship of symbols, the information that's presented needs to have an internal relationship (see 1.3.3).

The metaphor is what allows the reader to understand the rules of a world. If, for example, these rules are in a virtual reality environment (or simulated environment), allow the reader to understand their capabilities Some interaction designers term it "preconditions," but, semantics aside, these rules allow the reader to anticipate change, and they provide a redundant level of information that highlights differences.

The desktop metaphor is predictable because most of us know how a desk functions. Most of us understand pieces of paper and folders, trashcans, and the basic process of copying and pasting. But, as we saw from Ted Nelson's criticisms, the internal consistency isn't what it might be. It's worth citing a second time:

> *"We are told that this is a "metaphor" for a "desktop." But I have never personally seen a desktop where pointing at a lower piece of paper makes it jump to the top, or where placing a sheet of paper on top of a file folder caused the folder to gobble it up; I do not believe such desks exist; and I do not think I would want one if it did."*

The desktop is a metaphor for interaction. Others that we see today include radio dials for Internet audio listening devices, calculator push-buttons for numeric calculators, paint and canvas for drawing programs, and pages for text (it's curious to notice the lack of buildings and other spatial metaphors when we see them around us so much).

In summary, the metaphors that are chosen for interaction are difficult because the interaction of the computer screen rarely maps to the interaction of the act it's emulating. The whole reason there is a paint program is so that it can do things that paint and canvas cannot. The metaphor eventually breaks down when taken to its limited extremes. Additionally, interaction metaphor is based on a process of determining what the user does and how he or she understands it. It is a form of compression of information.

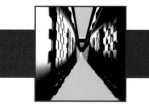

4.3: Narrative

With the pen in one's hand, narrative is a difficult art; narrative should flow as flows the brook down through the hills and the leafy woodlands, its course changed by every boulder it comes across and by every grass-clad gravelly spur that projects into its path; its surface broken, but its course not stayed by rocks and gravel on the bottom in the shoal places; a brook that never goes straight for a minute, but goes, and goes briskly, sometimes ungrammatically, and sometimes fetching a horseshoe three quarters of a mile around, and at the end of the circuit flowing within a yard of the path it traversed an hour before; but always going, and always following at least one law, always loyal to that law, the law of the narrative, which has no law.

With a pen in hand the narrative stream is a canal; it moves slowly, smoothly, decorously, sleepily, it has no blemish except that it is all blemish. It is too literary, too prim, too nice; the gait and style and movement are not suited to narrative. That canal stream is always reflecting; it is its nature, it can't help it. Its slick shiny surface is interested in everything it passes along the banks—cows, foliage, flowers, everything. And so it wastes a lot of time in reflections.

—Mark Twain

4.3.1: Principles

The writer's tool of foreshadowing, the painter's tool of foreshortening, and the interaction designer's tool of hierarchical representation (nesting menus) can be considered the same basic method of telescoping information so that a wide view is compressed into a narrow perspective. It's a means of presenting an entire topology.

A topologic exploration probably isn't a narrative. It might be considered a plot for simply architectural reasons of interface presentation, but without some sense of opinion or perspective—and, to be safe, a beginning and end—it amounts to little more than an exploration. But an exploration that has an implied opinion can be, as we've seen, a form of narrative, and in some cases interactive narrative. This is a role that characters serve in interactive narrative because setting and character work closely together.

  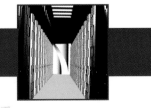  

Take a simple grass field. A single person walking around on the field is hardly a narrative of any interest. Even adding a couple of people and having them all wander around the field lacks a sense of narrative, even if there is competition and character involved.

Even if we give the people in this interaction among themselves a pigskin and start calling this topologic competition a football game, it still lacks narrative characteristics such as conflict, resolution, and suspense.

Two things, however, can quickly change this. A football game quickly becomes a story when a sportscaster is there to narrate, providing opinion on who is doing what and why at what times. The game, simply, needs an opinion or perspective to move it into a narrative realm. This is the role of the sportscaster; to insert opinion where there was only action. This brings the game to a level of narrative, not only enhancing the experience of the radio listener (the sound of shuffling shoes, torn sod, and grunting men wouldn't be terribly interesting), but also enhancing the experience for people who are, for example, watching the game on television. Sega's *NFL 2K* starts the game with a sportscaster's introduction, immediately introducing an element of narrative that helps simulate real play and simultaneously drops the reader into a narration of events in which they can participate. So the first is the introduction of narration—or opinion—on a verbal level.

Second, adding a camera that reinforces that sportscaster's opinion, moving the viewer from that objective god's-eye perspective to a point where individual perspective and focus are brought to particular actions provides a familiar sense of context and perspective. The camera is an interface that, like text, we're all at least familiar with (if not well-versed at using). The camera is the narrative interface to the 3D space, transporting the user there as if they were eyes. Sega went all-out in their camera capabilities for *NFL 2K*, underscoring the fact that they knew the camera was an important part of preserving the interest of the reader. There is a crowd of cameras that include "Close, Standard, Far, Isometric, Cinematic, Side, Top, View, and Blimp," along with interactive controls for replays and other moments in the game. These multiple forms of camera might even be thought of as "drop-down menus" in conventional 2D interfaces. So this second addition is the introduction of narration—or opinion—on a visual level.

A sportscaster and a camera won't necessarily make something interesting. There are several main elements that have been traditionally used by writers of fiction, but let's calcify these, for the sake of discussing the primary elements of writing a narrative, to two elements of motivation: investment, and interest.

Investment and interest are at the very heart of interactive narrative.

4.4: Interaction

```
// ANIMA simulation main loop.
Called once per tick

void
CAnmApplication::Simulate()
{
    // Any new input?
        PollSensors();

    // Process events generated
        by input
        HandleEvents();

    // Render a frame
        Render();
}


// Copyright (c) 2001
// by Tony Parisi
```

4.4.1: Interaction Principles

It was 1994. I was working with the Interactive Media Festival in San Francisco. My job was "webmaster," and the Festival's job was to work with an international jury of 15 experts of interactivity and, through this network of experts, research and display the best forms of interactive artwork in the world. The Festival, in its second year, was to be held in Los Angeles at the Variety Arts Center. Meanwhile, since it was the spring of 1994 and Internet hype was heated, people would fly in from Los Angeles to our San Francisco office so that they could "take a look at The Websites." In retrospect, it seems quite strange, this idea of flying somewhere to see the Internet.

That same year at a European web conference an idea for a 3D technology for the web was broached. This idea proposed that a language for 3D imagery that complemented and worked in conjunction with HTML be developed. Later that year, Mark Pesce persuaded *Wired* magazine to start a mailing list, and Tony Parisi got to work on writing a browser. Meanwhile, Silicon Graphics Inc, a giant among a rather wolfish flock, got wind of events early on, and with the help of Gavin Bell, introduced several versions of VRML that introduced "composability, scalability, and extensibility."

These efforts eventually blossomed into a community of programmers and engineers firmly resolved to see the realization of this dream.

Lisa Goldman, the Creative Director of the Interactive Media Festival (and one of the only people I've ever met who has 20/20 foresight), introduced Mark Pesce, Tony Parisi, and me. The four of us agreed that it would be interesting to see what interaction VRML could have with the Festival. This was considered a test-bed. Ambition is the folly of both youth and a new technology, so we decided to use it as a real-time Internet interface to the physical space of the Festival in Los Angeles. It was to be the first of over a dozen such art projects I have been involved with that integrate the virtual and the physical. In the meeting, we discussed the risk of the virtual eating the physical, and we all agreed that the physical space had to take precedence. The 3D website would be there to serve the physical space.

And we were told that a browser would be ready in time. We had six months.

I went back over to The WELL, a BBS I had worked at the previous year, and with the help of David Lewis and Annette Loudon managed to put together a team of over 30 volunteers. We imagined nothing less than The Gibsonian Dream. We worked late at night on steaming fresh VRML code, sending it to the mailing list and the folks at SGI who were simultaneously working on the VRML browsers. It was a timing effort in which both sides of this rather taped-together development effort were straining for the date of the Festival in Los Angeles. There were, after all, still no browsers, there was no budget, there were 30 volunteers working with untested code, and the project had attracted the baleful gaze of the *New York Times* and *Los Angeles Times*, among others. It's unnecessary to say that tensions were as high as our ambitions.

Some six months later, we had developed a fully accurate architectural version of the Festival that included modeled versions of each of the installations. Visitors to the site were able to drive through the building, look at the installations (through video cameras as well as the modeled VRML replicas), and messages to visitors at the Festival (who could also chat and email to Festival staff and visitors of the physical space in Los Angeles). This incredible team of volunteers did it all without ever even being able to go to the physical space itself.*

By the time I arrived in Los Angeles, on the first day I was there, I knew where the bathroom was without having to ask anyone. It was a strange sensation of "Preja-Vue."

As if that wasn't enough, we also built an artificial life visualization in VRML (that included a non-Euclidean Internet visualization) as well as a couple of other projects that helped describe the projects in the gallery.

Eventually, the Festival shut its doors and we spun Construct Internet Design out of that original volunteer effort of designers and programmers. Now, nine years later, I'm able to see that there were some basic lessons that we learned from the Interactive Media Festival. This early stage of building worlds, despite streaming video and anti-matter phaser cannons, provided several key elements of interaction:

1. Observe—The reader makes an assessment.
2. Explore—The reader does something.
3. Modify—The reader changes the system.
4. Change—The system changes the reader.

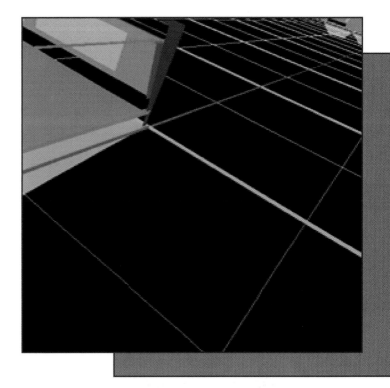

By using the rather disturbing combination of the Internet and interactive (real-time) 3D graphics of VRML, we fell into the solution more than intentionally created it. The installation at the Festival wasn't a narrative, but it was an architectural space that integrated with a networked version of the space. It was one of my early lessons about the design of physical space as it relates to digital interaction over the Internet.

Several members of this 34-person volunteer team went on to help Lisa Goldman and me form Construct: James Waldrop, Michael Gough, Annette Loudon, Adam Gould, and Todd Goldenbaum.

4.4.2: Designing the Interaction

Any narrative worth reading begins with an idea worth telling. The story has to be interesting. But the less the story and the interaction design are separated, the better the end result will become.

The narrative's structure and the design of the interaction should be two ingredients in a single recipe. In the best forms of interactive narrative, one can't take precedence over the other. This is an important point, so I'll say it again: In the best forms of interactive narrative, the story structure (things such as plot, timing, character, and story pacing) should have an equanimical relationship with the design of the interaction. Many interactive projects, such as websites, cellular technologies, and enhanced television shows, have decided to repurpose existing content and then hang the bells and whistles as if this will breathe a new life in it that wasn't there before. Just as it's a bad idea to fix soup ingredients and then add water when serving your dinner guests, interaction has to be integrated as part of the authorship process. This demands a kind of author who understands interaction design, story design, and the importance of multiple simultaneous perspectives. All this is to point out that some stories will be more suited to interaction design than others, and in the best situation, the interaction and the story inform each other.

There are as many possible forms of interaction design as there are stories, but some key, additive forms of interaction design and interactive components to consider include:
1. Adding ambient information
2. Adding perspectives
3. Increasing investment

These are a short list of options, not requirements. To expand this a bit:

1: Adding ambient information. An interactive narrative could add information and provide things to do. Moving through a place and looking for items that increase an understanding of that place, investigating what's already there, flipping switches, solving puzzles, learning systems, or even viewing pretty pictures can certainly be valid options. Consider Broderbund's classic, *Myst*. This is probably the simplest form of interaction that current-day interactive narratives contain, and so it's among the easiest forms of interaction to add in. The plot isn't altered, the tension of the story isn't increased, and the characters don't change. Many readers will find that this gives them a sense of exploration and the novelty of the exploration itself may prove interesting. Where architectural exploration adds information about the characters, provides backstory, or deepens the metaphor of the tale, it is most appropriately used.

2: Adding perspectives. An interactive narrative could provide multiple perspectives and different ways to look at the world of that narrative. Again, this is meant in both a dimensional and emotional sense. This is, as has been mentioned, the primary benefit to three-dimensional interactive imagery (such as architectural drive-throughs), but it's also a nifty means of building suspense, thickening the plot, and thinning out inhibitions that someone might have to affect the system in front of them. The best way to do this is to allow a reader to experience a story from the view of different characters. This assumes the existence of #1; otherwise, the new perspective isn't interactive.

3: Increasing investment. An interactive narrative could increase investment and draw readers deeper into the story the further they read. This is probably the single most effective method of making the reader feel interest, motivation, and that particular desire to turn the page. Investment is one of several commodities: a reader's time, a reader's resources, his attention when reading, his energy put into the process of interacting, his reputation among other readers who are in that same virtual space, or anything that a person might use to evaluate his own success.

Tomagochi, the *Sims*, and other virtual farms have been successful because we invest our time and attention to them, nurturing them, feeding them, watching them change. The time investment and the attention investment is what makes them valuable to us. It's our own value reflected back that causes us to then add more. This process is critical to note because it is the process of investment that allows someone to increase his interest, and his interest is what increases his investment. A good writer of interactive narrative understands how to create and sustain this cycle.

The investment and the form of the investment is generally the job of the author to determine. In literature and movies, it's an increased interest in the events and relationship of the events in the plot. In arena-based video games, it's simply staying alive (or killing the other guy, depending on how it's played). In something like *Dungeons and Dragons*, it's the acquisition of gold and the accumulation of hit points. In a good story, however, it's simply the means of discovering the solution to the problem that started the story in the first place.

But regardless of what method, motivation, or type of interaction the author chooses, the real heart of the interactive narrative is the relevance of the story to the people who are doing the reading.

4.5: Summaries and Outlook

...There are certain periods in history that we might call phase transitions, bifurcations or critical points. With respect to evolution, we discuss how there are certain elements that adapt to one another in some state, and somehow they come together and create a new function. It's called an exaptation.

—Jordan Pollack

4.5.1: Emerging Hybrids

Hybridization is a fundamental trend of technologic advancement. The television was the hybridization of movies and radio. Movies were the hybridization of theater and still-frame animation. Software, meanwhile, is integrating all of these forms to generate interactive narrative.

Therefore, interactive narrative comes from a long family line that includes ancestors named Speech, Writing, Theater, Painting, Photography, Radio, Video, and Software.

Software is far more suited to this process of hybridization than other media have been. Take the recent developments of the Internet. The web (specifically, its early incarnation as the Mosaic/Mozilla browser of the summer of 1993) is the hybridization of file transfer protocols (FTP), networked layout protocols (SGML), and image viewing protocols (JPG or GIF). Things have only gotten more tangled since then. We can now interact with real-time telerobotic sex machines hyperlinked to streaming audio and video feeds—operating on the other side of the globe (fortunately).

Meanwhile, the Internet, cell phones, televisions, movies, video games, and the Internet have been overlapping for some years now.* We're beginning to see the integration of several of these (*Tomb Raider* and the *Star Wars* series is certainly building large enough worldviews to accommodate the newly emerging multiplayer games of the coming years). Stories and games that use each of these media systems and tie them into a shared worldview will become increasingly powerful means of telling stories.

These forms of integration will come as little surprise to most stockbrokers who have already done a fine job of melding media to relay information and opinion. The rarified steppes of the stockbroker's world are a curious space to watch because the competition is so fierce and the transfer of information so distilled.

232

3D muds have been on the rise (if not in the oven) for the past decade. Worlds, Inc. was an early precursor to three-dimensional multiuser environments. These environments have been under development for close to 12 years now as multiple people sharing the same space have been one of the long-term promises of graphical cyberspace. The writings of Stephenson and Gibson did a fine job of kickstarting the imaginations of developers and writers, and the gradual improvement of 3D formats, protocols, and languages has been one means of instituting these ideas.

This idea of "Snowcrash," (an advanced and fully extended form of a multi-user three-dimensional VR environment) is, essentially, a hybrid that has enormous potential to integrate with other forms of media because we already understand how these media types are integrated into the real world. This basic template of the real world is what's allowed these ideas to take such a strong hold on the imagination. The challenge it presents is the articulation of new and imaginative spaces (because who wants to log into a version of the real world when the real world is just outside the door?) and understanding how media types such as text, video, audio, and 3D interfaces that live inside the existing 3D world will co-exist. Competitions in video game environments, such as *Quake* tournaments, may soon provide something similar to what we see in current real-world boxing matches. It doesn't seem an unrealistic possibility that video game tournaments may someday be played on national television—or something like it.

The possibilities appear large.

4.5.2: Emerging Trends in Development

Because this art form of narrative is so new—really at the very early days of existence—it's difficult for us to not only look at the existing state of the art form, but to make reliable predictions of what's down the road. The presence of the Internet has certainly had a marked effect on narrative because it allows people the opportunity to work with and against each other (arguably the central theme of all games). *Everquest* or the *A.I.* movie project couldn't have existed without it. Wireless technology has altered that basic social infrastructure and given it a new flavor of real-world integration, and this, in turn, has led to games like *Majestic* in which the cell phone, the fax, the landline, email, and webpages provide portals into a single piece of content that sustains the narrative.

But more than any of these is the desire for increased participation. The goal, as Doug Church puts it, is for the author's job to be secondary to the reader's job and for the world that is being expressed to be so full of interaction and so flexible that we are able to adopt the same modes of interacting with it that we use every day in the real world.

One way to achieve this is through built-in "simulation." This is done by allowing the environment to grow itself, rather than being written. It's a new authoring approach that solves some important problems.

Algorithmic Environments

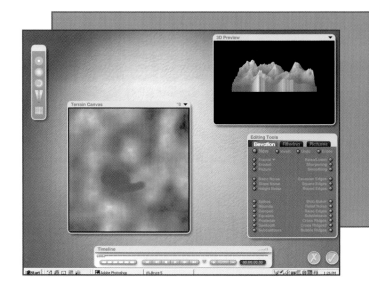

With environments becoming more complicated, richer, larger, and more interactive, the production costs of development increase. But so does the immersion. How can production value be added without increasing costs?

Let's consider two fundamentally different approaches to environment development: manual and procedural. Think of "manual" as sewing an environment together and think of "procedural" as growing one.

Manually built environments require someone sitting down at a modeling, drawing, or coding application, building a basic geometric element, and then assigning all of its graphical and behavioral properties. Let's take a hillside as an example. First, the hillside is modeled in a modeling application such as 3ds max or Maya (or imported, say), and then that hillside is given features such as trees, rocks, sand, or grass. These features need to then be integrated onto the bare model of the hill. Assuming all the trees are appropriately colored, they need to be placed. And then, once they are placed, they need to be recolored a little so they look natural together (it's not a believable model if all trees look that same). Maybe there's a little more rock on the north side of the hill. Maybe the trees don't look quite random enough. Maybe there's a bare patch of dirt, or some sticks lying on the ground. Next, we have some global parameters such as "Light" and "Sky Color" (characteristics in the code that ensure that if a character looks around, he will see the same color sky and the same degree of light as he would on the next hill). Other parameters are "Solidity" and "Gravity" (characteristics in the code that ensure that if a character runs up the hill, he actually follows the slope of the hill) and relative size. Once these values are assigned, then the designer takes that particular geometry and its affiliated lines of code and carefully, like a surgeon, inserts it into the larger environment.

This is a manual production process that requires building the thing and then assigning it properties by hand.

However, there is a procedural approach as well that provides more material with less overall effort. This is an approach that generates environments within a range of predetermined parameters. This means that rather than a landscape designer manually building the parts of the model that make up the surface of a hill and individual bushes (as in the previous example), that person instead determines general parameters and sees that those general parameters are expressed within a range of options to choose from. This is the difference between a landscape designer sitting down and generating the code and models from hand or simply saying "Computer, make me 20 hills with some trees on the south side and a few rocks down the north side. I will pick the one that looks the best when I see them and maybe try a few more."

The way that it works is conceptually simple with some dramatic implications. Imagine that each of the features of our hill is a value that can be expressed numerically: the number of trees, what percent are on the north side, what percent of the hill is covered with grass, what percent is covered with rocks. Every specific feature of this hill is something that is numeric. (It has to be if it lives in the computer.) Rather than having a designer try to generate the hill visually, smart developers are writing code that does this for them. The designer's job soon becomes one of assigning a range of values, or of choosing from the hundreds of hillsides that come back in a matter of seconds.* This not only allows the designer more time spent on the concentration of the design and less on the production, but it also begins to build the value of that shop that is doing the development.

Essentially, this algorithmic approach provides the designer the opportunity to make aesthetic decisions while leaving the computer with the mathematical gruntwork. It's hard for most companies to find the time to make an investment of this nature, but after having spoken with multiple design firms that have made this effort, this author has never heard a word of regret after having made the commitment.

It's worth noting that, after the designer has set the values for "Hill" and the application begins to churn out hill after hill after hill, there's territory to be explored. This has implications for the off-spring of the Snowcrash dreams of The Black Sun and The Metaverse; an enormous virtual city filled with people each engaged in their own narrative. Algorithmic, or procedural, approaches mean that someone driving down Main street can suddenly turn right, off the path, and keep going right for as long as he wants, and never come to the edge of the world. These days, the edge of the world is a point where the designer stopped building the model. Soon, the edge of the world will be where people haven't explored.

So the idea is to build a tool that generates a series of objects, and then ask the designer to choose from among those objects, informing their variables, so that a large range of well-designed material is generated in a short span of time.

When a good idea sinks in, its applications are wide. This can be done with architecture as well as landscapes, and with rooms as well as buildings. Characters, like buildings, are really just objects with visual and behavioral properties. So this procedural approach can be done with characters as well. In 1998, at Construct Internet Design, we began to fashion a tool called "Avagen" that allowed us to import metaball-based models and export fully real-ized polygon-based models. This "avatar generator" was intended as an investment in the production process that allowed a steep ramp in the sheer quantity of files that could be produced.

Eventually, we'll see similar developments with the personalities and brains of characters, and not just with the bodies.

Artificial Intelligence

Character is important to narrative, and few "ghost-town narratives" continue to be a success. People provide opinion and supply interest.

The *Dungeons and Dragons* narrative model spawned an approach to gaming that allowed potentially hundreds of people to interact in the same conceptual world. And, in the last few years, we've seen an increased attention being paid to "Massively Multiplayer Online Gaming." So it seems clear we enjoy playing games with each other.

But more than one developer has made mention that multi-user games will go the way of *Pong*, *Galaga*, and (sadly) *Zork*. There are several key issues that massively multiplayer games don't address. First is the fact that we all like to be in the spotlight to some degree. Being in the spotlight encourages a high level of investment and participation. By having only four or five players—as opposed to several thousand or a hundred thousand—collaborating or competing in the same environment, we don't slice up the spotlight of attention. This means that players will be more motivated to contribute more. This means that, if all goes well, they will enjoy the game more.

Second is the fact that in many games playing with people you know—like playing a game of chess—fosters a stronger suspension of disbelief. If, for example, you have five people all playing *Dungeons and Dragons*, and one starts to cause problems (throwing pepperoni, or overturning the table, say), that makes the interaction with the other people, and the very game itself, more difficult. So reducing the number of people in a narrative environment seems a trend that will appear on the horizon soon, as well. It not only changes the attention ratios of the readers, but it also allows for different levels and concentrations of game play. Dwell time, detail familiarity, attention span, and style are all things that contribute to the way that interactive narrative is read.

These two things conjure a world that is richer in interaction with people, but has fewer people in it. Not a contradiction at all, this indicates that the role of artificial intelligence such as chatterbots, talkbots, and other conversational characters are all becoming increasingly important and may well serve as fundamental a role in forms of visual narrative as architecture does today.

"NPCs," or "Non-Player Characters," are earning more attention from developers as an important part of game play. Perhaps it's time to rename them "Non-Reader Characters," but the introduction of alternative protagonists, or new antagonists, changes the design of the story so that it is more focused on the player and less on the designer. By introducing increasingly flexible components of narrative, the level of interaction also increases.

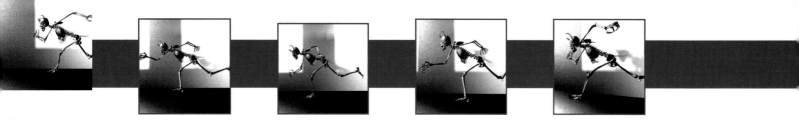

4.5.3 — Conclusion

For years, I launched invectives against the notion of "interactive television," pointing out that the stories on television broadcasts are inherently noninteractive. This, I believe, remains the case. Interactivity cannot be slapped on top of Buffy and her vampires and add anything other than interactive widgets, which really adds nothing to the show. However, the basic idea of plot (a series of events that takes place over time) can be integrated with interactivity (a series of user-participatory events that, also, take place over time).

This shift must happen during the authoring process. An "interactive narrative" is a form of narrative that allows someone other than the author to affect, choose, or change the events of the plot. In this scenario, the author's role becomes two-fold. First, the author must present a series of compelling events that increase readers' interest and investment. Second, the author must allow change and interpretation of those events. The author has to learn to work as both a writer and an interface designer.

By integrating interaction and narrative, readers become more interested in the story because they have more invested in it. We already have a deep box of tools given to us by the world of visual communication. By meshing these old tools of metaphor, style, perspective, and opinion, we can encourage and propel new art forms into existence, forms that will electrify readers' imaginations as film, television, print, telephony, and the networked computer converge into a single form.

The emergence of interactive narrative isn't a revolution. It's the rebirth of the existing art form of narrative as a Chimera, a living form whose body is composed of the forms that have come before it.

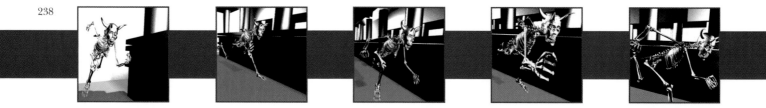

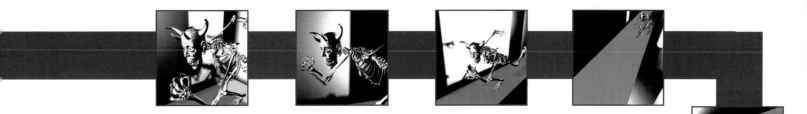

This is, as you can see, just the beginning.

About the Comic and Flipbook Narratives

Proof, despite its alcohol content (or depth of interactivity), is in the pudding.

I hope you noticed that in the upper corners of this book is a flipbook animation. If you didn't, please turn the page. This ties in with the comic cell narrative that runs along the bottom of each page. I also hope you noticed this. This narrative is a minimal example of the narrative form this book discusses. I say "minimal" because you can change the plot and the pacing, but, in this case, not a whole lot else. But it kept us entertained.

So this is an example of an interactive narrative that shows different levels of metaphor, redundancy, information compression, and varying degrees of time and pacing (we never figured out if this is a comic or an animation). We've tried to highlight how media types shape the depth and form of interaction. We've tried to present multiple perspectives (doing our best to follow a classic narrative arc), and, because the entire story contains no words, we forced ourselves to rely on imagery alone.

In this story, our character generates a "world," as it's called in VR circles. And, like many of us who involve ourselves in this work, our character gets stuck inside. The story runs parallel to the four parts of the book: Theory, 2D, 3D, and Practice. The story is, partly, about writing and the empty place where plot begins—making something from nothing, or nearly nothing. A rib and some spit, maybe. Writing a story starts, usually, with an existing problem, the invention of a problem, or a new idea altogether. In this story, all three are the case. The Bible's book of Genesis is the same story.

The part that we like is the character herself. Or himself (we're not sure which). Character is a critical part of any narrative. This character, however, is a special case. What you see on the pages of this book is only the graphic design of a form of interactive narrative called a conversational character—a form of "Artificial Intelligence" that is able to respond to humans in conversation and present a narrative through the words and images.

This development process and the character itself (named "St_Elmo") will be the subject of my next book, co-authored with Paco Xander Nathan. The book is due out in Fall of 2002. Please keep an eye on http://pause-effect.com for updates as we go.

All of these complicated contortions and schizophrenic schematics to the side, we hope that the story entertains as well as educates; despite the story's low-octane level of interactivity, we hope it helps the medicine go down.

Thanks for reading.

—msm

Adams, Henry. *Mont St. Michel & Chartres*. Penguin. New York, 1986.

Anderson, M., Carlsson, C., Hagsand, O., Stahl. *The Distributed Interactive Virtual Environment*. Swedish Institute of Computer Science, 1994.

Arnheim, Rudolf. *Visual Thinking*. University of California Press. Berkeley, 1969.

Bateson, Gregory. *Steps to an Ecology of Mind*. Ballantine. New York, 1972.

Benford, S., Lennart, E., Fahlén, E. *A Spatial Model on Interactivity in Large Virtual Environments*. Third European Conference on CSCW. Italy, 1994.

Bentham, Jeremy. *The Panopticon Writings*. Verso. London, 1995.

Bentley, Eric (Ed.). *The Theory of Modern Stage—An Introduction to Modern Theatre and Drama*. Penguin Books, 1972.

Bolter, Jay David. *Writing Space: The Computer, Hypertext, and the History of Writing*. Lawrence Erlbaum Associates, 1998.

Borges, Jorge Luis. *Labyrinths, Ficciones*. W.W. Norton and Co. New York, 1998.

Brooks, Jr., F.P. *Computer Architecture: Concepts and Evolution*. Addison-Wesley. Reading, 1997.

Calvino, Italo. *Invisible Cities*. (English edition translated by William Weaver), Harcourt Brace Jovanovich, Inc., New York, 1972.

Carter, Peter. *Mies Van Der Rohe at Work*. Phaidon Press Inc., 1999.

Chase, Gilbert. *The Music of Spain*. Dover Publications. NY. 1941.

Coleridge, Samuel T. *Biographia Literaria*. Rest Fenner. London, 1817.

Cotton, Bob & Oliver, Richard. *Understanding Hypermedia*. Phaidon Press Ltd., London, 1997.

De Santillana, Giorgio. *The Crime of Galileo*. University of Chicago Press. Chicago, 1955.

De Sola Pool, Ithiel (Ed.). *The Social Impact of the Telephone*. The MIT Press. Cambridge, 1981.

Dyson, George. *Darwin and the Machines*. Helix Books/Addison Wesley. New York, 1997.

Eagleton, Terry. *Ideology of the Aesthetic*. Cambridge, 1991.

Engeli, Maia. *Digital Stories: The Poetics of Communication*. Birkhäuser Publishers for Architecture, Basel. Berlin, 2000.

Ernst, Max. *Une Semaine De Bonte: A Surrealistic Novel in Collage*. Second Edition. Dover Publications. 1976.

Fahey, Liam & Randall, Robert M. *Learning from the Future: Competitive Foresight Scenarios*. John Wiley & Sons. New York, 1997.

Fraser, J. T. (Ed). *The Voices of Time: A Cooperative Survey of Man's Views of Time as Expressed by the Sciences and by the Humanities*. The University of Massachusetts Press. Amherst, 1966, 1981.

Gombrich, Ernst Hans. *Art and Illusion*. Bollingen Series #35. Princeton University Press. Princeton, 1980.

Gombrich, Ernst Hans. *Ideals and Idols: Essays on Values in History and in Art*. Phaidon Press. New York, 1994.

Gombrich, Ernst Hans. *Meditations on a Hobby Horse: And Other Essays on the Theory of Art*. Reprint Edition. Phaidon Press Inc., 1994.

Gombrich, Ernst Hans. *The Story of Art*. Lowe & B. Hould. Ann Arbor, 1989.

Held, Robert. *Inquisition*. Qua D'Arno, Florence, 1997.

Hubrich, Peter H. *Gustav Freytag's Ideologies*. Kronberg, 1974.

James, William. *Psychology*. World Publishing. New York, 1892.

Johnson, Steven. *Interface Culture*. HarperCollins Publishers. New York, 1997.

King, Stephen. *On Writing—A Memoir of the Craft*. Simon & Schuster Trade. New York, 2000.

Krueger, W., Bohn, C., Froehlich, H., Schueth, H., Strauss, W., Wesche, G., "The Responsive Workbench: A Virtual Work Environment." In *IEEE Computer*. Vol 28, No. 7, Pp. 42–48. 1995.

Laurel, Brenda (Ed.). *The Art of Human-Computer Interface Design*. Addison-Wesley. New York, 1990.

Laurel, Brenda. *Computers as Theater*. Addison-Wesley Publishing Company. New York, 1993.

Lessig, Lawrence. *Code and Other Laws of Cyberspace.* Basic Books. New York, 1999.

Levi, Eliphas (Translated by Arthur Edward Waite). *The History of Magic.* Rider and Company, London. Seventh Edition. 1957.

Linfert, Carl. "Hieronymus Bosch," English Translation Published by Thames & Hudson. Great Britain, 1989.

Manovich, Lev. *The Language of New Media.* MIT Press. Cambridge, 2001.

McCloud, Scott. *Understanding Comics (The Invisible Art).* Kitchen Sink Press, 1999.

McLuhan, Marshall. *Understanding Media: The Extensions of Man.* MIT Press. Cambridge, 1994.

McLuhan, Marshall & Fiore, Quentin. *The Medium Is the Massage.* Random House. New York, 1967.

McLuhan, Marshall. *The Mechanical Bride: Folklore of Industrial Man.* Vanguard Press. New York, 1951.

Mitchell, William J. *The Reconfigured Eye: Visual Truth in the Post-Photographic Era.* MIT Press. Cambridge, 1994.

Murray, Janet. *Hamlet on the Holodeck, The Future of Narrative and Cyberspace.* The Free Press. Boston, 1997.

Nelson, Ted. *Literary Machines.* Self-published, 1981.

O'Malley, C. *Computer Supported Collaborative Learning.* Springer Verlag. 1995.

Pesce, Mark. *VRML—Browsing and Building Cyberspace.* New Riders Publishing. Indianapolis, 1995.

Poe, Edgar Allan. *The Philosophy of Composition.* Matthews, Brander, ed. *The Oxford Book of American Essays.* Oxford, 1914.

Poster, Mark. *The Mode of Information. Poststructuralism and Social Context.* The University of Chicago Press. Chicago, 1990.

Pound, Ezra. *The ABC of Reading.* J. Laughlin Publishers. New York, 1960.

Pynchon, Thomas. *Gravity's Rainbow.* Penguin USA. New York, 1995.

Rosenberger, Tara M., & Smith, Brian K. Fugue. "A Conversational Interface That Supports Turn-Taking Coordination." 32nd Hawaii International Conference on Systems, 1998.

Ryan, T. A., & Schwartz, C. B. "Speed of Perception as a Function of Mode of Presentation." *American Journal of Psychology.* 69, 60-69. 1956.

Sadie, Stanley (Ed.). *The New Grove Dictionary of Musical Instruments.* London. Macmillan Press, 1987.

Saville-Troike, Muriel. *The Ethnography of Communication.* 2nd Edition. Basil Blackwell. New York, 1982.

Shaw, George Bernard. *The Quintessence of Ibsenism.* Dover, 1994.

Shedroff, Nathan. *Experience Design 1.* New Riders Publishing. Indianapolis, 2001.

Spiegelman, Art. *Maus, A Survivor's Tale.* Random House. New York, 1986.

Stephens, Mitchell. *The Rise of the Image the Fall of the Word.* Oxford Univ Press. Oxford, 1998.

Stockton, Francis Richard. "The Lady or the Tiger?" 1884.

Suler, John. "The Psychology of Avatars and Graphical Space in Multimedia Chat Communities." 1996. http://www1.Rider.Edu/~Suler/Psycyber/Psyav.Html.

Twain, Mark. *A Pen Warmed Up in Hell.* Harper and Row. New York, 1972.

Walker, John. *The Autodesk Files, Through the Looking Glass.* http://www.fourmilab.ch/autofile/www/autofile.html.

Wexelblat, A. "The Reality of Cooperation: Virtual Reality and CSCW." In *Virtual Reality: Applications and Explorations.* Academic Publishers, 1993.

White, Hayden. *METAHISTORY: The Historical Imagination in 19th Century Europe.* Boston & London. The Johns Hopkins University Press, Sixth Printing. 1987.

White, Hayden. *The Content of the Form: Narrative Discourse and Historical Representation.* Reprint Edition. Johns Hopkins University Press, 1990.

Reports of Gustav Freytag, please see Gustav Freytag Society and Gustav Freytag Archives, Berlin, c1954.

"4:33" (Cage), 184
3D muds, 233

A

A.I. Artificial Intelligence (movie), 4, 43
  game complement
    case study, 124, 131-138
    The Guide, 137
abdicating authorship, 54
abstracting
  abstraction of metaphor, 32
  characters, 87-88
  images, 88
Acropolis, 154
advertising
  click-thrus, 19
  use of narrative, 36
Age of Empires, 66, 68
"Aleph, The" (Borges), 5, 24
Alexander, Christopher, 170, 175
algorithmic environments, 234, 236
ambient information, 230
Ambient Machines (web site), 149
America Online, 18
  Harry Potter interactive vignettes, 19
  purchase of Time-Warner, 18
anamorphosis, 90
Angelico, Fra, 98-99
animation, 115
Annunciation, The (Angelico), 10, 98
  narrative imagery in, 98-100
Aquinas, Thomas, 10
architecture, 154
  interaction in, 174-176
  narrative in, 154-155, 171, 180
    Fort Scott military installation,
      171-173
    Holocaust Memorial, 155-156
  role of architect, 170-171
  virtual, 182
  walls, 174-176
Aristotle, 22
  definition of plot, 22
Assisi, Church of San Francesco, 11

B

Bain, Ed, 147
  interview, 147-148
Banja, 20, 82
  case study, 126, 144-146
Baptism of Christ, narrative imagery
  in, 101
Bateson, Gregory, 48
BBS (Bulletin-Board Service), 19
Beast, The. See Cloudmakers
Behaim, Martin, 13
Benayoun, Maurice, 181
  interview, 195-196
Borges, Jorge Luis, 5, 24
Bosch, Hieronymous, 103-104
Bovee, Michael, 64, 139
  interview, 139-140
Brooks, Jr., Frederick, 220
Brothers Karamazov, The
  (Dostoevsky), 23
Bulletin-Board Service (BBS), 19

C

Cage, John, 184
camera obscura, 13
cameras
  audience viewpoint, 163
  Cinematic Camera, 165
  fixed, 84
  floating, 84
  position, 80
  Theatric Camera, 163
    versus Cinematic Camera, 165
  in three-dimensional dataspace, 158
  use in building narrative, 225
  viewpoint in space, 158
case studies
  A.I.: Artificial Intelligence game
    complement, 124, 131
      author interview, 131-135
      reader interview, 135-138
  Banja, 126, 144-146
  Cloudmakers, 124, 131
      author interview, 131-135
      reader interview, 135-138
  Crutch, 125, 141

Deux Ex 2, 191-192, 194
Devil's Tramping Ground, The, 126,
  147-148
*Is God Flat, Is The Devil Round?, What
  About Me?*, 195-196
Jimmy Corrigan, 125, 143
La Noche de Santa Ines, 187-189
Liquid Stage, 125, 139-140
Memex Engine, 126, 149-151
Top Agent, 201-203
Ultima Online, 198-199
Virtools, 205-209
CD-ROMs, 59
characters, 28
  abstracting, 87-88
Chiaroscuro, 167
Choose Your Own Adventure books, 63
Church of San Francesco in Assisi, 11
Church, Doug, 54
Cimabue, Giovanni, 7
Cinematic Camera, 165
click-thrus, 19
closed systems versus open systems, 43
Cloudmakers
  case study, 124, 131
    author interview, 131-135
    reader interview, 135-138
  The Guide, 137
Collins, Kelly, 173
color in graphic design, 112
comic books
  foveal vision in, 94
  gutterspace, 90
  narrative in, 127
  in three-dimensional space, 128
Comic Chat, 81
comics books
command lines, 58
  versus graphical user interfaces, 58
composition in interactive design, 119
Computers as Theater (Laurel), 162
conflict, 92

constraints in design, 219
    customization vs. design, 221
    optimization vs. ubiquity, 220
    responsiveness vs. resolution, 220
context, 47
contrast in graphic design, 112
Crucifixion, The, narrative imagery in, 105-106
Crutch, case study, 125, 141
cubed information, 168
customization, 221

D

da Vinci, Leonardo, 99
Daguerre, L. J. M., 15
Dark Angel, 60
decision-making, 51
Denouement, 23, 27
design, 221
design constraints, 219
    customization vs. design, 221
    optimization vs. ubiquity, 220
    responsiveness vs. resolution, 220
Desis, 23, 27
desktop metaphor, 32
Deus Ex, 64, 218
Deus Ex 2, 213
    case study, 180, 191-194
Devil's Tramping Ground, The, case study, 126, 147-148
di Bondone, Giotto, 7-8, 10-12
    Perspectivist Approach, 12
    work in Church of San Francesco in Assisi, 11
dimensional imagery, 167
    capabilities, 168
    cubed information, 168
    juxtaposed information sets, 169
dimensional perspective, 6-7
Dramatic Arc, 3
Duchamp, Marcel, 108
Duchateau, Ludovic, interview, 205-209
Dylan, Bob, 50

E

Eastwood, Clint, 7
Edison, Thomas, 164
electronic media
    converting to digital form, 55
    non-linear participation in, 57
emotional perspective, 6-7
enhanced television, 59
environments, algorithmic, 234, 236
epiphany, 49, 91
episodic narrative, 61
    in television, 61
Epi_Editor, 216
Everquest, 19, 66, 192, 218
exploration, 44, 121
expressive narrative, 63

F

Fenlon, Pete, 131
Final Fantasy, 41
finger alphabets, 50
first person, 74, 161
    diminishing use of, 161
    floating cameras, 84
    importance of, 162
    versus third person, 80
fixed cameras, 84
fixed viewpoint, 163
floating cameras, 84
foreshadowing, 49, 91
    versus foreshortening, 157
foreshortening, 91
    versus foreshadowing, 157
forms of narrative, 4
Fort Scott military installation, 171-173
four steps of interaction, 227
foveal vision, 93
    in comic books, 94
Freed, James Ingo, 156
Freytag Triangle, 22
Freytag, Gustav, 22

G

Garden of Earthly Delights, The (Bosch), 103
genealogy of perspective, 7, 10-16
globe, creation of, 13
Goethe, 112
Goldman, Lisa, 228
Good, The Bad, and The Ugly, The, 7
graphic design, 111
    color, 112
    contrast, 112
    functionality, 111
    legibility, 111
    movement, 115
graphical user interfaces (GUI), 58
Gravity's Rainbow (Pynchon), 24
Greek epic narratives, 50
Greenaway, Peter, 185
Grunewald, Matthias, 105
GUI (graphical user interfaces), 58
    versus command lines, 58
    mouse-based, 58
Guide, The (*Cloudmakers*), 137
gutterspace in comic books, 90

H

Head Mounted Display (HMD), 169
Holocaust Memorial, 155-156, 184
Homer, 50
Hon, Adrian, interview, 135-138
Hugo, Victor, 69
Hunchback of Notre Dame, The (Hugo), 69
hybridization, 232-233

I

IF (interactive fiction), 73
images, 33
    abstracting, 88
    color, 112
    contrast, 112
    designing for narrative, 109-111, 116
    dimensional, 167-169
    generating meaning, 95
    graphic design, 111
    legibility, 111

lines of sight, 93
movement, 115
narrative in, 93-94
  Annunciation, 98-100
  Baptism of Christ, 101
  Crucifixion, The, 105-106
  examples, 96
  Las Meninas, 107
  Last Judgement, The, 103
  Nude Descending a Staircase, 108
  seeing versus remembering, 95
  Tablet of Isis, 97
non-verbal text, 33
perspective, dimensional imagery,
  167-169
production in computers, 34
sign-language, 34
time in flat imagery, 90
use with text, 34
  television, 34
value in narrative, 3

imitation of life, 28
"Immortal, The" (Borges), 5
impositional narrative, 63
indeterminacy, 43
information
  acquiring, 122, 177
  ambient, 230
  dimensional, 168
  discovering, 122, 178
  juxtaposed information sets, 169
  redistributing, 123, 179
  subdividing, 118
information patterns, 46
  context, 47
  precepts, 47
  repetition, 47
interaction
  in architecture, 174-176
  basic process, 44
    exploration, 44
    modification, 45
    observation, 44
    reciprocal change, 45
  design, 116, 120, 177
    acquiring information, 122, 177
    composition, 119
    discovering information, 122, 178

feedback, 118
  general versus specific, 116
  redistributing information,
    123, 179
  subdividing information, 118
designing, 230-231
  components, 230
elements of, 229
exploration, 121
four steps of interaction, 227
modification, 121
observation, 120
in system design, 228-231

Interaction Design Constraints, 38
interactive fiction (IF), 73
interactive narrative, 60
  blurring of roles of readers and
    writers, 26
  defined, 2
  determining quality and form, 62
  expressive, 63
  impositional, 63
  plot structures, 63-66
  versus traditional narrative, 2
interactive television, 238
interactivity, 37
  command line, 58
  designing decisions for, 51
  Interaction Design Constraints, 38
  non-linear participation in, 57
  principles of interaction, 39
    input/output, 39
    inside/outside, 40
    open/closed, 43
interest, 225
Interface Culture (Johnson), 26
Internet, 18
interviews, 124, 180
  Bain, Ed, 147-148
  Benayoun, Maurice, 195-196
  Bovee, Michael, 139-140
  Duchateau, Ludovic, 205-209
  Hon, Adrian, 135-138
  Lafia, Marc, 149-151
  Laukasto, Marko, 201-203
  Lee, Elan, 131-135
  Janin, Olivier, 145-146

Koster, Raph, 198-199
Kurki, Mitja, 201-203
McCloud, Scott, 124, 127-130
Novak, Maurice, 182-185
Pantin, Anita, 187-189
Smith, Harvey, 191-194
investment, 225
  increasing, 231
IonStorm design process, 213-214
  story testing, 215
  user testing, 215
*Is God Flat?, Is The Devil Round?, What
  About Me?* case study, 181, 195-196

J
James, William, 40
Janin, Olivier, 144
  interview, 145-146
Jimmy Corrigan, case study, 125, 143
Johnson, Steve, 26
Joyce, James, 51
juxtaposed information sets, 169

K
kinetoscope, 164
*Kiss Between May Irwin and John C. Rice,
  The*, 164
Koster, Raph, 63, 181, 214
  interview, 198-199
Kurki, Mitja, interview, 201-203

L
Lafia, Marc, 65, 149
  interview, 149-151
Last Judgement, The (Bosch), 104
  narrative imagery in, 103
Laukasto, Marko, interview, 201-203
Laurel, Brenda, 162
Laws of Motion (Isaac Newton), 15
Lee, Elan, interview, 131-135
legibility in graphic design, 111
Lewis, David, 229
linear narrative, 51
lines of sight, 93

Liquid Stage, 64
case study, 125, 139-140
Loudon, Annette, 229

M

Majestic, 233
Martini, Simone, 99
McCloud, Scott, 90
interview, 124, 127-130
McLuhan, Marshall, 67
meaning
generating
redundancy and differences in
metaphors, 110-111
generating in images, 95
generating through repetition, 100
Memex Engine, 65
case study, 126, 149-151
Meninas, Las (Velazquez), narrative
imagery in, 107
meta-messages, 48
metaphors, 30, 47, 109
abstraction of, 32
characters, abstracting, 87-88
desktop metaphor, 32
images, abstracting, 88
myths, 33
redundancy in, 110
generating meaning, 110-111
presenting differences, 110
in system design, 222-223
Microsoft Excel, 26
mimesis, 162
modification, 45, 121
modulated plots, 65
Montgomery, Ray, 63
morals, 29
mouse-based graphical user
interfaces, 58
movement in graphic design, 115
MUDs (Multi-User Domains), 179
Myst, 44
myths, 33

N

narration, 5
narrare, 5
versus writing, 29
narrative, 21
in advertising, 36
in architecture, 154-155, 171, 180
Acropolis, 154
Fort Scott military installation,
171-173
Holocaust Memorial, 155-156
articulation of time in, 50-53
suspense, 51
building, 223
cameras, 225
interest, 225
investment, 225
opinion, 224
turning readers into writers, 227
characters, 28
conflict, 92
Denouement, 23, 27
designing images for, 109-111, 116
graphic design, 111
Desis, 27
episodic, 61
in television, 61
forms, 4
frequency of use, 35
Freytag Triangle, 22
Greek epic, 50
in images, 93-94
Annunciation, 98-100
Baptism of Christ, 101
Crucifixion, 105-106
examples, 96
Las Meninas, 107
Last Judgement, The, 103
Nude Descending a Staircase, 108
seeing versus remembering, 95
Tablet of Isis, 97
imitation of life, 28
interactive, 60
blurring of roles of readers and
writers, 26
defined, 2
determining quality and form, 62
expressive, 63
impositional, 63
non-linear participation in, 57
plot structures, 63-66
versus traditional, 2
linear, 51
morals, 29
narration, 5
opinion, 29
Peripeteia, 23, 27
perspective in stories, 5
plot, 24
defined, 27
point of view, 73, 79
first person, 74
second person, 75
social interaction, 81
third person, 76
story problems, 24
symbols, 24
symbology of symbols, 24
in television, 36
temporary, 50
time, 24
in topology, 223
traditional versus interactive, 2
use of imagery in, 3
visual cues, 176
in websites, 18
writing, 49
Nelson, Ted, 32
network environments, designing, 219
Newton, Isaac, Laws of Motion, 15
NFL 2K, 224
Noche de Santa Ines, La, 180
case study, 187-189
nodal plots, 64
nodal story structure, 214
Novak, Marcos, 175, 180
Novak, Maurice, interview, 182-185
Nude Descending a Staircase (Duchamp),
narrative imagery in, 108

O

observation, 44, 120
open plots, 66
open systems
versus closed systems, 43
indeterminacy, 43

opinion
  morals, 29
  in narrative, 29
optimization, 220

Palace, The, 82
Pantin, Anita, 180
  interview, 187-189
Parisi, Tony, 228
Passion, The, 10
Pattern Language, A (Alexander), 170
patterns of information, 46
  context, 47
  precepts, 47
  repetition, 47
Peripeteia, 23, 27
perspective, 2, 231
  camera obscura, 13
  Chiaroscuro, 167
  dimensional, 6-7
  in dimensional imagery, 167-169
  "discovery" of, 7
  emotional, 6-7
  genealogy, 7, 10-13, 15-16
  Maurice Novak interview, 182
  Perspectivist Approach, 12
  protracted, 91
  role of, 2
  in stories, 5
  subjective, 16
  types, 6
  vanishing point, 6
  zooming, 162
Perspectivist Approach, 12
  principles of, 17
Pesce, Mark, 228
Pioneer 11, 49
Plankalkul, 57
plot, 24
  Aristotle's definition, 22
  defined, 27
  Denouement, 27
  Desis, 27
  Maurice Novak interview, 183
  modulated, 65

nodal, 64
open, 66
Peripeteia, 27
structures in interactive narrative, 63-66
timing in interactive narrative, 63
use-case scenarios, 28
Poe, Edgar Allan, 23
Poetics, The (Aristotle), 22
point of view, 73
  first person, 74, 161
    diminishing use of, 161
    floating cameras, 84
    importance of, 162
  second person, 75, 161
  shifting, 79
  social interaction, 81
  third person, 76, 161, 166
    versus first and second person, 80
    increasing use of, 161
principles of interaction, 39
  input/output, 39
  inside/outside, 40
  open/closed, 43
production metrics, 217
Pynchon, Thomas, 24

Ravenna Baptistry, 102
readers
  blurring of roles, 26
  defined, 26
  determining in system design, 218
  turning into writers, 227
reciprocal change, 45
redundancy in metaphors, 110
  generating meaning, 110-111
  presenting differences, 110
repetition, 47, 110
  generating meaning through, 100
resolution, 220
RespondTV, 218
responsiveness, 220
Rilke, Rainer Maria, 109
Rodin, Gustav, 109
Romeo and Juliet (Shakespeare), 24

saccadic eye movements, 94
Sanzio, Raphael, 13
second person, 75, 161
  versus third person, 80
Sega gaming platform, 165
Sermon, Paul, 41
Shakespeare Programming Language, 116
Shakespeare, William, 24
Shedroff, Nathan, 38
Shootout at the OK Corral, 7
sign-language, 34
Simnet, 19
Sims, The, 66, 166, 231
Smith, Harvey, 180, 221
  interview, 191-192, 194
Snow Crash (Stephenson), 233
social interaction, 81
software development
  relationship to writing, 25
  use-case scenarios, 27
Software Requirements Document (SRD), 217
Sonic the Hedgehog, 64
Sopranos, The, 60
space
  audience viewpoint, 158, 163
  camera viewpoint, 158
Spector, Warren, 191-192
Spider-Man, 61
SRD (Software Requirements Document), 217
Star Wars, 4, 232
Star Wars Rogue Squadron, 79
Starcraft Brood War, 166
Stephenson, Neal, 233
Stewart, Sean, 131
stories, morals, 29
story problems
  in narrative, 24
  Peripeteia, 23

story structure
  nodal, 214
  "string of pearls", 193, 214
story testing, 215
"string of pearls" story structure, 193, 214
Sullivan, Louis, 170
suspense, 51
Sutherland, Ivan, 169
symbology, metaphors, 47
symbols, 109
  metaphors, 30
  in narrative, 24
  symbology of symbols, 24
system design, 213
  algorithmic environments, 234, 236
  building the production metrics, 217
  defining requirements, 217
    Software Requirements Document (SRD), 217
  design constraints, 219
    customization vs. design, 221
    optimization vs. ubiquity, 220
    responsiveness vs. resolution, 220
  designing networked environments, 219
  determining readers, 218
  emerging trends, 233
  hybridization, 232-233
  interaction, 228-231
  IonStorm design process, 213-214
    story testing, 215
    user testing, 215
  narrative, building, 223
    cameras, 225
    interest, 225
    investment, 225
    opinion, 224
    turning readers into writers, 227
  Team ChMan design process, 216
  use of metaphors, 222-223

T

Tablet of Isis, 49
  narrative imagery in, 97
Tamara, 189
Team ChMan, 20
  design process, 216

Technique of Drama (Freytag), 22
Telematic Dreaming, 41
television, 34
  enhanced television, 59
  episodic narrative in, 61
  interactive television, 238
  use of narrative, 36
  viewing behavior, 56
temporary narrative, 50
text
  linearity of, 84
  use with images, 34
    television, 34
Theatric Camera, 163
third person, 76, 161, 166
  increasing use of, 161
  versus first and second person, 80
time
  articulation in narrative, 50-53
    suspense, 51
  in comic books, 90
  in flat imagery, 90
  linearity, 52
  Maurice Novak interview, 183
  in narrative, 24
  in plotting interactive narrative, 63
  sequential versus non-sequential, 52
  universality, 52
  as a volume, 52
Tomagochi, 231
Tomb Raider, 4, 41, 232
Top Agent, 181
  case study, 201-203
topology, 223
traditional narrative versus interactive narrative, 2
Turok, 79

U

Ubiquitous Computing, 181, 201
ubiquity, 220
Ultima Online, 19, 43, 63, 66, 181
  case study, 198-199
use-case scenarios, 27, 53
  versus plot, 28
user testing, 215

V

Van Eyck, Jan, 99
vanishing point, 6
  "discovery" of, 7
Velazquez, Diego, 107
viewpoint
  audience, 158, 163
  camera, 158
  fixed, 163
    versus moving, 163
  moving, 163
Virtools
  case study, 205-209
virtual architecture, 182
Virtual Places, 82
virtual reality, 180
visual cues, 176
VRML, 228

W

walls, 174-176
Ware, Chris, 51, 143
Waters, Muddy, 111
Weisman, Jordan, 131
Wexelblat, Alen, 219
Woodring, Jim, 81
Worlds Chat, 82
writers
  blurring of roles, 26
  defined, 26
writing, 49
  relationship to software development, 25
  versus narration, 29

X

X-Files, The, 60

Z

Z1 (calculator), 57
zooming, 162
Zuse, Konrad, 57

Cover

Photography: Gabriella Marks/triggerfinger.com
Illustration: Marvin Mann and Mark Stephen Meadows.

Interior Cover

Plate from "Underweysung der Messung,"
Manual on Perception and Measurement,
Albrecht Durer, 1572.

All chapter spreads by Marvin Mann and Mark Stephen Meadows.

Preface

Narrative projects and/or experiments by
Mark Stephen Meadows
crutch, part 1/9 (1995, internet)
buzerd, part 2/9 (1996, internet)
dendrite (1997, internet)
pill, part 4/9 (1999, print)
walkin comix (2000, architecture)

Page 02

St_Elmo Wireframes.
Illustration: Marvin Mann and Mark Stephen Meadows.

Page 04

Seven people sharing the same virtual and physical space.
Photo, Mark Stephen Meadows.
Hellboy Comic, ©2001 by Mike Mignola,
used with permission by Dark Horse Comics.
Hellboy Game, Courtesy of Cryo Interactive.
http://www.cryo-interactive.com/
Screen captures of A.I./Cloudmakers Internet Narrative
Courtesy of Microsoft.
   http://www.donu-tech.com/
   http://www.belladerma-srl-it.ro/
   http://www.coronersweb.org/eb2183.html
   http://www.spcb.org/
   http://www.bangaloreworldu-in.co.nz/

Page 06

Raphael Sanzio, The School of Athens,
1510-11, Vatican, Rome.
Filippino Lippi, Three Scenes From The Story of Esther,
c.1472, Louvre, Paris.

Page 08

Giotto di Bondone, Detail, Vision of Pope Gregory IX,
c.1300, Superior Church of Assisi.

Page 09

Giotto di Bondone, Detail, Resurrection of Lazarus from
Life of Saint Mary
Magdalene (Attributed to Giotto, Palmerino di Guido
and Others) c.1309, Superior Church of Assisi.
Giotto di Bondone, Detail, The Crib at Greccio,
c.1297-1300, Superior Church of Assisi.

Page 10

Giotto di Bondone, St. Francis Preaching Before Honorius
III by Giotto, c.1297-1300, Superior Church of Assisi.
Giotto di Bondone, The Resurrection of Lazarus,
(Attributed to Giotto, Palmerino di Guido and Others)
c.1309, Superior Church of Assisi.

Page 11

Intrados with Frescoes from the Upper Church of
Basilica of San Francesco,1277-1300, © Elio Ciol/corbis
View of Superior Church of Assisi with highlights of
painting positions, Assisi Archives /
Mark Stephen Meadows illustration.

Page 12

View of Superior Church of Assisi with highlights of
viewer positions, Assisi Archives /
Mark Stephen Meadows illustration.

Page 13

Camera Obscura photographs taken with traditional 16th
century technology. All photos, courtesy of Amélie
Padioleau. a.padioleau@netcourrier.com

Page 13

Cenni di Pepe, AKA Cimabue La Vierge et l'Enfant
en majesté entourés de six anges. c.1280, Louvre, Paris.
[Inset] Bellini, Giovanni, Madonna with Saints, 1505,
Church of St. Zaccaria, Venice.

Page 15

All images of 1850 period dageurreotypes.
Courtesy of Dennis A. Waters: www.finedags.com

Page 16

Earth at Night. Courtesy of Robert Simmon, NASA GSFC
http://antwrp.gsfc.nasa.gov/apod/ap001127.html

Page 17

Giotto di Bondone, The Dream of Pope Innocent III,
1297-1299, Superior Church of Assisi.
Giotto di Bondone, St. Francis Casting the Demons out
of Arezzo, c.1297-1300, Superior Church of Assisi.

IMAGE INDEX

250

Page 18

Powerlines of Nara. Photo, G. Marks|triggerfinger.com

Page 19

Banja, the face of future content-based communities. Courtesy of Team ChMan. http://www.banja.com/

Page 20

Banja. Courtesy of Team ChMan. http://www.banja.com/

Page 21

Definitions of narrative in French (Larousse), English (Merriam-Webster), and German (Cassel).

Page 22

Gustav Freytag's Dramatic Triangle.

Page 23

Gustav Freytag's Dramatic Triangle Subdivided for Novels and Novellas.
Gustav Freytag's Dramatic Triangle, sans Desis, as per Edgar Allen Poe.

Page 24

Excerpt from William Shakespeare's *Romeo and Juliet*.

Page 25

Different Forms of Contemporary Reading, composite, Mark Stephen Meadows.

Page 27

Use-Case Scenario, Example #1.

Page 28

The importance of opinion; "Lunch with Nun," Photo, Mark Stephen Meadows.

Page 29
[top row]

BarFly, Deux Ex, Courtesy of IonStorm.
matt@ooze.com in clever disguise.
Poet Stefen Starner, Photo, Carrie Jo Snyder.
[second row]

Banja's Poug, Courtesy of Team ChMan.
http://www.banja.com/
The D7VA, Courtesy of Marc Lafia
http://www.memexengine.com/
Mark Scheeff as Old Man Munghy.
Illustration, Mark Stephen Meadows.

[third row]

Padre. Painting, Mark Stephen Meadows.
Justin Hall, circa 1994. Photo, Daphne Strauss.
ASCII Character. Illustration, Mark Stephen Meadows.

Page 30

Microsoft Excel. Composite, Mark Stephen Meadows.

Page 32
[top row]

Apple Desktop Example.
Microsoft Desktop Example.
[bottom row]

Macintosh Desktop Example.
Linux Operating System Example.

Page 35

Magazine Stand, Republique, Paris. Thanks to Benoit and Baxa.
"Adam on the Air," Photo, G. Marks|triggerfinger.com

Page 36

"Monitors, Monitored." Photo, G. Marks|triggerfinger.com

Page 37

Hand ringing doorbell. Photo, G. Marks/triggerfinger.com
Typical train track. Illustration, Gabriella Marks

Page 39

MysteryMan ringing doorbell.
MysteryMan patiently waiting.
MysteryMan leaving.
All Photos, Gabriella Marks|triggerfinger.com

Page 40

She answers door. Photo, G. Marks|triggerfinger.com
In We Go. Photo, Gabriella Marks|triggerfinger.com

Page 41

Inside and Outside the skull modes of interaction. Illustration, Mark Stephen Meadows.

Page 42

Telematic Dreaming, Courtesy of Paul Sermon.

Page 43

The Hardcore interaction of Gambling.
Photo, Gabriella Marks|triggerfinger.com
The Beast A.I. game (entrypoints),
Courtesy of Microsoft Corporation.

http://www.donu-tech.com/
http://www.belladerma-srl-it.ro/
http://www.coronersweb.org/eb2183.html
http://www.spcb.org/
http://www.bangaloreworldu-in.co.nz/

Page 44
Hand ringing doorbell. Photo, G. Marks|triggerfinger.com

Page 45
MysteryMan ringing doorbell.
MysteryMan patiently waiting.
Someone answers door.
In We Go. All Photo, Gabriella Marks|triggerfinger.com

Page 48
Gregory Bateson, Theory of Mind, Ballantine Books,
New York, 1956, 1972, 1979

Page 49 - 52
"movement, light through time," Photos, Shelby Ring.

Page 53
Use-Case Scenario Example #2

Page 54
Passage Des Abbesses. Photo, Mark Stephen Meadows.

Page 55
European civic-broadcast radio, c.1930.
Photo, Mark Stephen Meadows.

Page 56
European civic-broadcast radio, c.1930.
Photo, Mark Stephen Meadows.

Page 57
Konrad Zuse Painting, Konrad Zuse's Z1.
Courtesy of Horst Zuse and http://www.epemag.com

Page 61
"Characterizing Commerce."
Photo, Gabriella Marks|triggerfinger.com

Page 64
Nodal Plot Structure Example.

Page 65
Modulated Plot Structure Example.

Page 66
Open Plot Structure Example.

Page 68
Three different forms of reading:
the library, the library, and the video game parlor.
Photos, Mark Stephen Meadows.

Page 69
Alternative possible narrative paths through
Hugo's Novel "Notre Dame."

Page 70
St_Elmo. Illustration, Marvin Mann
& Mark Stephen Meadows.

Page 71
Irenee, The Accordian Player, 2002, Paris.
Photos and Illustrations, Mark Stephen Meadows.

Page 72
St_Elmo on Le Grand Ecran, Paris.
Illustration, Marvin Mann and Mark Stephen Meadows.

Page 74
St_Elmo, First Person Camera Examples.
Illustration, Marvin Mann and Mark Stephen Meadows.

Page 75
St_Elmo, Second Person Camera Examples.
Illustration, Marvin Mann and Mark Stephen Meadows.

Page 76
St_Elmo, Third Person Camera Examples.
Illustration, Marvin Mann and Mark Stephen Meadows.

Page 77
Deus Ex, courtesy IonStorm.
The Dungeon Master hard at work.
Photos, Gabriella Marks|triggerfinger.com

Page 78
St_Elmo, Camera Examples. Illustration,
Marvin Mann and Mark Stephen Meadows.

Page 79
Turok: Evolution. Courtesy of Acclaim Entertainment, Inc.
and HighWater Group

Page 80
Mesdames Pernier and Dumas, Paris.

Page 81
Mesdames Dumas and Pernier, Paris.
Microsoft Comic Chat.

Page 82
Worlds Inc/Worlds Chat; thanks to Jeff Robinson and the kind folks at http://www.scamper.com/
Palace Chat; Thanks to Bruce Damer, DigitalSpace Corporation, http://www.digitalspace.com

Page 83
Banja's "Zelia" and "Butcher" Courtesy Team ChMan. http://www.banja.com

Page 85
"Conscience," An example of a one-frame narrative. Illustration, Mark Stephen Meadows.

Page 86
"Blokhed," & "Morning Walk" by Mark Stephen Meadows. Pill Character Development of "Pill" from concept to design, Mark Stephen Meadows.

Page 87
Examples of the Ryan/Schwartz approach to image recognition. [Note: These are not original images. Illustration, Mark Stephen Meadows.]

Page 89
Une Semaine De BontE : A Surrealistic Novel in Collage, by Max Ernst. Thanks to Dover Publishing.
February 1976. Second Edition.
Banja, Courtesy of Team ChMan.
"If I were king, nobody would be allowed to wear pants." Illustration, Mark Stephen Meadows.

Page 90
Scott McCloud's now-famous breakdown of comics' narrative treatment of time. Courtesy of Scott McCloud and Kitchen Sink Press.

Page 91
Example of Foreshortening, Andrea Mantegna, The Lamentation over the Dead Christ, c. 1490, Pinacoteca di Brera, Milan.
Example of Anamorphosis, Hans Holbein, The Ambassadors, 1533, National Gallery, London.
Example of Foreshortening, Eustache Le Sueur, The Return of Tobie, c.1640, Louvre, Paris.

Page 92
Example of Anamorphosis: Archangel, by William M. Cochran, Community Bridge.

http://www.sharedvision.org/
© 1998 William M. Cochran

Page 93
Example of foveal vision.
Illustration, Mark Stephen Meadows.

Page 94
Example of eye movement across a classic composition;
Leonardo da Vinci,
The Virgin and Child with Saint Anne,
c. 1510, Louvre, Paris.

Page 95
Rembrandt van Rijn, self-portrait, 1669 (last year of his life), National Gallery, London.
Pablo Picasso, Portrait of Ambroise Vollard, Paris, 1910, The Pushkin State Museum of Fine Arts, Moscow.
Vincent Van Gogh, self-portrait, 1889, Musee d'Orsay, Paris.

Page 96
Bembine Tablet of Isis, by J. Augustus Knapp & Manly P. Hall,
Philosophical Research Society, Inc., Los Angeles, CA

Page 97
Tarot Cards. Photo, Shelby Ring.

Page 98
Fra Angelico, The Annunciation;
Monastery of San Marco, Florence, c. 1437.
Museo Diocesano, Cortona 1432-43.
Museo di San Marco, Florence, c. 1442.

Page 99
Annunciations,
Martini, Simone, 1333, Uffizi, Florence.
Van Eyck, Hubert and Jan, Ghent Altarpiece
(Top Right Panel), 1432,
Cathedral of St Bavo, Ghent.
Da Vinci, c.1474, Uffizi Gallery, Florence.
Da Vinci, c. 1480, Louvre, Paris.

Page 100
Annunciations;
Boticelli, Sandro, The Cestello Annunciation,
c. 1489, Uffizi, Florence.
Solario AKA Andrea di Bartolo, 1506, Louvre, Paris.
Vasari, Giorgio , central panel c.1564-1567, Louvre, Paris.
Baldovinetti, Alesso, c. 1457, Uffizi, Firenze.

Braccesco, Carlo, Central Panel, c.1492, Louvre, Paris.
van der Weyden, Rogier, Middle Panel,
c.1460, Louvre, Paris.

Page 101
Annunciations;
Bouts, Dieric, (Upper Left Panel), c. 1450-1454,
J. Paul Getty Museum, Los Angeles.
Reni, Guido, c.1629, Louvre, Paris.
Carracci, Agostino, c.1570?, Louvre, Paris.
Daddi, Bernardo, c.1330, Louvre, Paris.

Page 102
The Baptistry Ceiling in Ravenna, Ceiling, walls,
and interior sketches.

Page 103
Hieronymus Bosch. Outer Wings (Cover),
Creation of the World.
Garden Of Earthly Delights (triptych),
c. 1504, Museo del Prado, Madrid.

Page 104
Hieronomous Bosch, Last Judgement (triptych), c. 1501,
Akademie der bildenden Künste, Vienna, Austria.

Page 105
Mathias Grünewald, The Crucifixion (Panel from the
Isenheim Altarpiece), 1515, Musee d'Unterlinden, Colmar.
Outer Wings of Altarpiece showing different display
positions of the series of triptychs.

Page 106
Mathias Grünewald, Crucifixion.
Showing Altarpiece positions 2 and 3.

Page 107
Diego Velázquez, Las Meninas, 1656, Prado Museum,
Madrid. Same, this time with divisions of depth.

Page 108
Marcel Duchamp, Nu Descendant un Escalier,
1912, Philadelphia Museum of Art.
Courtesy Artists Rights Society.
Muybridge, Edgar, Nude Descending Stairs, 1887,
© Hulton-Deutsch Collection

Page 109
Devils, Drinks, and Dancin - Examples of Iconography.
Photo, Gabriella Marks|triggerfinger.com

Page 111
Contrast Comparison (should be looked at quickly,
not studied).

Page 112
Color Chart Showing Goethe's color considerations.

Page 113
Subtractive and Additive Color Models.

Page 114
Retinal Fatigue and Complementary Color Example
(you have to stare at this one to make it work).

Page 115
Foreground and Background Color Example
(you have to stare for a while at this one, too).

Page 116
Hieronymus Bosch Last Judgement (triptych),
c. 1501, Akademie der bildenden Künste, Vienna, Austria.
Garden Of Earthly Delights (triptych), c. 1504,
Museo del Prado, Madrid.

Page 117-119
A comparison of magnifying information:
Adobe Photoshop Interface
and Banja's Cinematic Camera Interface.

Page 120
Iconography in interface.
The Role of Iconography in Religion.

Page 121
Chart showing the relationships between the steps of
interaction and their principles.

Page 122
Example of interactive reading - The Memex Engine -
http://www.memexengine.com/
Example of interactive reading -
Microsoft Windows operating system.

Page 123
How we differentiate forms of interactive reading
(namely input and output) with interface design.

2.5.1
Scott McCloud Interview. Frames from *Understanding
Comics, The Invisible Art.* http://www.scottmccloud.com/

2.5.2

Case Study One: Game Complement to *A.I.* (loosely called *The Beast* or *Cloudmakers*). Courtesy of Microsoft:
http://www.donu-tech.com/
http://www.belladerma-srl-it.ro/
http://www.coronersweb.org/eb2183.html
http://www.spcb.org/
http://www.bangaloreworldu-in.co.nz/
Thanks to the entire CloudMaker Community Screengrabs from Cloudmakers website. http://cloudmakers.org/

2.5.3

Case Study Two: Liquid Stage.
Liquid Stage/ Bovee Productions Screengrabs from Liquid Stage, Courtesy of Michael Bovee.

2.5.4

Case Study Three: Crutch.
Mark Stephen Meadows.
http://boar.com/crutch/

2.5.5

Case Study Four: Jimmy Corrigan,
The Smartest Kid on Earth.
Many thanks to Chris Ware and Fantagraphics Books.
http://www.fantagraphics.com/

2.5.6

Case Study Five: Banja.
Thanks to all the incredible staff and friends of Team ChMan for their help in putting more than a few images together.
http://www.teamchman.com & http://www.banja.com

2.5.7

Case Study Six: Devil's Tramping Ground.
Courtesy of Ed Bain and his own pack of diablos.
http://devilstrampingground.com/

2.5.8

Case Study Seven: Memex Engine.
Thanks to Marc Lafia & crew. http://memexengine.com/

Page 154

Redrawing of the Acropolis Floorplan showing approach and lines of sight upon entrance
(note: Mark Stephen Meadows redrawing based on Le Corbusier, Kleinm & traditional drawings).

Page 155

Athens, sunrise. Photo, Sami Sarkis. © copyright 1999-2002 Getty Images.
Las Vegas, sunset. Photo, Robert Glusic.
© copyright 1999-2002 Getty Images.

Page 156

Comparison of two buildings: 14th Street Entrance Holocaust Museum, Washington DC, Front Entrance, Mauthausen Concentration Camp, Mauthausen, Austria. Photo-illo, Mark Stephen Meadows.

Page 157

A classic theater still in use.
Photo, Mark Stephen Meadows.

Page 158

Modern Theater-goer. Photo, Fred Charles
© copyright 1999-2002 Getty Images.

Page 159

Person crossing street a la Brenda Laurel.
Photo, Gabriella Marks|triggerfinger.com

Page 160

Six examples of how architecture affects what we do.
Photos, Gabriella Marks|triggerfinger.com, Shelby Ring, and Mark Stephen Meadows.

Page 161

Depiction of first-person camera.
Depiction of second-person camera.
Depiction of third-person camera.
All illustrations by Mark Stephen Meadows
with Banja Example.

Page 162

The Hartsville Vidette, c 1848. Courtesy of Hartsville Chamber of Commerce Trousdale County, Hartsville, Tennessee, USA

Page 163

Opening of Lord of the Rings, Gaumont Grand Ecran, Paris, France. Photo, Mark Stephen Meadows.

Page 164

Opera de Paris, Palais Garnierm, Paris, France.
Photo: Mark Stephen Meadows.
The Kiss, 1886, Edison Mfg. Co./S. Lubin, 1896.

Page 165
Plate from "Underweysung der Messung," Manual on Perception and Measurement, Albrecht Durer, 1572. Age of Empires, Courtesy of Ensemble Studios and Microsoft.

Page 166
Age of Empires, Courtesy of Ensemble Studios & Microsoft.

Page 167
Marcos Novak's Liquid Architecture. An example of a virtual building in which things like gravity and ground don't exist. Courtesy Marcos Novak.

Page 168
The St_Elmo City, Marvin Mann & Mark Stephen Meadows.
Cyberspace, Marvin Mann.

Page 169
The Distasteful Future of The Cube, Marvin Mann & Mark Stephen Meadows.
Overlay of Classic Mercator Projection and an original hand-drawn Mercator Map.

Page 170
Banja's Chat entry cave showing multiple architectural options. Banja Chat, in action.

Page 171
The Knife-Christmas Outlet, near Mobile Alabama. Photo, Mark Stephen Meadows.
The Denfert-Rochereau Catacombs, Paris, France. Photo, Mark Stephen Meadows.

Page 172 -173
Fort Scott National Park and its interface. Photos, Mark Stephen Meadows.

Page 174
Examples of how architecture guides interaction; North Station, Paris. Photos, Mark Stephen Meadows.

Page 175
Orthogonal map of Paris's eighth district, c. 1740. A very non-othogonal map of Marcos Novak's Paracube project. Courtesy Marcos Novak.

Page 176
Deus Ex 2, Courtesy of IonStorm Studios.
Coke Machine Interfaces. Photos, Mark Stephen Meadows.
Elevator Interface (with train dashboard). Photo, Mark Stephen Meadows.

Page 177
Floorplan (redrawn) of the Old British Library Reading Room, British Museum, London.

Page 178
The Richard LeNoir Sunday Market, Paris. Photo, Mark Stephen Meadows.

Page 179
Paris Metro. Photo, Mark Stephen Meadows.
Banja on his merry way. Courtesy Team ChMan.
Chartres Cathedral (an incredible example of an interactive narrative in its own right floorplan (redrawn) showing entry passage and presentation.

3.5.1
Marcos Novak Interview.
Many thanks to Marcos for his help and providing these images of his Transarchitectures - buildings that float. http://www.centrifuge.org/marcos/

3.5.2
Case Study One: La Noche de Santa Inés.
The lovely Anita Pantin, her cohorts, and montages of La Noche in question.

3.5.3
Case Study Two: Deus Ex 2.
Harvey Smith, IonStorm, Steve Powers, and Deus Ex. http://www.deusex.com/

3.5.4
Case Study Three: Is God Flat / Is The Devil Round / What About Me?
Snapshots of Monsieur Benayoun's work, Z-A's profiler interface, and various installations that he and his company have produced. http://www.benayoun.com/

3.5.5
Case Study Four: Ultima Online.
Maps and screenshots from the multiplayer world of Ultima Online. http://www.uo.com/

3.5.6
Case Study Five: Top Agent.
Snapshot of the characters & interface of Orchimedia's (now Small Planet) Top Agent. http://www.orchimedia.com/

3.5.7

Case Study Six: Virtools Development Toolset.
Bertrand Duplat, Ludovic Duchateau, Nicolas Galinotti,
Romain Sididris - The Cerebral Cortex of Virtools,
The Behavior Company. Snapshots of Projects, interfaces,
and Monsieur Duchateau. (Courtesy of Virtools with
additional thanks to http://www.incandescence.com/)
http://www.virtools.com/

Page 212

Work in progress; structural reinforcements at the
intersection of Rue Des Martyr and Rue La Vieuville,
Paris, France. Photo, Mark Stephen Meadows.

Page 214

The Dock of Deus Ex. Courtesy of IonStorm.

Page 215

Screenshots & interface of Deus Ex. Courtesy of IonStorm.

Page 216

Team ChMan's Episode Editor ("Epi_Editor") Interface.
How they build their narratives. Courtesy of Team ChMan.

Page 217

Example of a Software Requirements Document (SRD).

Page 218

Two network diagram examples of different design
and complexity levels.

Page 219

Examples of interface design that introduce interaction
constraints. Photomontage, Mark Stephen Meadows.

Page 221

The customizable avatar interface from
Marc Lafia's Memex Engine.

Page 222

The 2001 Renaissance Faire of Larkspur, Colorado.
Photos, Sally Meadows-Shanks.

Page 224

Microsoft's Age of Empires, at its earliest,
least narrative point.
Microsoft's Age of Empires, at a later stage in
which investment and interest are increasing.

Page 226

The cycle of investment and interest. Job Seeker's Notice
Board, 1945. A bulletin board on the Rhein-Strasse
advertises jobs. Photo, Ramage, Frederick
© Hulton-Deutsch Collection/CORBIS

Page 228

The Virtual Reality Modeling Language logo as
originally designed by Kevin Hughes.

Page 229

Early Construct Internet Design architecture.
Architectural design, Mark Lawton, aka Kronos.

Page 230

The End of the Line. Photo, Mark Stephen Meadows.
Screencaptures from Myst, Courtesy of Cyan. From
upper-left to lower-right:
View out of the lighthouse in Stoneship Age.
Sirrus' bedroom in Stoneship Age.
Sirrus' bedroom in Channelwood Age.
The telescope in Stoneship Age. © Cyan.
http://www.myst.com/

Page 231

Screencaptures from Turok, first-person cameras XBox
Platform Implementation.
Courtesy of Nintendo and Highwater.

Page 234

Screenshots of Bryce-a present-day approach to
algorithmic modeling and envionment development.

Page 235

Screenshots of Bryce.

Page 236

Stranger in a Strange land, Tokyo.
Photo, Gabriella Marks|triggerfinger.com

Page 237

St_Elmo in the Spotlight of Attention.
Marvin Mann and Mark Stephen Meadows.

Page 239

Giotto di Bondone, Stigmata of Saint Francis:
Saint Francis Preaching to the Birds, 1300, Louvre, Paris.

Page 240

The St_Elmo Bone-frame, Marvin Mann and
Mark Stephen Meadows.

Solutions from experts you know and trust.

www.informit.com

- OPERATING SYSTEMS
- WEB DEVELOPMENT
- PROGRAMMING
- NETWORKING
- CERTIFICATION
- AND MORE...

Expert Access.
Free Content.

New Riders has partnered with **InformIT.com** to bring technical information to your desktop. Drawing on New Riders authors and reviewers to provide additional information on topics you're interested in, **InformIT.com** has free, in-depth information you won't find anywhere else.

- ■ **Master the skills you need, when you need them**

- ■ **Call on resources from some of the best minds in the industry**

- ■ **Get answers when you need them, using InformIT's comprehensive library or live experts online**

- ■ **Go above and beyond what you find in New Riders books, extending your knowledge**

As an **InformIT** partner, **New Riders** has shared the wisdom and knowledge of our authors with you online. Visit **InformIT.com** to see what you're missing.

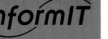

www.informit.com

www.newriders.com

Publishing
the Voices
that Matter

OUR BOOKS

OUR AUTHORS

SUPPORT

| ::: web development | ::: graphics & design | ::: server technology | ::: certification |

NEWS/EVENTS

PRESS ROOM

EDUCATORS

ABOUT US

CONTACT US

WRITE/REVIEW

You already know that New Riders brings you the Voices that Matter. But what does that mean? It means that New Riders brings you the Voices that challenge your assumptions, take your talents to the next level, or simply help you better understand the complex technical world we're all navigating.

Visit www.newriders.com to find:

▶ Never before published chapters

▶ Sample chapters and excerpts

▶ Author bios

▶ Contests

▶ Up-to-date industry event information

▶ Book reviews

▶ Special offers

▶ Info on how to join our User Group program

▶ Inspirational galleries where you can submit
  your own masterpieces

▶ Ways to have your Voice heard

New Riders

0735710783
Nathan Shedroff
US$45.00

0735711658
Hillman Curtis
US$45.00

073571102X
Jakob Nielsen & Marie Tahir
US$39.99

0735711747
John Lenker
US$40.00

0735711704
Andrew Chak
US$45.00

VOICES THAT MATTER™

From conception, to completion,
and beyond, New Riders brings
you the Voices that Matter in
creative media project strategy
and design.

New Riders

VOICES THAT MATTER

VISIT OUR WEB SITE

WWW.NEWRIDERS.COM

On our web site, you'll find information about our other books, authors, tables of contents, and book errata. You will also find information about book registration and how to purchase our books, both domestically and internationally.

EMAIL US

Contact us at: **nrfeedback@newriders.com**

- If you have comments or questions about this book
- To report errors that you have found in this book
- If you have a book proposal to submit or are interested in writing for New Riders
- If you are an expert in a computer topic or technology and are interested in being a technical editor who reviews manuscripts for technical accuracy

Contact us at: **nreducation@newriders.com**

- If you are an instructor from an educational institution who wants to preview New Riders books for classroom use. Email should include your name, title, school, department, address, phone number, office days/hours, text in use, and enrollment, along with your request for desk/examination copies and/or additional information.

Contact us at: **nrmedia@newriders.com**

- If you are a member of the media who is interested in reviewing copies of New Riders books. Send your name, mailing address, and email address, along with the name of the publication or web site you work for.

BULK PURCHASES/CORPORATE SALES

If you are interested in buying 10 or more copies of a title or want to set up an account for your company to purchase directly from the publisher at a substantial discount, contact us at 800-382-3419 or email your contact information to corpsales@pearsontechgroup.com. A sales representative will contact you with more information.

WRITE TO US

New Riders Publishing
201 W. 103rd St.
Indianapolis, IN 46290-1097

CALL/FAX US

Toll-free (800) 571-5840
If outside U.S. (317) 581-3500
Ask for New Riders
FAX: (317) 581-4663

New Riders

WWW.NEWRIDERS.COM